Jake Huntor

Exam Literacy

A guide to doing what works (and not what doesn't) to better prepare students for exams

Crown House Publishing Limited

www.crownhouse.co.uk

First published by
Crown House Publishing Ltd
Crown Buildings, Bancyfelin, Carmarthen,
Wales, SA33 5ND, UK
www.crownhouse.co.uk

and

Crown House Publishing Company LLC
PO Box 2223, Williston, VT 05495, USA
www.crownhousepublishing.com

First published 2018.

Crown House Publishing has no responsibility for the
persistence or accuracy of URLs for external or
third-party websites referred to in this publication,
and does not guarantee that any content on such
websites is, or will remain, accurate or appropriate.

British Library Cataloguing-in-Publication Data

A catalogue entry for this book is available
from the British Library.

Print ISBN 978-178583198-0
Mobi ISBN 978-178583353-3
ePub ISBN 978-178583354-0
ePDF ISBN 978-178583355-7

LCCN 2018943079

Printed and bound in the UK by
TJ International, Padstow, Cornwall

Pages 79, 105–107, 109–111 – AQA material is reproduced by permission of AQA. Pages 116, 168–169 – CGP material is reproduced by permission of CGP Books. Page 10, extract © Wiliam, Dylan (2016). 'Learning Styles: What Does the Research Say?', *Deans for Impact* [blog] (28 April). Available at: https://deansforimpact.org/learning-styles-what-does-the-research-say/. Used with permission of Deans for Impact. Pages 16, 17, extracts © Rose, Nick (2015). 'Can We Teach Students Effective "Revision Skills"?', *Evidence Into Practice* [blog] (8 February 2015). Available at: https://evidenceintopractice.wordpress.com/2015/02/08/can-we-teach-students-effective-revision-skills/. Page 17, extract © Powley, Ruth (2015). 'Meaningful Manageable Revision', *Love Learning Ideas* [blog] (25 March). Available at: http://www.lovelearningideas.com/blog-archive/2015/3/25/meaningful-manageable-revision. Used with permission. Page 27, tweet – used with permission of Hélène Galdin-O'Shea. Page 27, tweet – used with permission of Julia Smith. Page 28, extract © Tierney, Stephen (2016). 'It's the High Stakes Accountability Not the Testing', *@LeadingLearner* [blog] (3 May). Available at: https://leadinglearner.me/2016/05/03/reduce-high-stakes-accountability-not-testing/. Used with permission. Pages 28–29, extract © Christodoulou, Daisy (2014). 'Why Teaching to the Test is So Bad', *The Wing to Heaven* [blog] (19 January). Available at: https://thewingtoheaven.wordpress.com/2014/01/19/why-teaching-to-the-test-is-so-bad/. Used with permission. Page 29, tweet – used with permission of Tom Bennett. Pages 34, 88, 98, extracts © Brown, Peter C., Henry L. Roediger and Mark A. McDaniel (2014). *Make It Stick: The Science of Successful Learning*, Kindle edn (Cambridge, MA: Harvard University Press). Used with permission of Harvard University Press. Page 39, extract © Emeny, William (2016). 'A Week Working at UCLA in the Bjork Learning and Forgetting Lab', *Great Maths Teaching Ideas* [blog] (26 August). Available at: http://www.greatmathsteachingideas.com/2016/08/26/a-week-working-at-ucla-in-the-bjork-learning-and-forgetting-lab/. Used with permission. Pages 40, 43, 68, 90, 96, extracts © Didau, David (2015). *What If Everything You Knew About Education Was Wrong?* (Carmarthen: Crown House Publishing). Used with permission of David Didau. Page 43, extract © Caviglioli, Oliver (2017). 'My researchED Cheshire Presentation', *HOW2* (19 March). Available at: http://linkis.com/teachinghow2s.com/bl/BfbYM. Used with permission. Page 44, extract © Williams, Dan (2017). 'Cognitive Load Theory', *furtheredagogy* [blog] (20 May). Available at: https://furtheredagogy.wordpress.com/2017/05/20/cognitive-load-theory/. Used with permission. Page 58, tweet – used with permission of Knikki Hernandez. Page 70, extract © Fiorella, Logan and Richard E. Mayer (2015). *Learning as a Generative Activity: Eight Learning Strategies That Promote Understanding* (New York: Cambridge University Press). Used with permission. Page 72, extract © Willingham, Daniel (2009). *Why Don't Students Like School?* (San Francisco, CA: Jossey-Bass). Used with permission of Wiley. Pages 82–83, extract © Morgan, Kelly (2011). 'Teaching with Worked Examples – Save Learner Time and Effort While Increasing Performance!', *Kelly Morgan* [blog] (10 February). Available at: http://kellymorganscience.com/teaching-with-worked-examples-save-learner-time-and-effort-while-increasing-performance/. Used with permission. Page 84, extract © Ashman, Greg (2017). 'Cognitive Load Theory – "The Single Most Important Thing for Teachers to Know"', *Filling the Pail* [blog] (27 January). Available at: https://gregashman.wordpress.com/2017/01/27/cognitive-load-theory-the-single-most-important-theory-for-teachers-to-know/. Used with permission. Page 93, extract © Herbert, Wray (2012). 'Two Cheers for Multiple-Choice Tests', *Association for Psychological Science* (29 March). Available at: http://www.psychologicalscience.org/index.php/news/full-frontal-psychology/two-cheers-for-multiple-choice-tests.html. Used with permission of the Association for Psychological Science. Page 95, extract © Stock, Phil (2016). 'Five Strategies for Encouraging More Effective Independent Study', *Must Do Better* [blog] (24 March). Available at: https://joeybagstock.wordpress.com/2016/03/24/five-strategies-for-encouraging-more-effective-independent-study/. Pages 98–99, extract © Emeny, William (2015). 'Building Interleaving and Spaced Practice Into Our Pedagogy', *Great Maths Teaching Ideas* [blog] (1 February). Available at: http://www.greatmathsteachingideas.com/2015/02/01/building-interleaving-and-spaced-practice-into-our-pedagogy/. Used with permission. Page 108, extract © Smith, Megan and Yana Weinstein (2016). 'Learn How to Study Using . . . Elaboration', *The Learning Scientists* [blog] (5 July). Available at: http://www.learningscientists.org/blog/2016/7/7-1. Used with permission of the Learning Scientists. Pages 111–112, extract © Rogers, Ben (2017). 'Retrieval Practice and Sentence Practice All in One!', *Reading for Learning* [blog] (7 October). Available at: https://readingforlearning.org/2017/10/07/retrieval-practice-donows-are-great-but-lets-not-forget-sentence-practice/. Used with permission. Page 114, extract © Williams, Dan (2016). 'Making Maths Work', *furtheredagogy* [blog] (4 April). Available at: https://furtheredagogy.wordpress.com/2016/04/04/making-maths-work/. Used with permission. Page 121, questions 1–7 © Harris, Robert (2014). 'Learning Strategy 5: Self Explanation', *VirtualSalt* (27 February). Available at: http://www.virtualsalt.com/learn5.html. Used with permission. Page 123, correspondence – used with permission of John Sweller. Page 155, blog comment – used with permission of Anthony Radice. Page 156, extract © Fordham, Michael (2017). 'Resisting the Pull of the Generic: Knowledge, Specificity and Teaching', *Clio et cetera* [blog] (20 October). Available at: https://clioetcetera.com/2017/10/20/resisting-the-pull-of-the-generic-knowledge-specificity-and-teaching/. Used with permission. Page 159, extract © Conti, Gianfranco (2017). 'Patterns First – Why You Should "Ditch" Word Lists, Traditional Grammar Rules and . . . Your Textbook', *The Language Gym* [blog] (21 May 2017). Available at: https://gianfrancoconti.wordpress.com/2017/05/21/why-you-should-ditch-word-lists-and-traditional-grammar-rules/. Used with permission. Page 160, extract © Boxer, Adam (2017). 'The Retrieval Roulette', *Adam Boxer* [blog] (4 May). Available at: https://achemicalorthodoxy.wordpress.com/2017/05/04/the-retrieval-roulette/. Used with permission. Page 163, tweet – used with permission of Andrew Old. Page 163, FACE concept – reproduced by permission of Deborah O'Connor. Pages 163–164, extract © Sherrington, Tom (2015). 'FACE It. A Formula for Learning', *teacherhead* [blog] (19 September). Available at: https://teacherhead.com/2015/09/19/face-it-a-formula-for-learning/. Used with permission. Pages 175–176, quote and retrieval practice challenges grid – reproduced by permission of Kate Jones. Pages 176–177, extracts © Adragna, Rachel (2016). 'Be Your Own Teacher: How to Study with Flashcards', *The Learning Scientists* [blog] (18 February). Available at: http://www.learningscientists.org/blog/2016/2/20-1. Used with permission. Page 180, multiple choice question – reproduced by permission of Craig Barton. Page 181, extracts © Christodoulou, Daisy (2013). 'Closed Questions and Higher Order Thinking', *The Wing to Heaven* [blog] (6 October). Available at: https://thewingtoheaven.wordpress.com/2013/10/06/closed-questions-and-higher-order-thinking/. © Christodoulou, Daisy (2015). 'Assessment Alternatives 1: Using Questions Instead of Criteria', *The Wing to Heaven* [blog] (7 June). Available at: https://thewingtoheaven.wordpress.com/2015/06/07/assessment-alternatives-1-using-questions-instead-of-criteria/. Used with permission. Pages 186–187, extract © Tharby, Andy (2014). 'Memory Platforms', *Reflecting English* [blog] (12 June). Available at: https://reflectingenglish.wordpress.com/2014/06/12/memory-platforms/. Used with permission. Page 188, worked example sentences grid – reproduced by permission of Grainne Hallahan and Freya O'Dell. Pages 201–202, tables – reproduced by permission of Dawn Cox. Page 212, extract © Conti, Gianfranco (2015). 'Self-Efficacy – the Most Neglected Motivational Factor in Foreign Language Instruction', *The Language Gym* [blog] (30 May). Available at: https://gianfrancoconti.wordpress.com/2015/05/30/self-efficacy-the-most-neglected-motivational-factor-in-the-foreign-language-classroom/. Used with permission. Pages 214–215, extract © Harvard, Blake (2017) 'Easy Application of Spaced Practice in the Classroom', *The Effortful Educator* [blog] (22 October). Available at: https://theeffortfuleducator.com/2017/10/22/easy-application-of-spaced-practice-in-the-classroom/. Used with permission. Page 217, extract © Henderson, Bruce B. (2015). 'Learning is Thinking and Thinking as Learning: A Review of *Learning as a Generative Activity: Eight Learning Strategies That Promote Understanding* by Logan Fiorella and Richard E. Mayer', *PsycCRITIQUES*, 60(37). Available at: https://www.apa.org/pubs/highlights/psyccritiques-spotlight/PSQ_a0039516.pdf. Used with permission.

Foreword by Professor John Dunlosky

Department of Psychological Sciences, Director, Science of Learning and Education Center, Kent State University

Learning is difficult. Or at least, learning anything novel and complex is difficult. There is no way around it. So much so that any technique which is described as 'it makes learning easy' almost certainly does not hold true, because learning is not easy and it cannot be made easy. What makes matters worse is that students and teachers can mistake fast-and-easy progress with actual learning success when, in fact, many strategies that give rise to fast progress also lead to fast forgetting. And by using ineffective techniques and schedules for learning, students (and teachers) may inadvertently be making it more difficult to reach their learning goals. All of this can be frustrating, both for teachers who seek to help their students retain what they have learned and for students who want to succeed but too often find themselves struggling.

What is the solution? That is, in order to reduce frustrations and ultimately improve student achievement, how should instructors teach and how should students guide their own learning? If you have ever asked questions like these, do not put down this book – because in *Exam Literacy* Jake Hunton provides the answers in an easy-to-read volume that will inspire teachers and students alike. His perspective is especially noteworthy. After spending many years experiencing the same frustrations while teaching students foreign languages, Jake realized he needed to make some changes, and in order to do so he turned to empirical evidence (the hardcore research that indicates what really works) about which learning techniques are most effective and how to use them with fidelity.

Some of what he learned you may find surprising, such as that some of the most effective techniques can be implemented in the classroom, yet many teachers do not know about these techniques or how to use them effectively. One reason for teachers' limited knowledge can be traced back to the textbooks used to educate teachers – recent surveys in the United States and in the Netherlands indicate that the majority of these textbooks do not even mention these techniques!

To help spread the great news, Jake provides a user's guide to some of the most effective techniques, and he does so in a humorous and engaging manner that will be accessible to any interested reader. So, if you want to gain insight into how to improve your students' learning (or even your own), then read on – this book will no doubt become an invaluable resource for you and anyone who embraces lifelong learning in school and beyond.

Acknowledgements

When I started thinking about writing this book I came up with the title, 'Exam Literacy: How to Beat the Exam'. Are you cringing as much as I am? I am extremely grateful to David Bowman at Crown House not only for his constant support but also for his gentle rejection of that title.

I began by writing a guide for the steps students could follow, including how to download exam papers, specifications, mark schemes and examiner reports. Oh, and how to right-click and make a folder for each set of documents. Initially, it hurt a bit when the more I read, the more I realised I didn't know, and how writing a guide about how to organise exam material into folders and build up a store of tips and tricks from examiner reports didn't feel particularly relevant any more.

I am also grateful to all those involved in education – the teaching community, the teacher-bloggers and tweeters – including, of course, those who have been so helpful and supportive in allowing me to refer to their work; in particular, Dr Yana Weinstein from the Learning Scientists, Professor John Sweller, David Didau and, of course, Professor John Dunlosky. All of them have acted as my unwitting psychologists in helping to rein in my levels of bias to more tolerable levels. That is my own view though, and I'm sticking to it.

I am not wrong either to say a huge *merci*, *danke* and *gracias* to the Crown House Publishing team, my brilliant editor, Emma Tuck, and my family – former head teacher Mum, Debbie; deputy head teacher brother, Jude (@judehunton); his wife and MFL teacher, Mariana (@srahunton); my Dad, Colin, and his wife, Gill; my wife, Emily, and, of course, my wonderful son, Tristan.

Thank you also to the four wonderful schools – and their fantastic, hard-working staff and students – in which I have had the pleasure of working and training: the Grove School in Market Drayton, Alsager School in Cheshire, Arthur Terry School in Sutton Coldfield and Heart of England School in the West Midlands.

Contents

Introduction

In 1997, at Easter, I copied out new notes while looking at my old notes from my GCSE business studies textbook.

In 1999, I stared at the notes I had made in class for A level geography.

In March 2003, I sat on a train rereading notes from a lecture on Spanish morphology.

In April 2005, I highlighted passages from a book on psychometric testing.

This was all in preparation for exams at which I might have done better.

I sat these exams not knowing that there might be more effective ways of studying when away from the classroom, ways which might help to make studying more effortful yet rewarding.

I didn't know how much I didn't know when revising or restudying.

A three-hour block of time copying out of the textbook felt like good, old-fashioned, solid revision which should serve me well. There was a tangible product to my revision which meant I felt like I was going to do very well in the exam because, of course, how couldn't I, what with all that observable product at the end of my studying?

The strategy of copying out the notes and looking at the notes made it feel as if I was doing something productive. I would judge how well I had studied by the length of time I had dedicated to doing it.

I'm not sure what I expected from staring at the notes I had made in A level geography – perhaps that the key terms and definitions would evaporate off the page, go through a process of condensation and fall as precipitation, percolating into my long-term memory.

Rereading lulled me into a nice, fuzzy sense of comfortable cognitive ease. I confused familiarity with my notes with checking whether I actually knew the material when they weren't there.

Highlighting passages from a book on psychometric testing also lulled me into thinking that I knew the material much better than I did.

None of these study strategies were as effective as they might have been had I known more about techniques that could have told me what I knew, or didn't know, and perhaps helped to better embed what I wanted to embed in my long-term memory.

In 2007, I taught some lessons where I limited teacher-talk time to no more than 20 minutes.

In 2008, I managed to finish teaching my GCSE language course by Easter to allow some time at the end to revise. The course was based on the textbook and taught in a blocked order of topics.

In 2009, I gave the students plenty of past papers to do at home plus vocabulary to learn, but I didn't think to teach them any strategies on how they could study away from the classroom.

As both student and teacher, I didn't know what I didn't know – and some of what I did know was based on fragments of what I had been told was right, so there were a few urban myths among my thinking (the excellent *Urban Myths about Learning and Education* hadn't been written back then.[1])

When I first started thinking about writing this book three years ago, I admit that, as well as an analysis of potentially more effective study skills, I also began to consider ways that I could be more creative with exam materials. How about a card sort to match up comments from examiner reports with questions on the exam papers? How about designing a PowerPoint with the exam paper question, the mark scheme and the examiner report? How about students designing their own exam paper at an early stage in the course? How about cutting up sample answers and then giving the students a time limit to match the answers with the grades? How about teaching students how to use an online exam paper generator and setting a homework in which they create a question for their friend to complete? And so on.

I knew that exams were important when I started teaching, but I'm shocked to recall how little else I knew about them. I didn't know they were the source of so much debate and controversy. I didn't realise that an educational fault line runs right down the exam room and through wobbly, graffiti-daubed desks. Exams good, exams bad; exams too much, exams not enough. It took me a long time to see the political debate around exams. And to be honest, I'm not sure that I fully engage with it now.

The focus has changed a little since I started writing this book, so while there are a few references here and there to summative testing, it is more of a discussion about learning strategies which *might* work more effectively versus those that *might* not, with an overlap between the classroom and possible transfer to outside the classroom. I stress *might*: they are learning strategies which have shown promise versus the ones that have shown less promise.

---

1   See Pedro De Bruyckere, Paul A. Kirschner and Casper D. Hulshof, *Urban Myths about Learning and Education* (London: Academic Press, 2015).

The book is written from the point of view of a teacher who wants to know more about effective learning strategies and how (or if) they transfer away from the classroom. Some of the areas covered include:

■ Outsourcing study skills versus teachers teaching them within their subject domain.

■ Study skills/learning strategies which have been identified as those which might be less effective than others.

■ Study skills/learning strategies which have been identified as those which might be more effective than others.

■ Potential examples of how the techniques which might be more effective could look.

■ The overlap between learning strategies in the classroom and away from the classroom.

I'm grateful to all the researchers and bloggers out there while I have been researching this book. There is always so much to read and so much to learn that even when you feel you are finally satisfied something new comes along – another study, another blog, another way to challenge your thinking – that you question what you believed in and start rethinking and rewriting again. My own bias and I have disagreed a number of times throughout.

I hope you enjoy the debate.

Part 1
The Debate

Chapter 1

Testing and Revising: The Evidence

There are no magic potions to reach for when exam season approaches. There is no Asterix and Obelix 'Getanexamfix' druid. Unfortunately, as far as I know, there are no magic exam beans either. The next new initiative might not be a panacea but, in fact, another way to foster an atmosphere of pernicious accountability and 'support' a teacher out of the profession.

Nor are there any silver bullets to ensuring student academic success. Sometimes, though, the talk of exam success and students getting excellent grades can conjure up images of exam factories – huge, cold, industrial complexes where students are drilled in Victorian-style classrooms, writing out arithmetic on slate grey iPads.

When I started teaching I had no real understanding of how the memory works and even less of a clue about cognitive science. I thought that pace in the classroom was key (partly through received wisdom and partly through my own vanity: 'If you want to see great pace in lessons then go to Jake's classroom!').

This was both comical and sad, as I really did think that doing things quickly would impress observers and keep the students engaged. It did impress observers, but I don't know if it actually helped to engage the students.[1] I fear it didn't because when I started working at a new school, I began teaching lessons at such a brisk pace that the students complained they couldn't understand as I was speaking and doing things too quickly. Fears of account-ability fuelled my hyperactivity and led to little or no time for the students to understand the material or process it properly.

Pace became a 'tick-box' item in lesson observations, added to the list of 'things we must see in a lesson observation', such as differentiation. This sometimes led to three different sets of worksheets for clearly identifiable groups of students who, no matter how much stealth you could put into surreptitiously organising the class into 'higher ability', 'middle ability' and 'lower ability', the students would always know. In the end, both the students

---

1   See, for example, ch. 11 of Ruth Colvin Clark and Richard E. Mayer's *E-Learning and the Science of Instruction: Proven Guidelines for Consumers and Designers of Multimedia Learning*, Kindle edn (Hoboken, NJ: John Wiley, 2016), loc. 4526–4883.

and I became embarrassed by the whole thing. I now know that my own understanding of differentiation was rather ill-founded and not based on 'responsive teaching'.[2]

I also conducted mini-plenaries (perhaps it's just the terminology that's a problem, since if they were considered as 'retrieval practice' then mini-plenaries might be thought of more positively) and peer assessment without any awareness of the potential for the Dunning–Kruger effect – that is, the cognitive bias in which individuals who are unskilled at a task mistakenly believe themselves to possess greater ability than they do. An alternative, perhaps somewhat cruder, definition is that you're too incompetent to know that you are incompetent.

I'm not necessarily saying that pace was, and is, a bad thing; just that because I had picked up that it impressed people, it became one of the things I would do when being observed, and also something to look out for when I was required to do lesson observations. Seeking to confirm a prejudiced view was a skew that I never even knew I had.

It felt strange, nonetheless, that in my observed lessons where I limited teacher-talk time and ensured my pace was good, I was given mostly outstanding; yet I always felt that the students learned more from me standing at the front and teaching in a slower and more didactic manner, followed up by some guided practice. This was the style I reverted back to when teaching *sans* observer, especially when the exam season loomed large.

Giving students summative tasks to improve a summative outcome was also something I believed would help them to learn better over time: if I test them on the big thing in the way they are tested in exams, they will definitely get better at that big thing. This approach influenced the thinking behind a card sort I devised which involved matching up examiner reports and mark schemes.

As a language teacher, I also used listening tasks from textbooks and past papers to try to improve students' listening skills on a later summative listening test. It felt like I was doing my job, primarily because that was how I understood it *should* work from my teacher training. The fact that students' working memories were being overloaded because the listening exercises were too complex and the skill had not been broken down did not occur to me. (One of the advantages of deliberate practice – where a skill is broken down into smaller tasks – is that there is less of a load on working memory.)

By designing writing tasks which were summative assessments and then expecting students to improve on their next summative assessment, I was confusing learning and performance. Daisy Christodoulou (@daisychristo) notes that learning is about storing

---

2   For more on this see David Didau's (@DavidDidau) blog on differentiation: 'What Do Teachers Think Differentiation Is?', *The Learning Spy* [blog] (24 April 2017). Available at: http://www.learningspy. co.uk/research/teachers-think-differentiation/.

detailed knowledge in long-term memory whereas performance is about using that learning in a specific situation.[3] The two have very different purposes.

In a blog post on enhancing students' chances at succeeding at listening, Gianfranco Conti (@gianfrancocont9) raises the following issues:

Teachers do not teach listening skills, they quiz students through listening comprehensions, which are tests through and through;

They usually do not train students in the mastery of bottom-up processing skills (decoding, parsing, etc.).[4]

Rather than focusing on breaking down the skill of listening to ensure the students had mastered bottom-up processing skills, I instead played them extract after extract of a listening comprehension from a textbook. I wasn't aware that breaking down the skill would have been effective in building the students' listening skills because the practice looks different from the final skill. It's similar to using past papers to improve students' grades – it doesn't necessarily work.[5]

Maths teacher David Thomas (@dmthomas90) describes how over-focusing on exams can take the joy out of learning in the classroom. He observes that were it possible to teach assessment objectives directly then it would make sense for every piece of work to be a 'mini-GCSE exam', but this isn't possible as they are focused on generic skills, and these skills 'can only be acquired indirectly: by learning the component parts that build up to make the whole such as pieces of contextual knowledge, rules of grammar, or fluency in procedures'. Furthermore, 'these components look very different to the skill being sought – just as doing drills in football practice looks very different to playing a football match, and playing scales on a violin looks very different to giving a recital'.[6]

---

3   Daisy Christodoulou, *Making Good Progress? The Future of Assessment for Learning* (Oxford: Oxford University Press, 2016), pp. 42–43.

4   Gianfranco Conti, 'How to Enhance Your Students' Chances of Succeeding at Listening (Part 1)', *The Language Gym* [blog] (3 October 2016). Available at: https://gianfrancoconti.wordpress.com/2016/10/03/how-to-enhance-your-students-chances-of-succeeding-at-listening-part-1/. See also Steven Smith and Gianfranco Conti, *The Language Teacher Toolkit* (n.p.: CreateSpace, 2016).

5   There's a cracking Alex Quigley (@HuntingEnglish) blog post on the problem with past papers which he refers to as practising 'the big game': 'The Problem with Past Exam Papers', *The Confident Teacher* [blog] (8 April 2017). Available at: http://www.theconfidentteacher.com/2017/04/the-problem-with-past-exam-papers/.

6   David Thomas, 'How Exams Took the Joy, and the Learning, Out of Our Classrooms', *David Thomas' Blog* [blog] (29 May 2017). Available at: http://davidthomasblog.com/2017/05/how-exams-took-the-joy-and-the-learning-out-of-our-classrooms/.

The idea of being 'exam literate' might sound superficial (e.g. knowing key parts of the mark scheme or building up a store of key points from the examiner report), but in fact it is about spending time adopting some of the tenets of deliberate practice and building up mental models in each domain.

Just as adopting a deliberate practice model does not look like the final task, so exam literacy does not look like the final exam. I remember thinking that I was quite clever to come up with a homework task early on in a Year 12 Spanish course which got the students to design their own exam papers, and another time when I designed practice tasks which mirrored the exact style of the questions the students would face in their writing exam (even mimicking the dotted style of the lines on which students would write their answers!). I mistakenly thought that if they were familiar with the format of the paper then there would be no surprises in the exam.

The relative merits of different approaches has been a common topic of debate on Twitter and in the edublogosphere over the last few years. For example, there is a great chapter by Olivia Dyer (@oliviaparisdyer) on drill and didactic teaching in Katharine Birbalsingh's *Battle Hymn of the Tiger Teachers*,[7] and plenty of wonderful blog posts setting out common-sense approaches combined with aspects of cognitive science, as well as how to best plan a curriculum. A great place to start might be to have a look at any one of the Learning Scientists' blog posts.[8]

The education debate seems to have been shifting towards questioning what was once generally accepted about how best to teach in the classroom and, more pertinently for this book, learning strategies that are backed up by evidence about how students can learn more effectively. Things also seem to be moving towards not so much *how* to teach but *what* to teach.

It's tempting to think that everyone has moved on from learning styles and the like when you listen to the Twitterati, but myths masquerading as sound evidence may still be prevalent.[9] (Incidentally, Dylan Wiliam, writing on the Deans for Impact blog with reference to learning styles, says: 'it could be that the whole idea of learning-styles research is misguided because its basic assumption – that the purpose of instructional design is to make learning easy – may just be incorrect'.[10]) The idea that learning strategies which are designed to make it easier for the learner may actually be inhibiting learning, as well as the

7   Olivia Dyer, 'Drill and Didactic Teaching Work Best'. In Katharine Birbalsingh (ed.), *Battle Hymn of the Tiger Teachers: The Michaela Way* (Woodbridge: John Catt Educational, 2016), pp. 28–39.
8   See http://www.learningscientists.org/blog/.
9   See, for example, David Didau's blog, 'What Do Teachers Believe?', *The Learning Spy* [blog] (16 March 2017). Available at: http://www.learningspy.co.uk/research/what-do-teachers-believe/.
10 Dylan Wiliam, 'Learning Styles: What Does the Research Say?', *Deans for Impact* [blog] (28 April 2016). Available at: https://deansforimpact.org/learning-styles-what-does-the-research-say/.

idea that making certain conditions more demanding for learners could help their learning, feature a number of times in this book.

The first exam results that I had with a class were good, solid results: a set of meat-and-potato results that I had spent two years cooking up using a mix of trial and error, received wisdom and slavishly following the textbook (the scheme of work). Learning and performance were quite often confused using my own brand of end-of-the-lesson-pseudo-football-manager-encouragement-speak, with 'Great performance in today's lesson, guys!' featuring quite prominently.

The fact that after the exam some students came to speak to me about the paper – telling me some of the words they could remember but asking me what many other words that *I knew I had taught them* meant – forced me to question why curriculum coverage had been paramount. I *had* to finish that textbook chapter on transport before the students' study leave could begin (what happens if *gare routière* comes up on the exam?). Revision could not, and should not, take place before I had covered all of the topics in the textbook.

Tired of feeling like I hadn't done my job if the students couldn't recall or recognise words in their exams, I dared to abandon the textbook and do a little basic research on the vocabulary that had come up consistently in previous exams. Alongside teaching the topics, I started to practise and test language that I thought would be beneficial to the students, and practised and tested this content no matter what topic they were studying. (This took a simple form – projecting the list onto a whiteboard, covering up the meanings of words and phrases and then calling out the Spanish and waiting for the students to shout out the English, whole-class retrieval-style.)

When the students found that they could actually recall things in assessments and mini low stakes tests that they couldn't do before, I felt a little more emboldened. I didn't share this strategy with anyone other than the teachers in my family and, of course, the students themselves. The results for this class were excellent. The class had frighteningly high predicted grades but the final results made the local papers![11] I include this not to boast, but to demonstrate the impact of choosing to reject a dogmatic mentality about having to finish the textbook at all costs and instead ensuring the students had actually learned something.

OK, I admit that the proxy for that improvement was the exam, but what was going on in the lessons in the lead-up to the exam did not reflect the exam task. (Dare I be so bold as to claim that it was a sort of stumbled upon crude version of deliberate practice?) For example, rather than setting more and more past reading papers to try to improve the

11 See Rhiannon Hilton, Alsager School GCSE Results, *Crewe Chronicle* (31 August 2011). Available at: http://www.crewechronicle.co.uk/news/local-news/alsager-school-gcse-results-5607224.

students' reading paper marks, what became the norm was practising and testing short phrases and vocabulary (which I had identified as enabling the students to achieve a sort of semi-automaticity with their reading comprehension) at spaced intervals across the course.

The shift was based on trial and error and a questioning of accepted practice. Following the class's excellent exam results, I couldn't explain with any evidence other than the results themselves and the students' own anecdotal comments about how they could remember more language now or why what I had done had worked better to create the right conditions for them to succeed.

When I found out that there were concepts like 'spaced practice' and 'retrieval practice' (perhaps it was a sort of bias on my part to hunt them down as a way to confirm why I was doing what I was doing), I found an evidence base for what I had been doing. I just didn't know why it was working in the context of the students' improved knowledge (and improved results). I did then, and still do somewhat, bandy the terms around a fair bit, believing I have found the answer.

An army of like-minded practitioners, the researchED-ers, are also honing in on sorting the eduwheat from the pseudochaff. David Didau tweeted the last line of Dylan Wiliam's presentation slide at researchED Washington in 2016: 'All teachers & leaders need to be critical consumers of research.'[12] When I started my PGCE, even teacher-led research could take the form of discussing learning style questionnaires with students. One shudders to think. We were all passive consumers of this 'research' and what came to us from teacher training materials, never really asking for additional evidence of impact. I don't know why I didn't feel able to be more critical at the time – perhaps the fear of appearing arrogant or overly negative in front of more experienced colleagues or a consciousness of my lack of knowledge. Probably a mix of the two. I was doubtless a victim of groupthink bias.

There is always some sort of evidence to suggest that an initiative has worked, but what evidence is the right evidence? Of course, much depends on what you think the purpose of education is as to what evidence is relevant.[13] If you believe that one of the main purposes of education is to help to make learners cleverer, then having some evidence which shows how one approach might work better than another (under certain conditions) seems an eminently sensible place to start.

---

12 See https://twitter.com/LearningSpy/status/792373570634743809/photo/1. See also Dylan Wiliam, 'Why Teaching Isn't – and Probably Never Will Be – a Research-Based Profession'. Presentation at researchED Washington, Columbia Heights Education Campus, Washington, DC, 29 October 2016.

13 Sue Cowley has written an interesting blog post on this: 'What Works for What?', *Freeing the Angel* [blog] (28 February 2017). Available at: https://suecowley.wordpress.com/2017/02/28/what-works-for-what/.

Dr Gary Jones (another researchED-er) says, 'disregarding sound evidence and relying on personal experience or the popular ideas of educational gurus, consultants and bloggers is daily practice. Indeed, a major challenge for educational leaders is to distinguish between "popular" ideas and those "that work".' He goes on to name a number of ideas 'whose use is not justified by research'. One of the practices is 'Encouraging re-reading and highlighting to memorise key ideas.'[14]

This practice featured in a review of study skills by John Dunlosky and colleagues in which ten different study techniques designed to boost student learning were analysed.[15] These were elaborative interrogation, self-explanation, summarisation, highlighting/underlining, the keyword mnemonic, imagery for text, rereading, practice testing, distributed practice and interleaved practice.

Some of the above strategies are designed to support learning facts, some to improve comprehension and some to do a bit of both. The strategies identified as being most effective across a range of materials were practice testing and distributed practice.[16] Other strategies that were rated as promising but require more research were interleaved practice, elaborative interrogation and self-explanation.

Returning to Dylan Wiliam's session at researchED, as part of his presentation he included the following bullet point: 'in education, the right question is, "Under what conditions does this work?"' This, I think, would seem pretty apt for all of the techniques discussed in the Dunlosky review. Elaborative interrogation, for instance, is referred to as being more effective with factual information. You can always refer to some sort of evidence to make a point, of course, but it comes back to the question: what evidence is the right evidence?

In addition to the strategies referred to already by Jones in *Evidence-Based Practice*, the other approaches identified in the Dunlosky review as being less effective study skills were summarisation, the keyword mnemonic and imagery for text.

I didn't know about any of this during the first few years of teaching, and perhaps without Twitter I may have missed further opportunities to engage with the ideas in the review as well as the thought-provoking blogs and tweets out there.[17] For example, this helpful

---

14 Gary Jones, *Evidence-Based Practice: A Handbook for Teachers and School Leaders* (n.p.: Gary Jones and CEBMa, 2016), p. 5.

15 John Dunlosky, Katherine A. Rawson, Elizabeth J. Marsh, Mitchell J. Nathan and Daniel T. Willingham, 'Improving Students' Learning with Effective Learning Techniques: Promising Directions from Cognitive and Educational Psychology', *Psychological Science in the Public Interest*, 14(1) (2013), 4–58. Henceforth, this study will be referred to as the 'Dunlosky study' or 'Dunlosky review'.

16 I will refer to *practice testing* and *retrieval practice* interchangeably throughout the book. They both serve the same function (to be explored in more detail later): bringing information to mind.

17 EduTwitter has helped more than any course I've ever been on – try @TeacherToolkit – and Ross Morrison McGill's blog post for a good starting point: '10 Tips for Tweeting Teachers', *Teacher Toolkit*

tweet from Carl Hendrick (@C_Hendrick), head of learning and research at Wellington College, pointed me in the direction of a YouTube clip featuring Professor Dunlosky and associate professor Joe Kim: 'Every teacher should watch this: John Dunlosky – "Improving Student Success: Some Principles from Cognitive Science"'.[18]

Engaging with Research

According to Gary Davies (@gazbd), one of the reasons why teachers don't engage with research is because they 'don't feel as if engaging with research is *worth* their time'.[19] Davies goes on to say that this is a problem with the research, not a problem with the teachers. One of the causes of a lack of engagement is teachers' lack of expertise in assessing and evaluating research and in becoming researchers themselves. Davies adds: 'we cannot trust education researchers to do the right research or to think about the implications for classroom practice'.

In the comment section on the same blog, Alex Quigley suggests that there are lots of sources that can bridge the gap between the research evidence and teachers interested in developing their classroom practice through evidence-based practice. He recommends Barak Rosenshine's 'Principles of Instruction: Research-Based Strategies That All Teachers Should Know' as being 'useable and accessible'.[20]

Perhaps one of the biggest issues is that academic educational research cannot always be translated into a meaningful and teacher-friendly classroom version. I'm not a researcher and don't claim to be. I'm commenting on the research I've read from a teacher's point of view. There are enough 'perhaps', 'mights' and 'maybes' in this book to suggest that I might be hedging my bets, but the number of times they're used should convey that I'm making no wild claims that X or Y is a panacea. It's more about wanting to be research informed. Also, if all the talk about research and evidence can help to moderate the potential for bias and foster a more considered view, then perhaps that's no bad thing.[21]

(1 August 2014). Available at: https://www.teachertoolkit.co.uk/2014/08/01/10-tips-for-tweeting-teachers-by-teachertoolkit/.

18 See https://twitter.com/C_Hendrick/status/847735442350891008.

19 Gary Davies, 'Why Don't Teachers Engage with Research?', *Gary Davies* [blog] (5 June 2016). Available at: https://doctorgaz.wordpress.com/2016/06/05/why-dont-teachers-engage-with-research/.

20 See Barak Rosenshine, 'Principles of Instruction: Research-Based Strategies That All Teachers Should Know', *American Educator* (Spring 2012), 12–39. Available at: https://www.aft.org/sites/default/files/periodicals/Rosenshine.pdf.

21 I like to keep a copy of Daniel Kahneman's *Thinking, Fast and Slow* (London: Allen Lane, 2011) close at hand.

By the way, this book is intended to be a synthesis of ideas from some of the amazing writers and bloggers out there – a compendium of approaches that might help with more effective learning strategies – of course, interspersed with my own views.[22] (Any mistakes or accidental misrepresentations are mine.)

A brilliant report by Nick Rose and Susanna Eriksson-Lee from TeachFirst, entitled *Putting Evidence to Work*, made a distinction between evidence-based practice and evidence-informed practice. With regard to evidence-based practice, the example they use to define this is: 'A head teacher deciding whether to buy in a specific reading intervention package based on an EEF summary of an RCT suggesting the programme's effectiveness.' Whereas with evidence-informed practice, the example is: 'A teacher implementing spaced retrieval practice within their regular classroom teaching based on findings from cognitive science; or a teacher trying to improve the quality of feedback given to pupils based on the general guidance from the EEF toolkit.'[23]

That said, this tweet from PGCE tutor Daryn Egan-Simon is well worth bearing in mind: 'Prediction: Cognitive science will become the next educational fad to be misinterpreted & poorly implemented in schools across the country.'[24] A tweet from one of the Learning Scientists in response is also worth repeating: 'Not on our watch! @AceThatTest'.[25]

In 2015, Geoff Petty, author of *Teaching Today* and *Evidence-Based Teaching*, wrote an informative piece entitled 'The Uses and Abuses of Evidence in Education' referring, among other issues, to the types of bias to be aware of and a possible way of attaining quality assurance over the kinds of evidence that we use to benefit our own practice.[26] Petty describes how triangulating evidence between qualitative and quantitative research and the most effective teachers (in terms of a value-added measure) may be the best way to ascertain what might be most effective.

In a blog post, the writer Nick Rose (@Nick_J_Rose) analyses a number of generic study skills, including mnemonics, summarising and self-testing. Rose describes an experience in one of the schools in which he taught where an outsourced company was brought in to teach Year 11 students effective study skills. I can empathise with Rose when he says

---

22 A big thanks in particular to Andrew Old (@oldandrewuk) for all the work on the Echo Chamber, which has been like a library for me.
23 Nick Rose and Susanna Eriksson-Lee, *Putting Evidence to Work: How Can We Help New Teachers Use Research Evidence to Inform Their Teaching?* (London: TeachFirst, 2017). Available at: https://www. teachfirst.org.uk/sites/default/files/2017-10/Putting_Evidence_to_work_2017.pdf, p. 6.
24 See https://twitter.com/darynsimon/status/885203409133023232.
25 See https://twitter.com/pimpmymemory/status/885239290317373443.
26 Geoff Petty, 'The Uses and Abuses of Evidence in Education' (April 2015). Available at: http:// geoffpetty.com/wp-content/uploads/2015/04/The-uses-and-abuses-of-evidence.pdf.

that he 'wasn't particularly convinced the costly exercise improved the quality or effectiveness of revision that our students undertook after the event'.[27]

Rose argues that teaching generic mnemonic strategies, such as those used on the study skills day, independently of showing students how they could be transferred to their own subjects, is problematic. He cites a study by David Perkins and Gavriel Salomon on transfer of learning in which they state: 'In areas as diverse as chess play, physics problem solving, and medical diagnosis, expert performance has been shown to depend on a large knowledge base of rather specialized knowledge … General cross-domain principles, it has been argued, play a rather weak role'.[28] The nature of each subject that students study at school is arguably highly situated and consequently domain specific. This can make things difficult to pin down in terms of transferable learning from one domain to the next – unless each teacher in each subject domain teaches the skills to the students themselves.

Study Skills

In a vast meta-analysis on the 'Effects of Learning Skills Interventions on Student Learning' in 1996, John Hattie, John Biggs and Nola Purdie reviewed 51 studies in which interventions designed to improve student learning involving one or a number of different study skills were analysed. They evaluated various studies where interventions outside normal teaching circumstances tried to improve learning. They found that the further away from usual teaching practices these interventions were, the more difficult it was to identify any measurable results. They concluded that situated cognition (i.e. knowledge constructed within and linked to the social, cultural and physical context of an activity), apart from training for simple mnemonic recall, is recommended where activities are within the same domain as the subject being studied and promote a high degree of active learner involvement and metacognitive awareness.[29]

The lack of transfer across subject domains is seemingly a key issue. Modelling strategies with the content from the subject domain that is to be revised, with the subject expert

---

27 Nick Rose, 'Can We Teach Students Effective "Revision Skills"?', *Evidence Into Practice* [blog] (8 February 2015). Available at: https://evidenceintopractice.wordpress.com/2015/02/08/can-we-teach-students-effective-revision-skills/.

28 See David N. Perkins and Gavriel Salomon, 'Transfer of Learning' [contribution to the *International Encyclopaedia of Education*, 2nd edn (Oxford: Pergamon Press)] (1992). Available at: http://jaymctighe.com/wordpress/wp-content/uploads/2011/04/Transfer-of-Learning-Perkins-and-Salomon.pdf.

29 John Hattie, John Biggs and Nola Purdie, 'Effects of Learning Skills Interventions on Student Learning: A Meta-Analysis', *American Educational Research Association* 66(2) (1996), 99–136 at 99, 102.

teaching how students might apply the learning strategy, obviously relies on an expert's knowledge of that domain. This is in contrast to the way that costly specialist intervention companies teach revision strategies: modelling how certain techniques (e.g. memory palace technique, loci method) might work to help Year 11 students remember key details from a part-time actor's invented story about a red car travelling at 40 mph towards Birmingham on a Saturday afternoon at 3 p.m.

I share Rose's view about revision gurus and companies failing to explain to students how revision strategies actually transfer to the various subject domains that the students take at GCSE. I also agree with deputy head teacher Ruth Powley (@powley_r) when she observes that 'Revision strategies should be subject-specific'. She adds:

Evidence Into Practice suggests here that, 'the sorts of "study skills" events (which schools often outsource to external providers) are unlikely to have any positive impact on student outcomes. A better plan might be to teach teachers the various mnemonic techniques and encourage them to find examples of where the ideas might be profitably applied within their own subject domain.'[30]

Before having read lots of blogs and studies on this, I wondered if all of this was a straw man. It probably is, of course, for those schools which don't outsource their revision techniques.

Therefore, the examples provided in this book are domain-specific models (or snapshots) of the learning strategies, designed by subject teachers in the domain in which they are modelled and completed by an erstwhile GCSE student (yours truly!). The modelling of how the answers could look when using elaborative interrogation and self-explanation alongside subject content represent my interpretations of applying these techniques (trialled using my own limited domain knowledge).

Then again, perhaps it is too simplistic to talk in terms of domains as solely subjects. In a podcast led by maths teacher, *TES* maths adviser and host of the Mr Barton Maths Podcast, Craig Barton (@mrbartonmaths), with TeachFirst maths teacher and Up Learn's director of education, Kris Boulton, Boulton discusses what constitutes a domain, wondering whether maths is a domain or whether geometry is a domain within maths.[31] Having said that, it

30 Ruth Powley, 'Meaningful Manageable Revision', *Love Learning Ideas* [blog] (25 March 2015). Available at: http://www.lovelearningideas.com/blog-archive/2015/3/25/meaningful-manageable-revision. See also Rose, 'Can We Teach Students Effective "Revision Skills"?'.
31 Craig Barton, 'Kris Boulton – Part 1: Planning Lessons, Engelmann and Differentiation', *Mr Barton Maths* [podcast] (17 July 2017). Available at: http://www.mrbartonmaths.com/blog/

still makes sense that the subject teacher who has expertise in these domains (within a domain) is the one to lead on teaching the students how to apply a technique to support their learning away from the classroom.

Practice Testing and Transfer

In *What If Everything You Knew About Education Was Wrong?*, David Didau defines 'transfer' as 'applying knowledge learned in one situation to a new situation'.[32] In *What Every Teacher Needs to Know About … Psychology*, Didau and Nick Rose go on to discuss context and transfer, referring to 'far transfer': 'So-called "far transfer" between different subject domains – the idea that you could learn the skill of analysis in history and then apply it to physics – is much more difficult than is often supposed.'[33]

In terms of a study skill which might transfer across several domains' worth of content, how about a type of practice testing (aka retrieval practice) known as a free recall test or 'brain dump'. This will be discussed in more detail later, but put simply it is about reading some content, putting the content out of sight and then writing out everything you can recall from memory with no prompts. Couldn't this relatively simple technique transfer across a multitude of domain content?

In 'When and Where Do We Apply What We Learn?', Susan Barnett and Stephen Ceci present a taxonomy for far transfer.[34] Six of the factors referred to involve the context in which transfer takes place, one of which is transfer from one knowledge domain to another. The example given on the taxonomy for 'near transfer' in the knowledge domain is mouse versus rat. The 'far transfer' is science versus arts. The authors point out that physics and chemistry would most likely have more aspects in common than physics and English, and would therefore be nearer to each other in transfer terms.

So, are students who are delivered outsourced revision sessions being as well catered for in terms of the transfer of learning strategies as they would be if their teachers (i.e. domain-specific experts) were teaching them how to apply the learning strategies? It's straw man time again.

kris-boulton-part-1-planning-lessons-engelmann-and-differentiation/.

32 David Didau, *What If Everything You Knew About Education Was Wrong?* (Carmarthen: Crown House Publishing, 2015), p. 238.

33 David Didau and Nick Rose, *What Every Teacher Needs to Know About … Psychology* (Woodbridge: John Catt Educational, 2016), p. 63.

34 Susan M. Barnett and Stephen J. Ceci, 'When and Where Do We Apply What We Learn? A Taxonomy for Far Transfer', *Psychological Bulletin*, 128(4) (2002), 612–637 at 623.

Practice testing or retrieval practice has been established in the edublogosphere for a while, so readers may already know it's nothing new. However, in the context of the Dunlosky review, it is worth bringing together some of the references on practice testing and the whys and wherefores as to its gold-star rating in the authors' summary paper, 'What Works, What Doesn't'.[35]

In *What If Everything You Knew About Education Was Wrong?*, Didau discusses the benefits of the testing effect.[36] Put simply, testing students is not limited to simply getting them to sit an exam under test conditions. The process of getting them to retrieve information (testing their retrieval) benefits retention in the longer term, helping to cement that knowledge. Throw in some feedback and it's a potentially powerful practice strategy.

In *Making Good Progress*, Daisy Christodoulou describes quizzing as being a beneficial tool which allows both teacher and student to find out if they have grasped something or not. Christodoulou also refers, as does Didau, to the view that testing through recall of information strengthens memory itself and improves understanding.[37]

Alex Quigley (@HuntingEnglish) discusses practice testing in *The Confident Teacher* (acknowledging that retrieval practice doesn't sound quite as threatening as practice testing), where he compares retrieval practice with a study skill already mentioned: rereading. By getting students to do a sort of free recall test at the start of the lesson (for more on this see Chapters 3 and 4), writing out everything they can remember (retrieval practice) – versus rereading notes and copying them out – Quigley points out that it is the more effortful retrieval that leads to greater encoding in long-term memory. While retrieval without notes is harder in the first instance, the act of retrieval leads to the information being more strongly embedded in the long-term memory. It is a 'deliberate difficulty'.[38]

While the example that Quigley refers to is classroom based, clearly the same process could be applied away from the classroom for a student who is revising: reading notes one day, leaving a little time for the forgetting to kick in and then writing down everything they can remember about the topic as a free recall test. This could then be followed at a later point by looking back at the notes and identifying any misconceptions in the information they have written down during the free recall test. Finally, they can test if what has been retrieved during the free recall test transfers by completing some practice questions, testing the material retrieved during the free recall test or, perhaps even better, seeing if the

35 John Dunlosky, Katherine A. Rawson, Elizabeth J. Marsh, Mitchell J. Nathan and Daniel T. Willingham, 'What Works, What Doesn't', *Scientific American Mind*, 24(4) (2015), 46–53.
36 Didau, *What If Everything You Knew About Education Was Wrong?*, pp. 233–246.
37 Christodoulou, *Making Good Progress?*, pp. 169–170.
38 Alex Quigley, *The Confident Teacher: Developing Successful Habits of Mind, Body and Pedagogy*, Kindle edn (Abingdon: Routledge, 2016), loc. 3441.

material tested in the free recall test can be applied to another area in the same domain or even transfer it to another domain – the dream!

It could also take the form of revision homework. While we're touching on homework, it's worth mentioning a blog by Joe Kirby (@joe__kirby) which suggests some brilliant ideas for revision and self-quizzing.[39]

While retrieval practice is not a panacea, perhaps teaching students what it means and how to use it alongside domain-specific knowledge could be a positive move towards promoting a learning strategy which might transfer to students working at home or later on in life.[40] It is certainly more effective than one-, two- or three-off generic revision skills teaching provided by an outsourced company.

Generative Learning and Revision

In *Learning as a Generative Activity*, Logan Fiorella and Richard E. Mayer define generative learning as 'helping learners to actively make sense of the material so they can build meaningful learning outcomes that allow them to transfer what they have learned to solving new problems'. They go on to clarify that it is 'a process of sense making, in which you try to understand what is presented by actively selecting relevant pieces of the presented information, mentally organizing them, and integrating them with other knowledge you already have'.[41] The authors set out the stages of generative learning that learners go through, with learners initially selecting the pertinent material to deal with, arranging it into 'a coherent cognitive structure in working memory',[42] and finally integrating the material with previous knowledge from long-term memory.

The idea of helping the learner to understand the material is a key theme in *Learning as a Generative Activity*. Perhaps it is no coincidence, therefore, that elaborative interrogation is regarded as a promising revision technique by Dunlosky et al. Some of the techniques discussed in the Dunlosky review, and in *Learning as a Generative Activity*, involve elaboration and are essentially 'ways of translating the lesson into another form of representation'.[43]

39 Joe Kirby, 'A 5 Year Revision Plan', *Pragmatic Education* [blog] (3 May 2015). Available at: https://pragmaticreform.wordpress.com/2015/05/03/a-5-year-revision-plan/.

40 See the excellent blog from Greg Ashman: 'When Quizzing Fails', *Filling the Pail* [blog] (13 May 2016). Available at: https://gregashman.wordpress.com/2016/05/13/when-quizzing-fails/.

41 Logan Fiorella and Richard E. Mayer, *Learning as a Generative Activity: Eight Learning Strategies That Promote Understanding* (New York: Cambridge University Press, 2015), pp. vii, viii.

42 Fiorella and Mayer, *Learning as a Generative Activity*, p. viii.

43 Fiorella and Mayer, *Learning as a Generative Activity*, p. 2.

Asking why and encouraging students to elaborate on their answer is also mentioned as part of a whole-school revision strategy by one of the authors of *Making Every Lesson Count*, Shaun Allison (@shaun_allison), in his blog post on 'Supporting Learning Through Effective Revision Techniques':

> ... we remember things when we have to think about them. So when supporting students with revision we should be doing more of the following:
>
> ▪ Testing.
>
> ▪ Spacing it out.
>
> ▪ Keep asking 'why'?
>
> ▪ Building on what they know.
>
> ▪ Getting them to explain their steps in problem solving.[44]

The idea that there is some sort of elaboration which creates meaning to something being revised through connecting new information to existing knowledge is key. Indeed, without some form of hard mental effort the effects of retrieval practice may be diminished. Nick Rose observes that 'the testing effect disappears where there is no mental effort involved in the retrieval'.[45]

In *Cognitive Psychology*, E. Bruce Goldstein, in a section on how to study more effectively, also refers to elaboration – that is, 'thinking about what you are reading and giving it meaning by relating it to other things that you know' – as an important aspect of studying.[46]

---

44 Shaun Allison, 'Supporting Learning Through Effective Revision Techniques', *Class Teaching* [blog] (29 January 2015). Available at: https://classteaching.wordpress.com/2015/01/29/supporting-learning-through-effective-revision-techniques/.

45 Nick Rose, 'Germane Load: The Right Kind of Mental Effort?', *Evidence Into Practice* [blog] (26 January 2016). Available at: https://evidenceintopractice.wordpress.com/2016/01/26/germane-load-the-right-kind-of-mental-effort/.

46 E. Bruce Goldstein, *Cognitive Psychology: Connecting Mind, Research, and Everyday Experience* (Belmont, CA: Cengage Learning, 2010), p. 187.

Aims and Aspirations

The intention of this book is to discuss what has been shown to work more and less effectively as set out in the Dunlosky review and present how some of the more effective techniques could look. I have also included references to strategies discussed in *Learning as a Generative Activity*, as well as potential ways of elaborating on the content through modelling generative learning activities.

There is some overlap between the strategies discussed in the Dunlosky review, *Learning as a Generative Activity* and the brilliant Learning Scientists' 'Six Strategies for Effective Learning'.[47] For instance, self-explanation is discussed in the Dunlosky review and in *Learning as a Generative Activity*. Interestingly, summarisation is not recognised as such an effective technique as practice testing in the Dunlosky review, but it is included in the strategies which promote generative learning in *Learning as a Generative Activity*. As summarisation has not made the cut in the Dunlosky review as a top-mark technique, I have not included it alongside the high-to-middling impact techniques in Chapter 4.

---

47 See http://www.learningscientists.org/downloadable-materials/.

The strategies from the three crossover sources are set out in the table below.

Dunlosky et al.: 'Improving Students' Learning with Effective Learning Techniques'	The Learning Scientists: 'Six Strategies for Effective Learning'	Fiorella and Mayer: *Learning as a Generative Activity*
1. Practice testing (high rating)	1. Spacing	1. Learning by summarising
2. Distributed practice (high rating)	2. Retrieval practice	2. Learning by mapping
3. Elaborative interrogation (medium rating)	3. Elaboration	3. Learning by drawing
4. Self-explanation (medium rating)	4. Interleaving	4. Learning by imagining
5. Interleaving (medium rating)	5. Concrete examples	5. Learning by self-testing
	6. Dual coding	6. Learning by self-explaining
		7. Learning by teaching
		8. Learning by enacting

Another observation is that in the Dunlosky review, imagery for text did not meet the criteria for a top rating, but dual coding is referred to by the Learning Scientists and learning by imagining features as a technique to foster generative learning.

In fact, while we're here, one of the Learning Scientists' strategies which is not referred to explicitly in the Dunlosky review or in *Learning as a Generative Activity* is concrete examples – that is, teaching abstract examples as concrete examples. Here is a domain-specific strategy (created by Joan Fuller, head of computer science at Heart of England School in

Solihull) which helps to show how an abstract concept could be delivered by referring to a concrete example. Domain-specific examples created by domain experts; well, I couldn't have created this example myself, could I?

The Domain Name System (DNS)

The domain name system is just like a postcode.

Postcode, e.g. TR19 7AA

A postcode gives a structured label to a complicated and long building address

It also groups together several buildings which are near to each other to make it easy to find and deliver post and parcels

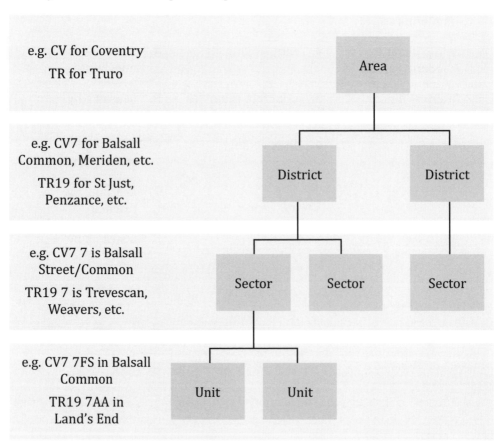

Domain name, e.g. www.landsend-landmark.org.uk

A domain name gives a structured label to a complicated IP address for a web based resource (e.g. a webpage)

It also groups together web information in a way that makes it easy to find and see a web based resource

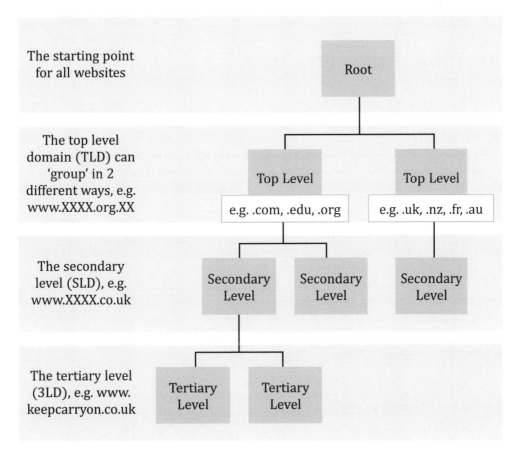

The starting point for all websites — Root

The top level domain (TLD) can 'group' in 2 different ways, e.g. www.XXXX.org.XX — Top Level (e.g. .com, .edu, .org) / Top Level (e.g. .uk, .nz, .fr, .au)

The secondary level (SLD), e.g. www.XXXX.co.uk — Secondary Level / Secondary Level / Secondary Level

The tertiary level (3LD), e.g. www. keepcarryon.co.uk — Tertiary Level / Tertiary Level

The idea here is that using the specific example of a postcode (which students should already be familiar with), and linking this to the newly encountered idea of a domain name, should help to make this more abstract concept stick better. There might be worse things one could do than go through the scheme of learning highlighting abstract examples across the course and looking at how these might be matched to a concrete example that novice learners might already know about.

Techniques like elaborative interrogation, self-explanation, practice testing and so on are modelled on short sections of content in Part 2. Of course, when using elaborative inter-rogation and self-explanation of the GCSE content, my own answers represent quite personal interpretations from someone else using the same techniques. While these have been checked by the teachers of the subjects with whom I have trialled the techniques (to avoid any erroneous or ludicrous sounding statements), they are my own answers based on my prior knowledge of the content.

Revision versus Teaching

There is an overlap in this book between techniques to use when teaching revision skills explicitly and when teaching students the strategies in relation to domain-specific exam-ples in order for them to practise using them independently away from the classroom. The sections on practice testing, interleaving and distributed practice all feature references to teaching, and not solely on how the students might use the strategies away from the classroom.

In fact, interleaving and distributed practice are only fleetingly referred to in terms of how the students might adopt them when working independently. And that could be the point. Could we scrap breakfast club intervention sessions and after-school revision ses-sions where students are mass-fed a diet of last-minute revision concepts, and instead concentrate all of our efforts on teaching using a spaced and interleaved curriculum, so the students actually forget very little throughout the course? There is, of course, an argu-ment for not bothering with revision sessions at all – backing up John Tomsett's (@ johntomsett) view that extra revision sessions are used in schools 'so staff could "cover their backsides" if results were poor'.[48] It's an interesting point.

In her blog, RE teacher and senior leader Dawn Cox (@missdcox) says that she knows of schools and teachers that are banning revision sessions with a view to integrating a spaced learning model instead: 'I know that there are teachers/schools that are working on a spaced learning model and those that ban all "revision" sessions out of lesson time but reading this has reminded me of how effective it might be to choose option 3'.[49] Option 3 is planning the content through spaced learning.

48 John Tomsett quoted in Billy Camden, 'Headteacher Scraps "Mad" Year 11 Revision Classes to Protect Pupil Mental Health', *SchoolsWeek* (4 March 2016). Available at: http://schoolsweek.co.uk/head teacher-scraps-mad-year-11-revision-classes-to-protect-pupil-mental-health/.

49 Dawn Cox, 'Ditch Revision. Teach It Well', *missdcoxblog* [blog] (9 January 2016). See https://missdcoxblog.wordpress.com/2016/01/09/ditch-revision-teach-it-well/.

Head of geography Mark Enser (@EnserMark) wrote a brilliant piece for the *TES* on out-of-hours revision sessions.[50] In the article, Enser refers to the shared resource that is student grades and how competition can lead to an additional workload burden on top of the already onerous demands on the profession. In my view, the problem seems to be that intervention has become a catch-all for extra revision classes and not a judicious and well-planned feature which involves something more considered than 'intervention sessions' for all Year 11 students a few weeks after they have started the year, which are really just additional lessons. Reducing period 6 lessons might be a more sane and supportive way to help support teachers' well-being. Of course, this may all be unachievable because of the nature of the 'accountability stick'.[51]

So, perhaps a hybrid model where spaced and interleaved curriculums – which have in-built revisiting and recapping techniques, like spaced retrieval practice alongside the teaching of domain-specific revision techniques, which could be applied by students when they are away from the classroom – might be the model to adopt. This is very different from how I used to think of revision as a newly qualified and recently qualified teacher – in other words, cramming in after-school revision classes and finishing up the course as quickly as possible in order to do extra revision sessions towards the end.

ResearchED legend Hélène Galdin-O'Shea tweeted this in response to Dawn Cox's session at Teaching and Learning Takeover 2016: 'LET'S DITCH THE WORD REVISING AND LET'S CALL IT LEARNING AND REVISITING FROM THE START.'[52] Two responses to her tweet sum up the problem with the term 'revision' very well: 'It's long been known in Higher Education that "revision" is a euphemism for learning'[53] and 'Studying this for Masters revision is the study of information learned before …'[54]

Even if revision is something which should be part of the curriculum, and not tagged on hurriedly and frantically in a race to fulfil the dictates of a textbook or scheme of work, there are still learning strategies which research and cognitive science principles suggest might be more effective than others and could be used by students away from the classroom. While ensuring that the curriculum encompasses spacing, interleaving, practice testing and so on (with the goal of avoiding the need to include revision sessions following the first GCSE lesson with a group) is important, it is perhaps just as important that the

---

50 Mark Enser, 'Schools Must Say "No" to Out-of-Hours Revision Sessions, for the Collective Good of the Profession', *TES* (10 December 2017). Available at: https://www.tes.com/news/school-news/breaking-views/schools-must-say-no-out-hours-revision-sessions-collective-good.

51 Tom Sherrington, 'Accountability "Stick" Is Taking Us to the Brink: Time for Radical Change', *teacherhead* [blog] (13 December 2017). Available at: https://teacherhead.com/2017/12/13/accountability-stick-is-taking-us-to-the-brink-time-for-radical-change/.

52 See https://twitter.com/hgaldinoshea/status/787252216897863680.

53 See https://twitter.com/ded6ajd/status/787316452885954560.

54 See https://twitter.com/tessmaths/status/787317642717724677.

students know how to use these learning strategies when working independently. So, for the purposes of this book, whenever the term 'revision' is mentioned it will refer to students adopting learning strategies to use independently.

Exams and Testing

An exam paper represents a sample of the subject domain. It doesn't, and can't, measure everything that has been taught and learned. Stephen Tierney (@LeadingLearner) suggests that the issue is not with testing and tests but with the high stakes accountability associated with the testing. In other words, the problem is the drive to be better than last year's set of results: 'The tests have become the proxy measures by which your worth as a school, through league tables and inspections, is judged; similarly for the teacher. Leaders under pressure end up doing daft things.'[55] However, the fear of the consequences of a set of poor exam results is an unfortunate, if powerful, motivator, and perhaps relates back to John Tomsett's remark about staff covering their backsides.

Daisy Christodoulou has written about this with reference to Daniel Koretz's book *Measuring Up*.[56] She sets out Koretz's list of reactions to the high stakes test, the potential impact it can have on students and how the perception of memorisation can be altered:

1. Working more effectively 2. Teaching more 3. Working harder 4. Reallocation 5. Alignment 6. Coaching 7. Cheating.

Koretz says that 1–3 result in genuine gains, 7 always results in false gains and 4–6 can result in either genuine or false gains depending on how they are used. Reallocating time generates false gains if you are taking time away from things that are also an important part of the domain. Alignment is when you match the teaching to the test syllabus. 'Coaching refers to focussing instruction on small details of the test, many of which have no substantive meaning.'

I think all three of these tactics are used in the most damaging ways in English schools. When it comes to coaching, I have often noticed how pupils who cannot

55 Stephen Tierney, 'It's the High Stakes Accountability Not the Testing', *@LeadingLearner* [blog] (3 May 2016). Available at: https://leadinglearner.me/2016/05/03/reduce-high-stakes-accountability-not-testing/.

56 Daisy Christodoulou, 'Why Teaching to the Test is So Bad', *The Wing to Heaven* [blog] (19 January 2014). Available at: https://thewingtoheaven.wordpress.com/2014/01/19/why-teaching-to-the-test-is-so-bad/. See also Daniel Koretz, *Measuring Up: What Educational Testing Really Tells Us* (Cambridge, MA: Harvard University Press, 2009).

tell you one date from history are able to tell you the number of marks available for each question on a history exam paper. This is perhaps one reason why memorisation gets such a bad name. Memorisation of the right things – for example, times tables and verb tales – is extraordinarily valuable, but memorisation of the wrong things – for example, marks to minute ratios and exam cheats and hints – is clearly not.[57]

I think this helpfully illustrates how easy it can be to skew the focus towards the short-term performance goal. Focusing too much on the component parts of the exam at the expense of the knowledge across the course is the issue. Finding a balance between exam preparation and practice testing of knowledge seems to be the ideal.

In *Leverage Leadership*, in a passage dedicated to his thoughts on 'teaching to the test', Paul Bambrick-Santoyo writes:

One frequent objection to data-driven instruction is that a focus on assessment amounts to empty 'teaching to the test'. From this point of view, data force teachers to choose between 'real' teaching and irrelevant test preparation. If the assessments a school uses are not rigorous enough, or if they are not aligned to what students need to know, then this is a valid critique. However, when interim assessments are well constructed and college ready, they are *an unparalleled resource* in driving student learning ... data-driven instruction is not about teaching to the test: it is about testing the teaching.[58]

Perhaps it is more about testing the learning, with the emphasis on testing the teaching coming via the high stakes accountability. Tom Bennett remarks, 'I'm against PRP [performance-related pay] and tables etc. But tests? Come on. Tests are an important way we check learning.'[59] Martin Robinson describes a possible way of reducing the fear factor surrounding tests, 'How to not panic so much? Well, maybe more testing, low stakes, as part of regular teaching and learning could help.'[60]

57 Christodoulou, 'Why Teaching to the Test is So Bad'.
58 Paul Bambrick-Santoyo, *Leverage Leadership: A Practical Guide to Building Exceptional Schools* (San Francisco, CA: Jossey-Bass, 2012), p. 34.
59 See https://twitter.com/tombennett71/status/727051321841455105.
60 Martin Robinson, 'Don't Panic About Tests', *Trivium21c* [blog] (17 May 2016). Available at: https://martinrobborobinson.wordpress.com/2016/05/17/dont-panic-about-tests/.

For what it's worth, my own view on language exams is this: I teach my students to understand how to use languages and aim to foster engagement in learning languages through promoting interest in what they're learning about. I want my students to be cleverer at learning languages. However, I also recognise that there has to be a measurement of both my teaching and the students' learning, so my assessment method in the lead-up to the students' final exam is based on conducting some assessments which reflect the nature of the final exam. I have found that this has helped to promote students' self-efficacy – their sense that they can actually do well in languages.

However, I try not to sacrifice their learning and narrow the curriculum to only focus on what is externally assessed, and I adopt spaced retrieval practice of language that would transfer across topics so the students are exposed to techniques which should help them to retain language that they can use no matter what topic is being assessed. How's that for sitting on the fence? Maybe it is a consequence of teaching a subject which seems to struggle to recruit for numbers,[61] or maybe it is a by-product, but both the students and I sometimes conflate success in languages with being able to get good results.

Perhaps effective learning strategies like retrieval practice can help to reduce the stakes ahead of exams. As Martin Robinson says, low stakes testing in class as part of teaching and learning could be a way of reducing test anxiety (as could low stakes testing as part of a student's revision plan away from the classroom), as well as being a more effective learning strategy as part of a spaced and interleaved curriculum.

In the next chapter, we will focus on the learning strategies designed to prepare students for high stakes testing – the domain-specific techniques and aspects of curriculum design which may help to avoid after-school revision sessions after the first lesson in Year 10.

---

61 See Katherine Sellgren, 'Harsh Marks "Put Pupils Off Languages"', *BBC News* (18 April 2016). Available at: http://www.bbc.co.uk/news/education-36027905.

Chapter 2
Memory and Forgetting

When I was an NQT teaching my first GCSE French group, I made it a mission to make as many PowerPoints as possible. It almost became a hobby to make as many wonderfully designed, colourful and engaging PowerPoints with French, German and Spanish words and phrases bouncing in and out and off-screen, and sometimes back on screen. This filled up a lot of summer holidays.

My time was directed towards building many decorative resources and ensuring that I completed the course. The textbook *was* the course. It became a familiar pathway: I must make sure that I have covered all of the language from the textbook by at least April. My colleagues and I agreed. We just had to finish the course. Then we had done our job.

'Phew!' I would say just before the Easter holidays, with the students' books full of language they had noted down throughout the past few months in the order that the textbook dictated. I watched as students turned the final few pages of their textbooks and on to that last topic of the tourist office and lost property. All I needed to do was to set a textbook reading and writing task on this topic, and then I could tick off the curriculum coverage.

Following the reading and listening exams for this group, some of the students came to find me. They said they had found them hard. I couldn't resist retrieving from my pigeon hole the paper they had just toiled over to go through some of the answers with them. I picked out words that I knew that I had taught them either earlier in the year or in Year 10.

'Sir, what does *gare routière* mean?' was a question that a number of them asked me. This was incomprehensible to me. I could remember teaching them the word: 'Don't you remember? It's bus station. We did that in Year 10.' There were a number of other items of vocabulary or other areas of the language which came up on the paper which I knew they had been taught but that the students had not retained. I could remember the students writing the word down and understanding the meaning of the word in the lesson. This didn't make much sense to me.

It was a while later when it began to dawn on me that the students were forgetting things and not retaining everything that I wanted them to learn. They *appeared* to be learning what I was teaching them in the lesson but then forgetting a fair amount of this when they were faced with an exam.

When training to be a teacher I had learned nothing about the Ebbinghaus forgetting curve, for instance, nor anything about memory itself (let alone the goal-free effect in cognitive load) and the implications of all of this for the classroom.[1] While it may be familiar to many readers, it might still be worth a little forage into the forgetting curve and the work of Ebbinghaus as a starting point for looking at cognitive load theory and the implications of overloading working memory.

Hermann Ebbinghaus was a German psychologist who is generally recognised as being the first to carry out experiments into remembering and forgetting. In 1885, he published *Über das Gedächtnis: Untersuchungen zur experimentellen Psychologie*, which was translated into English as *Memory: A Contribution to Experimental Psychology*.

One of Ebbinghaus's key findings was the forgetting curve which illustrates how memory declines over time. He measured how, unless regular revisiting of the content that we want to learn takes place, we forget what we have learned very quickly.

Ebbinghaus forgetting curve

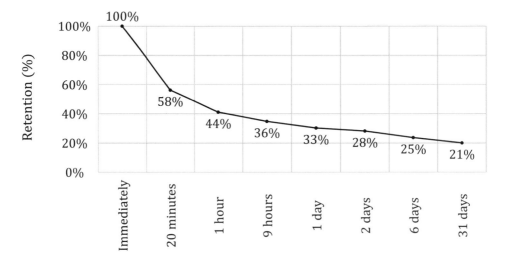

If only 20% or so of the material from each topic that I was teaching was retained by my students without revisiting it, but their performance in individual lessons looked good (with me proving that the students could recall and apply the knowledge I had imparted throughout the lesson towards the end of the lesson), then I could say that I was doing my

---

1   For more on this see the chapter on working memory in Didau and Rose, *What Every Teacher Needs to Know About … Psychology*, pp. 34–42.

job in the here-and-now (i.e. in the classroom) but not over time to ensure the knowledge was retained for the there-and-then (i.e. in the exam).

Clearly, it would be wrong to assume that nearly 80% of all material initially learned is forgotten after 31 days. The implications of a sweeping generalisation like that depend on many different factors.[2] In the words of David Didau: 'what we need to accept is that forgetting is endemic and predictable – everyone forgets at broadly similar rates over time'.[3] But as a general guide to how forgetting impacts on revision and learning, I think it is pretty significant. (I should add that this section does not attempt to be a psychology textbook. It represents my reflections on what I didn't know about memory and learning when I started teaching.[4])

There is a caveat to Ebbinghaus's work: Benedict Carey points out that Ebbinghaus used short groups of letters that were nonsense syllables, and thus were not connected to anything else, which might explain why they were quickly forgotten.[5] However, even if his work was not based on particularly meaningful content, I think that it still sparks an interesting discussion on the phenomenon of forgetting.

Kris Boulton has alluded to a 'mudslinging curriculum'.[6] In other words, there is so much content to get through across the curriculum that it is taught in a shallow way, moving rapidly from one topic to the next, meaning that much of what is taught has been forgotten by the following year. Boulton likens it to slinging mud at a wall and hoping that some of it sticks.

Finding out about the forgetting curve was a revelation (along with just how often we need to revisit something in order for it to stick[7]), as was discovering ways to make what you wanted the students to know stick for longer.

---

2   See, for example, Jo Cook, 'Is It About Time We Forget Ebbinghaus?', *HRZone* (30 September 2014). Available at: http://www.hrzone.com/talent/development/is-it-about-time-we-forget-ebbinghaus.
3   See Didau, *What If Everything You Knew About Education Was Wrong?*, pp. 190–191.
4   For some more in-depth information on learning and memory see www.lastinglearning.com. In a very interesting blog post, Sue Gerrard (@suzyg001) responds to a request for more information on long-term memory limitations by suggesting Alan Baddeley, Michael Eysenck and Michael Anderson's *Memory* (Hove and New York: Psychology Press, 2009). See also Sue Gerrard, 'Cognitive Science: The Wrong End of the Stick', *logicalincrementalism* [blog] (25 October 2017). Available at: https://logicalincrementalism.wordpress.com/2017/10/25/cognitive-science-the-wrong-end-of-the-stick/.
5   Benedict Carey, *How We Learn: The Surprising Truth About When, Where and Why It Happens*, Kindle edn (London: Macmillan, 2014), loc. 532–541.
6   Barton, 'Kris Boulton – Part 1'.
7   For more information on this see Graham Nuthall's *The Hidden Lives of Learners* (Wellington: New Zealand Council for Educational Research Press, 2007).

Ebbinghaus's research also includes the notion of spacing out repetition of the material to ensure that it is retained for longer. Each time to-be-learned material is revisited by retrieving it from memory, the knowledge of the material is brought back up to 100%, with the recollection of that material being strengthened such that the forgetting of the material is slowed.

In *Make It Stick*, Peter Brown, Henry Roediger and Mark McDaniel state that 'we know from empirical research that practicing retrieval makes learning stick far better than reexposure to the original material does. This is the testing effect, also known as the retrieval-practice effect.'[8] In *Small Teaching*, James Lang emphasises that in order to retrieve knowledge you have to practise the retrieval of that knowledge.[9]

All of this had significant implications on how I prepared my students for their exams and, of course, beyond. As an NQT, I had been teaching a topic according to the textbook, then moving on to the next topic in the textbook, then the next and so on, until the students sat their exams. However, this blocked practice method of teaching was not preparing the students for their exams (let alone beyond) as effectively as it could. I was sufficiently convinced to change my practice to ensure that I would revisit (i.e. space out), practise and test the material that I wanted them to learn, and that I would be revisiting this material, practising it and testing it with the students no matter what topic we were covering. At the time, this was all based on a hunch and had nothing to do with any awareness of the research.

So, I was now teaching a topic but also including essential long-term memory retrieval practice of the material that I wanted the students to learn, which led to their memory of the course content being strengthened. By combining a frequency analysis of the language that regularly appeared in questions on past papers, I found the time to teach *and* test the students on this language, no matter what topic I was teaching.

At first this was led by previous exam papers (and has since changed to include less exam-specific language and a broader range of content and a focus on developing listening skills). My thoughts at the time went as follows:

1. Analyse all of the exam papers and look for common language that comes up again and again as essential knowledge in order to answer the question correctly, as well as any language which will aid understanding of how to answer the question.

---

8   Peter C. Brown, Henry L. Roediger and Mark A. McDaniel, *Make It Stick: The Science of Successful Learning*, Kindle edn (Cambridge, MA: Harvard University Press, 2014), loc. 456.

9   James M. Lang, *Small Teaching: Everyday Lessons from the Science of Learning*, Kindle edn (San Francisco, CA: Jossey-Bass, 2016), loc. 523.

2. Put this language onto several presentation slides. (PowerPoint was just a means to present the stuff I wanted the students to know, so out went the overly detailed and decorative PowerPoints. It could just as well have been a sheet of paper with a list of language that I put under a visualiser or perhaps a customised textbook.)

3. Design ways of practising this language knowledge with the students which encouraged them to think about the meaning of the material.

4. Find the time to practise and test this language knowledge (which was unconnected to the topic I was teaching). Giving up on the prescribed order of starter, main and plenary format was somewhat scary initially.

5. Employ retrieval practice (testing the students' recall) of the key exam language, no matter what topic I was teaching.

I didn't know why I was doing this. I just started questioning why I had to be a slave to how the textbook had presented the material (and consequently the scheme of work) and to teach it in this imposed, arbitrary order.

I found that, after a while, the students' marks were markedly better than the previous year's had been when they started completing past papers, homework and also with tasks in class (where I no longer felt the need to start again with reference to language structures that I knew I had taught earlier in the year). They were also more proficient at comprehending the language and there were fewer instances of them looking up word after word in the dictionary when reading target language texts.

I have now started to shift from my initial emphasis on past paper structures. For example, in a recent Key Stage 3 curriculum model in my current school our goal has been mastery of a domain, and an exam is a perfectly valid way to measure how far our students have achieved this mastery.[10]

In the edublogosphere, discussions on memory and cognitive science abound. There's an excellent blog post by Joe Kirby on scientific curriculum design. He not only discusses quizzing (testing) as a means to learning, but also how the research shows that spacing and quizzing of previous content can be effective on student learning.[11] There's more on the testing effect to help with revision and making it stick in Chapter 4.

---

10 Daisy Christodoulou touches on this in *Making Good Progress?*, p. 145.
11 Joe Kirby, 'Why Don't Students Remember What They've Learned?', *Pragmatic Education* [blog] (16 November 2013). Available at: https://pragmaticreform.wordpress.com/2013/11/16/memory/.

Retrieval Space versus Storage Space

In *What If Everything You Knew About Education Was Wrong?*, David Didau says that 'everything we've ever encountered has a retrieval strength (how easily we can recall that thing right now) and a storage strength (how well we know something …). Retrieval strength correlates with our ability to recall information when we want it, and storage strength is simply how deeply embedded individual items are in schemas.'[12]

The distinguished professor of psychology at the University of California, Robert Bjork, illustrates the difference between retrieval strength (RS) and storage strength (SS) with the example of trying to remember the address of a person you wish to visit. Going over and over the address will give it high RS for immediate use but it is unlikely to have high SS because you will not use it again, and RS decreases over time.

I think all of this is important for a number of reasons. One of the main reasons is that it shows the ludicrousness of the whole idea of trying to ascertain any measurement of progress by getting learners to recall stuff in the same lesson, immediately after knowledge and skills have been imparted, when retrieval strength is still high.

So, time for some anecdotal evidence to illustrate how to 'play the system' of demonstrating progress in lessons through harnessing the effects of high retrieval strength. I spoke to an MFL teacher a few years ago who felt under the cosh in their school because they weren't deemed to be showing enough progress in the all-important 20-minute 'progress window' (thankfully the profession seems to have moved on somewhat). Recently, the teacher had been receiving 'requires improvement' for their lessons, despite having been there for some time and previously receiving 'good' and 'outstanding' ratings.

I suggested an approach to demonstrate progress to the lesson observer:

1. Choose which vocabulary you want to show that the students have made progress in (e.g. the words for school subjects).

2. Set up your success criteria at the start of the lesson (e.g. 'To be able to recognise the meaning of at least eight to ten words in French for school subjects').

3. On a PowerPoint slide, cover up the meanings of the vocabulary. Ask the students how many words they know the meaning of at this point in the lesson. Make sure they note this down and show you (and the observer).

---

12 Didau, *What If Everything You Knew About Education Was Wrong?*, p. 191.

4. Uncover the meanings and teach the language, making sure the students are engaged (mainly centred on behavioural engagement to the detriment of the psychological engagement which might take place during generative learning strategies, for instance).

5. Cover up the meanings on the PowerPoint slide again.

6. Ask the students to write down as many meanings as possible and then uncover them so they can mark their work.

7. Get the students to show you how many words they now know the meaning of and compare this with how many they could recognise before. (Make sure the observer is well aware of the progress that has been made during the lesson.)

There you have it: rapid and sustained progress in the eyes of the observer. And it worked too – depending on how you define 'worked'.

The teacher told me that the observer was impressed with how much progress the students had made and things became a little easier for the teacher concerned. I knew then that things had got a bit ridiculous; I just didn't know why they were a bit ridiculous. I had no evidence to counter someone's skew that this sort of 'progress' had to be seen in lessons.

I had been doing a similar thing in my own lessons as well – for example, setting objectives based on proving what students could recall in that lesson. The idea that we can assign some level of micro-measurement of learning right there and then takes control culture to a level that would be funny if livelihoods didn't depend on having to show that progress had been made and satisfy the box-ticker. Manufactured accountability in order to be compliant towards the bias of others is the antithesis of trust. Of course there has to be professional accountability, but the idea of 'intelligent accountability' seemed far away.[13]

In the excellent *Mark. Plan. Teach.*, Ross Morrison McGill refers to Lucy Crehan's (@lucy_crehan) insightful book *Cleverlands*, in which she notes that schools and the systems in them have the capability to change cultures.[14] This is just one source which makes me think that the days of the pernicious accountability culture may be numbered.

As I understand it now, it was all about setting the right success criteria for retrieval. Great, we could prove that students were able to retrieve language that had been imparted

---

13 See David Didau, 'Intelligent Accountability', *The Learning Spy* [blog] (4 October 2015). Available at: http://www.learningspy.co.uk/featured/intelligent-accountability/.

14 Ross Morrison McGill, *Mark. Plan. Teach.: Save Time. Reduce Workload. Impact Learning.*, Kindle edn (London: Bloomsbury Education, 2017), loc. 169; Lucy Crehan, *Cleverlands: The Secrets Behind the Success of the World's Education Superpowers* (London: Unbound, 2016).

during a lesson, even though the superficial coverage wasn't deep enough to actually embed it. But it was enough to see off an observer and keep your nose clean, so that's all right then.

This also ties in to planning. In a podcast with Craig Barton, Kris Boulton asserts that the lesson itself is an incorrect unit of time around which to plan. In other words, the longer the amount of time over which teaching can take place, the more successful it will be. He suggests that if we are thinking about planning individual lessons then we are probably only operating at about 5% of our potential.[15]

The reason I'm focusing on this apparent need to show that students can recall something at the end of the lesson is not only to show how silly it is, but also to illustrate what a poor indicator of learning current retrieval strength is; it is, in fact, an indicator of current performance.

What students could recall in those lessons showed simply that: what they could recall in the lesson. It didn't tell us whether what they were doing in the lesson was going to be adapted and transferred to an exam in a few months' time, let alone to other situations or domains after the exam. The emphasis should be on ensuring that students' storage of key material is secure, and that they can retrieve this with ease when they need to beyond the here-and-now. Nowadays, even this may seem like a straw man.

In terms of effective revision, if students can retrieve something easily – that is, if they have high retrieval strength of something they've just revised – then revising it again straight away and massing it is going to feel easy. Perhaps that's why rereading, or at least massed rereading, can elicit the illusion of fluency: the students easily retrieve information from something they've just reread and therefore feel that the revisiting is working.

If the retrieval strength lowers, then revisiting will become harder and impact more greatly on storage strength. In other words, allowing time to forget during revisiting or revision lowers the retrieval strength, but following the forgetting the storage strength increases again upon revisiting.[16]

William Emeny (@Maths_Master), author of *The Magic of Pineapples: A Brain Tingling Adventure Through Amazing Mathematics* and *100 Things Awesome Teachers Do*, spent a week at the Bjork Learning and Forgetting Lab in Los Angeles and wrote an informative summary of his findings. He comments on the positive gains for retrieval strength and storage strength each time something is retrieved from memory:

15 Barton, 'Kris Boulton – Part 1'.
16 See a guest post from Dr Veronica Yan (@EdScientists), a professor at the University of Texas at Austin, on 'Retrieval Strength vs. Storage Strength', *The Learning Scientists* [blog] (8 May 2016). Available at: http://www.learningscientists.org/blog/2016/5/10-1.

You need to retrieve learning a number of times with a spacing gap to build storage strength.

Gains in storage strength (depth of understanding) are much greater if done so after you have had time to forget your previous learning (i.e. done from low retrieval strength). Conversely, if you try to get gains in conceptual understanding by retrieving something from the point when it is already 'automatic', the gains are minimal; you do it 'without thinking' and because you don't think, you don't link it to other things in your memory. As Bjork puts it, 'teachers need to realise forgetting is the friend of learning'.

The implication of these ideas (which have been verified experimentally) is that if you want 'deep learning' (high storage strength), you need to build it over time through revisiting topics a number of times when you find them difficult, but not impossible, to retrieve from your memory. Put bluntly, sustained learning is not a rapid gain, but instead requires a number of revisits over time. Mid-term planning to revisit concepts a number of times is essential if you want your students' learning to be sustained. Telling them once and expecting them to remember it is futile.[17]

Retrieval Strength, Desirable Difficulties and Cues

In summarising Daniel Willingham's paper, 'What Will Improve A Student's Memory?', Durrington High School's *Research Bulletin* suggests that 'we rarely recall information from memory directly; instead, we rely on cues'. The article adds that 'it is not time or decay that leads to the inability to retrieve something from memory; in fact, the cause is usually the poor quality of the cues we have at our disposal'.[18] It goes on to describe the need to help our students to form distinctive memories.

17 William Emeny, 'A Week Working at UCLA in the Bjork Learning and Forgetting Lab', *Great Maths Teaching Ideas* [blog] (26 August 2016). Available at: http://www.greatmathsteachingideas. com/2016/08/26/a-week-working-at-ucla-in-the-bjork-learning-and-forgetting-lab/.
18 Durrington High School, 'What Will Improve a Students' Meomory [sic]?', *Research Bulletin*, Issue 8, Spring 2 (2016). Available at: https://twitter.com/atharby/status/699211606102839296. See also Daniel Willingham, 'Ask the Cognitive Scientist: What Will Improve a Student's Memory?', *American Educator*, 32(4) (2008), 17–44. Available at: https://www.aft.org/sites/default/files/periodicals/ willingham_0.pdf.

Developing an array of cues to help students to retrieve key content is a powerful learning strategy. Daniel Willingham's notion of memory as the 'residue of thought' is just as applicable for students planning their revision as for a teacher planning their revisiting.[19] (We will return to this aspect of making memories distinctive in Chapter 3.)

Robert Bjork coined the term 'desirable difficulties', which has received a fair bit of airtime among the Twitterati. It features prominently in Nicholas Soderstrom's *Study Smart*,[20] and is referred to a number of times in David Didau's *What If Everything You Knew About Education Was Wrong?*, where he observes:

Bafflingly, if we want to improve learning we might have to reduce performance by introducing what Professor Robert Bjork calls 'desirable difficulties'. It turns out that making it more difficult for students to learn means that they actually learn more! Maybe increasing difficulty during the process of encoding might have a positive impact on our ability to retrieve information.[21]

Didau goes on to explain what some of these desirable difficulties might be and a number of them also feature in the Dunlosky review, *Learning as a Generative Activity* and the Learning Scientists' six strategies – for example, interleaving, practice testing and spacing material out. There's a pattern emerging here: if it's too easy then you're doing it wrong!

The idea of retrieval, and the ease with which a learner can retrieve what they need in order to do well in an exam, might be a good place to start with a revision strategy for students away from the classroom – that is, making the key points of each subject more recallable when in the exam.

Robert and Elizabeth Bjork describe another element of desirable difficulties which relates directly to exam revision and might grate with anyone who has ever recommended using the same nice, quiet room for revision. They cite a 1978 study by Steven Smith, Arthur Glenberg and Robert Bjork in which it was found that changing the venue for revision actually led to greater retention of the material.[22]

---

19 Willingham, 'What Will Improve a Student's Memory?', p. 18.
20 Nicholas C. Soderstrom, *Study Smart: 10 Ways to Master the SAT/ACT Using the Science of Learning* (n.p.: Lasting Learning Press, 2016).
21 Didau, *What If Everything You Knew About Education Was Wrong?*, p. 216.
22 Elizabeth L. Bjork and Robert Bjork, 'Making Things Hard on Yourself, But in a Good Way: Creating Desirable Difficulties to Enhance Learning'. In Morton A. Gernsbacher and James Pomerantz (eds), *Psychology and the Real World: Essays Illustrating Fundamental Contributions to Society* (New York: Worth, 2009), pp. 59–68. Available at: https://bjorklab.psych.ucla.edu/wp-content/uploads/sites/13/2016/04/EBjork_RBjork_2011.pdf. See also Steven Smith, Arthur Glenberg and Robert Bjork,

Working Memory and Cognitive Load

The Working Memory Model

I am grateful to psychology teacher Grace Theay, who has written a short piece about the working memory model:

The working memory model was put forward by Alan Baddeley and Graham Hitch who said that short-term memory is an active processor which contains several different components. These components work together to allow us to work on a task that requires storing information as we go along. This could be applicable to maths, for example, when you have to work on a sum. Let's say the sum is (50 + 25) x 3. First you would work out the 50 + 25, hold 75 in your working memory and then do the final part of the sum. The model itself can appear quite daunting and complex to a non-memory specialist (and my A level psychology students when they see it for the first time!) but I will try to break it down as simply as I can.

The model looks like this:

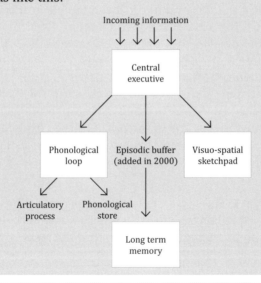

'Environmental Context and Human Memory', *Memory & Cognition*, 6 (1978), 342–353. There is a very useful passage on this in a section on 'The variation effect' in Didau and Rose, *What Every Teacher Needs to Know About … Psychology*, p. 65.

Information comes first to the central executive. When I am describing this to my students I liken it to the CEO of a company. The information comes in and the central executive is the part of the working memory model (WMM) that pays it attention. The central executive has very limited capacity (so it can't handle being bombarded with information) and is not able to store any information. Therefore it needs to pass it to one of the other components or 'slave systems'. Again, when I am teaching this I liken the slave systems to departments in the CEO's company that he passes the work along to once it has been 'processed'.

The slave systems are made up of the phonological loop and the visuo-spatial sketchpad. These also have a very limited capacity. The phonological loop deals with auditory information (e.g. the voice of a teacher). This is further divided into the phonological store which holds any words you hear (like an inner ear) and the articulatory process which is used for rehearsing words you hear or see (like an inner voice). The other slave system is the visuo-spatial sketchpad. This stores visual and spatial information and is used when you are planning a spatial task (like how to draw a shape or navigate around a route). Again, this storage is only temporary.

The slave systems are able to 'dual task', meaning you can work on a visual and auditory task at the same time (e.g. listen to a piece of music by Debussy and draw a shape). The slave systems can do this effectively as they are not being overloaded. However, they are less effective at dual tasking when the task requires more than one visual or acoustic task. An example of this would be a very word-heavy PowerPoint that you want students to read, while at the same time you are talking to them. In this instance, students have far too much trying to be processed in their phonological loop and they will end up only processing one of them. This would explain why when you are getting your students to copy from the board and listen to you speak, they have trouble with it and usually block out the sound of your voice altogether!

In 2000, the model was revised slightly to incorporate the episodic buffer. This was added as Baddeley realised that there was nowhere acknowledged in the previous model that allowed us to store the visual and acoustic elements that we need when we are working on a task. The episodic buffer therefore stores information for a very brief period, integrates it and also sends it to the long-term memory.

This model is tricky and can seem fairly complex; however, understanding working memory will really help your students to learn more effectively. It's worth reading more about as you really will see the benefits in your lessons. Good luck!

Didau says the following with regard to working memory:

Working memory is synonymous with awareness. The act of paying attention, of reading these words or listening to a colleague complain about their class' lack of homework, fills up our working memory ...

In the 1950s, George Miller defined the limits of short-term memory as 7 + 2 items. This means that most of us can retain a seven digit telephone number without too much effort but anything longer is problematic.[23]

In a session on dual coding at researchED Cheshire in 2017, former head teacher and designer of the brilliant HOW2s (visuals of teaching approaches, including the set of six cognitive science strategies for effective learning referred to by the Learning Scientists), Oliver Caviglioli (@olivercavigliol), suggests that George Miller's 'magical' number seven has actually proved to be lower following more recent research.[24] He notes:

In later years, Miller admitted to the title being a joke. After all what is the word 'magic' doing in a scientific paper? And if scientific, why so imprecise (plus or minus two)? Nonetheless, this figure has been taken as true for decades. Today, you'll still find people quoting the number, ignorant of its origin, yet proclaiming it as a certainty.

More recently – well, over 16 years ago now – Cowan and colleagues have discovered the limits of our working memory to be nearer four. As a tip-of-the-hat tribute to Miller, you'll notice the repetition of the in-joke of using the term 'magic' once more.[25]

23 Didau, *What If Everything You Knew About Education Was Wrong?*, p. 184.
24 George Miller, 'The Magical Number Seven, Plus or Minus Two: Some Limits on Our Capacity for Processing Information', *Psychological Review*, 63(2) (1956), 81–97.
25 Oliver Caviglioli, 'My researchED Cheshire Presentation', *HOW2* (19 March 2017). Available at: http://linkis.com/teachinghow2s.com/bl/BfbYM.

Caviglioli also refers to *The Unified Learning Model*, in which working memory forms pretty much the entire subject – the book's premise is that without working memory there will be no learning.[26] In *The Unified Learning Model*, Shell et al. relate working memory to motivation; I will return to this later.

In *What Every Teacher Needs to Know About … Psychology*, Didau and Rose describe the various sub-components of working memory. As we have already seen, two of these components are the phonological loop and the visuo-spatial sketchpad. The phonological loop processes auditory information and the visuo-spatial sketchpad processes visual and spatial information.

To maximise the limitations of working memory and help to alleviate cognitive overload, we can take advantage of the fact that auditory and visual/spatial information are processed in different parts of the working memory. So, for example, giving students a series of pictures or diagrams while also explaining what is happening can be more effective in helping them to remember the explanation than one or the other.[27]

In a blog post on cognitive load and what teachers can do to reduce it, Dan Williams (@ FurtherEdagogy), author of *English and Maths in Your Pocket*, says:

Activate prior knowledge before sharing new information with students – Our long term memory is said to have a number of organised patterns of knowledge (known as schema). Each schema acts as a single item in working memory, so can be handled easier than having lots of new, isolated information.[28]

In *Efficiency in Learning*, Ruth Clark, Frank Nguyen and John Sweller discuss making the best use of working memory resources through maximising the visual and auditory sub-components of working memory. The improved cognitive efficiency which results from using both visual and auditory explanation is referred to as the 'modality effect'.[29] Tasks which rely too heavily on one area may overload working memory.

26 Duane F. Shell, David W. Brooks, Guy Trainin, Kathleen M. Wilson, Douglas F. Kauffman and Lynne M. Herr, *The Unified Learning Model: How Motivational, Cognitive, and Neurobiological Sciences Inform Best Teaching Practices* (New York: Springer, 2010), p. 13.
27 Didau and Rose, *What Every Teacher Needs To Know About … Psychology*, pp. 39, 47.
28 Dan Williams, 'Cognitive Load Theory', *furtheredagogy* [blog] (20 May 2017). Available at: https://furtheredagogy.wordpress.com/2017/05/20/cognitive-load-theory/.
29 Ruth C. Clark, Frank Nguyen and John Sweller, *Efficiency in Learning: Evidence-Based Guidelines to Manage Cognitive Load*, Kindle edn (San Francisco, CA: Pfeiffer, 2006), loc. 1093.

Playing a clip alongside an audio narration may therefore be a better bet than playing a clip with text on it and then also talking over it! I used to spend the small hours making scrolling PowerPoints with lots of text and visuals which I would then talk over – basically repeating what was on the slides – because I believed that trying to cram in as much information as possible was key. (This also applied to my learning mats: a more experienced colleague told me they were 'very busy' which I took as a compliment at the time!)

The idea of imposing 'extraneous load' on learning resources and instruction was new to me. In *Efficiency in Learning*, the authors state that extraneous load uses up mental resources on tasks which have no relevance to the key learning goal.[30] The 'less is more' approach may have sometimes seemed counter-intuitive to me when I was creating revision help sheets. The desire to immerse a learner in content seemed to make more sense, as at least everything they might need was right there in front of them. But if something can be understood on its own – like a diagram on a worksheet, for instance – then adding additional text might be counterproductive. Clark et al. warn that experts sometimes want to give as much information as possible and, because they are experts in the domain, they don't suffer from the same cognitive load as learners.[31]

In *E-Learning and the Science of Instruction,* Clark and Mayer point out that people have 'dual channels', in that they process visual information through a different channel from auditory information.[32] This was a revelation for me.

To sum up the learning strategies discussed so far, rereading and highlighting are not as demanding as practice testing. Moreover, they are revisiting and revision techniques which may lull the learner into thinking that they have revised or revisited effectively when, in fact, they may be experiencing the fluency illusion.

In the next chapter we explore those techniques which the Dunlosky review revealed to be less effective: highlighting, rereading, summarising, the keyword mnemonic and imagery for text.

---

30 Clark et al., *Efficiency in Learning: Evidence-Based Guidelines to Manage Cognitive Load*, loc. 438–447.
31 Clark et al., *Efficiency in Learning*, loc. 1732.
32 Clark and Mayer, *E-Learning and the Science of Instruction*, loc. 1361.

Chapter 3
What *Might Not* Work As Well

Highlighting/Underlining

Ergonomics and anthropometrics

In order for a designer to design a successful product for their target market they need to consider both ergonomics and anthropometrics. Ergonomics is the study of people and how they interact with their environment. Anthropometrics is the study of the human body and the collection of measurements and data from it. Designers can use these measurements and ergonomic information to help them design products that are useful, user-friendly and intuitive to use.

Timbers

There are three categories of timber available to designers when designing and making products. These all have different properties and different uses. Softwoods, such as pine, are known as coniferous trees, and they are generally fast growing in cooler climates; whereas hardwoods, such as teak, are known as deciduous trees and are more expensive due to them being slower growing in warmer climates. Finally, there are manufactured boards, such as plywood and MDF, which are man-made and come in much larger sheets than natural timbers.

Plastics

There are two main categories of plastics, thermoplastics and thermosetting plastics. Thermoplastics can be heated and formed many times. This is because their polymer chains are not crossed linked, and when heat is added the chains can move freely past one another. In contrast, thermosetting plastics have a complex, crossed-linked structure meaning that they can only be heated and formed once. Thermoplastic plastics are more common in schools and include acrylic, PVC and polypropylene. Examples of thermosetting plastics include phenol formaldehyde and melamine formaldehyde.

Picking up a highlighter pen while reading the above text (written by head of design and technology Debbie Barwell) and choosing to highlight (or underline) six of the key ideas (or six words or six sentences) from the text would be one way to use this technique.

So, I might choose to highlight the definitions of ergonomics and anthropometrics in the first paragraph (perhaps in two different colours). In the next paragraph, I might highlight the names of the softwoods mentioned along with a characteristic like 'fast growing in cooler climates'. Then, in the third paragraph, I might highlight the terms 'thermoplastics' and 'thermosetting plastics' and 'can be heated and formed many times'.

Another option would be for someone else to highlight the key ideas for me and then hand me the text to highlight some more. Reading someone else's highlightings/under-linings and perhaps adding a bit here or there once I've processed their highlightings, might induce a comfortable feeling of fuzzy cognitive ease.

Or, if someone else had highlighted one key idea in the text and then I read it, this might be a potential way to recall the one idea that stands out from the other non-highlighted ideas more easily (this is known as the isolation effect and is referred to in the Dunlosky review[1]). So, perhaps I might just highlight the definition of ergonomics and anthropomet-rics and leave it at that, then sticking it on my bedroom wall to stare at while my mind wanders off elsewhere.

Or I could highlight some key sections, leave it a day or a week while I read notes on a passage from a revision guide on a different subject, and then go back to highlight some more – that is, spacing the highlighting. I could then do a test on the material, writing in my own words what is missing into a passage in which the highlighted text has been blanked out.

Or I could highlight/underline the words 'designer', 'successful', 'consider both ergonomics and anthropometrics', and then look back at the text five minutes later to highlight some more, then the same again the following day – that is, massing the highlighting.

Finally, I could change the interval between each highlighting session before choosing to either highlight some more text or reread what I have previously highlighted – for exam-ple, highlighting the six key words in the previous paragraph, leaving it a day, studying a different subject and then coming back to review and highlight, say, three more from the ergonomics and anthropometrics' passage. Then leaving it a week and highlighting three more, then leaving it a month and rereading and so on. Expanded spacing, highlighting and rereading!

1   Dunlosky et al., 'Improving Students' Learning with Effective Learning Techniques', p. 19.

The theory that if there were six ideas highlighted/underlined in this text then that might promote the recall of these ideas later on during a test is an attractive sounding proposition for the proponents of popping a highlighter into your pocket ahead of a planned revision session. However, the highlighter seems to have been a little maligned of late, with the fluorescent fellows taking some serious flack.

The Dunlosky review discusses previous studies involving the use of highlighting as a study skill.[2] This includes an experiment which involved three groups of students studying articles from *Scientific American* and *Science*, with one group (the control group) simply reading the material, another group highlighting as much or as little of the material as they would like (the active highlighting group) and the final group who read previously highlighted texts but did not highlight these themselves (the passive highlighting group). On a final multiple choice test, neither the active highlighting group nor the passive highlighting group performed better than the control group.[3]

However, there are aspects of highlighting/underlining which, when compared with rereading, have been shown to aid students' recall of the highlighted material. Dunlosky et al. refer to a 1975 study involving one group of students tasked with underlining a single, important sentence per paragraph, with the control group being asked to simply read the passage. The group tasked with underlining one important sentence per paragraph recalled a lot more material than the group who did not.[4]

So, what are the implications for classroom revisiting and revision? Perhaps if highlighting/underlining is used judiciously (i.e. highly selective highlighting/underlining) then the strategy might be effective. This may relate back to the isolation effect which we encountered earlier.

However, selective highlighting may demand a certain level of prior knowledge among the students in order for them to do it effectively (what if they're highlighting the wrong bit?). Dunlosky et al. suggest that potentially this makes highlighting less helpful to those students who know less about the subject matter.[5] If a domain expert had highlighted one sentence which they believed to be the most relevant, and then handed it to a relative novice, at least the selection would have been made by someone with subject expertise.

Why doesn't highlighting work as well as other techniques? We have established that if we want our students to remember things then they have to think hard about the material

---

2 Dunlosky et al., 'Improving Students' Learning with Effective Learning Techniques', p. 19.
3 Robert L. Fowler and Anne S. Barker, 'Effectiveness of Highlighting for Retention of Text Material', *Journal of Applied Psychology*, 59(3) (1974), 358–364.
4 John P. Rickards and Gerald J. August, 'Generative Underlining Strategies in Prose Recall', *Journal of Educational Psychology*, 67(8) (1975), 860–865.
5 Dunlosky et al., 'Improving Students' Learning with Effective Learning Techniques', p. 20.

– that is to say, they need to practise recalling or recognising the material. (This ties in quite nicely with practice testing in the next chapter.)

If there's very little thinking going on about the material that is being highlighted (i.e. if there's very little hard cognitive work), then you are unlikely to remember it. This is perhaps why, if highlighting does have any benefits, then it is when fewer, more valuable points are highlighted in a text than when using a whole rainbow's worth of highlighter pens.

Having said that, as David Didau suggests, thinking hard may not actually be a good indicator of learning.[6] He refers to a passage in *Making Good Progress*, in which Daisy Christodoulou discusses Paul Kirschner, John Sweller and Richard Clark's paper, 'Why Minimal Guidance During Instruction Does Not Work'.[7] It is argued that problem solving places demands on working memory which are connected with solving the problem; consequently, you can be thinking hard about solving a problem but that thinking may not sufficiently change long-term memory.

In *Cognitive Load Theory*, John Sweller, Paul Ayres and Slava Kalyuga discuss the goal-free effect and how means-end analysis may not promote learning. In other words, focusing on solving one specific goal using what is provided in a problem may result in a cognitive load which is not relevant to learning. For instance, the authors describe an experiment contrasting means-ends (specific goal given) and goal-free learning in relation to mathematics. The goal group had a traditional 'find the distance' type question and the goal-free group were asked to come up with the value of as many variables as they could. The way in which the goal-free group worked suggested that it was a much more effective strategy.[8]

The goal-free effect is also referred to in Craig Barton's *How I Wish I'd Taught Maths*, including some excellent examples which refer to slight tweaks in wording which change the task from a goal-specific task to a goal-free task.[9] I have included some other examples below of how this might work. With thanks to maths teacher Dan Frankton for designing these.

6   David Didau, 'Further Problems with the "Thinking Hard" Proxy for Learning?', *The Learning Spy* [blog] (11 January 2017). Available at: http://www.learningspy.co.uk/learning/problems-thinking-hard-proxy-learning/.

7   Paul A. Kirschner, John Sweller and Richard E. Clark, 'Why Minimal Guidance During Instruction Does Not Work: An Analysis of the Failure of Constructivist, Discovery, Problem-Based, Experiential, and Inquiry-Based Teaching', *Educational Psychologist*, 41(2) (2006), 75–86.

8   John Sweller, Paul Ayres and Slava Kalyuga, *Cognitive Load Theory (Explorations in the Learning Sciences, Instructional Systems and Performance Technologies)*, Kindle edn (New York: Springer, 2011), loc. 1396–1441.

9   Craig Barton, *How I Wish I'd Taught Maths: Lessons Learned from Research, Conversations with Experts, and 12 Years of Mistakes*, Kindle edn (Woodbridge: John Catt Educational, 2018).

In the first example below, the goal-specific task would be to 'Find angle EBD'. If a novice were attempting this problem they may resort to means-end analysis, whereby in order to arrive at the solution to the problem they would have to coordinate a number of different sub-steps in their fragile working memories to move towards the goal. It is possible that this demanding level of coordination would lead to cognitive overload and, therefore, despite the thinking hard, may not actually lead to a change in long-term memory and an ability to transfer what they have learned to another problem.

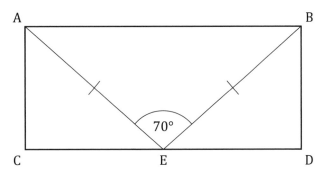

So, a simple tweak to make the problem goal-free and allow the novice to think hard, but in a way which doesn't adopt this means-end analysis is, according to the example given by Barton, to change the task instruction to 'Find as many angles as you can'. In this way, the novice is not constrained in terms of the sub-steps that have to be coordinated in working memory, and instead they are free to process steps for whichever angles they wish to work out.

Barton observes that examples do not have to be limited to geometry and includes an additional illustration from a different area of maths. Maths teacher Dan Frankton has also offered the following example:

A man wants to relay his patio with slabs measuring 60 cm by 60 cm. Each slab cost £5. A diagram of his garden is below.

	2.4m	
Patio		Grass
4.8m		

The goal-specific problem might be for the learner to answer, 'How much does it cost?', whereas the goal-free effect might be worded in the same way that Barton worded his example in *How I Wish I'd Taught Maths*: 'What can you work out?'

The idea of thinking hard, but only in the right way, puts a slightly different angle on simply saying that all revision should be hard and involve lots of demanding thinking. Therefore, another reason why highlighting might not work as well as other techniques is that students may be thinking hard about the highlighting but not the ideas in the text.

In an interview with Aubrey Francisco, the cognitive psychologist Henry Roediger describes how spaced retrieval practice can be a powerful learning tool. Roediger explains that retrieval practice is more effective than highlighting because it involves active output of that information, which in turn leads to knowing that piece of information better: 'what retrieval practice does is to help us practice getting information out of memory, to actively use information. Retrieval practice is part of active learning. Normal study activities like underlining, highlighting and rereading do not promote retrieval practice.'[10]

The same point is made on the StudyRight website which asserts that highlighting requires neither input nor output, therefore making it an ineffective study skill.[11]

Some of the comments to a blog post on highlighters by Alex Quigley champion the use of the highlighter but not as a revision tool.[12] Author, history teacher and education researcher, Harry Fletcher-Wood (@HFletcherWood), comments:

I agree that highlighters have no real merit in terms of memory and revision. However, they are very useful in 'active reading:' a great tool to have students start organising their ideas, to keep in mind what they're looking for in a text and to have ideas ready-organised and easily identifiable in discussions/ writing.

As a revision tool which does not involve information retrieval, highlighting has a low utility. If a student is spending the majority of their revision time highlighting then there may well be problems. Over-zealous highlighting might be diverting revision time away

---

10 Aubrey Francisco, 'Ask the Cognitive Scientist: Retrieval Practice' [interview with Henry L. Roediger], *Digital Promise* (15 October 2014). Available at: http://www.digitalpromise.org/blog/entry/ ask-the-cognitive-scientist-retrieval-practice.

11 See http://www.studyright.net/blog/highlighting-a-textbook-taking-notes/.

12 Alex Quigley, 'Why I Hate Highlighters!', *The Confident Teacher* [blog] (17 January 2015). Available at: https://www.theconfidentteacher.com/2015/01/hate-highlighters/.

from them using techniques which have been shown to work more effectively – like retrieval practice, for example.

The Dunlosky review cites a 2009 study by cognitive psychologists Jeffrey Karpicke, Andrew Butler and Henry Roediger.[13] They examined the study habits of 177 college students, asking them to name the strategies they used during studying and whether they would practise retrieval or reread after studying a textbook chapter. The majority of the students surveyed cited rereading as being their study skill of choice following an initial reading of a chapter of a textbook. According to Dunlosky et al., the choice of highlighting over other study skills is perhaps the main cause for concern, not because it necessarily prevents learning but because it stops students using that time to employ much more fruitful strategies.[14]

In a 1996 paper entitled 'Highlighting Text as a Study Strategy: Beyond Attentional Focusing', Reinhard Lindner, Wayne Gordon and Bruce Harris set out to discover if there was any benefit in using differently coloured highlighters, with one group using two highlighters – yellow for the main ideas and green for supporting ideas.[15] Their aim was to see if getting students to think about dividing the information into categories of importance would have a greater impact on learning, and also to identify whether the impact on learning came during the highlighting phase or afterwards when reviewing learning. In the two experiments that were carried out, despite a small increase in retention measured in the two-highlighter group, the experiments did not show a statistical significance.

In the second experiment, on an immediate test the two-highlighter group had the lowest mean score compared with the other three groups (i.e. control group, red pencil, one-highlighter). Interestingly, the researchers reflect that this lack of effect on the immediate test (in the delayed test, the two-highlighter group came second behind the one-highlighter group) could be because of a novelty effect of using the highlighters. They also suggest that if there was to be a potential benefit from using highlighting to organise ideas, rather than just to draw attention to them, then students would need some training in the practice.

This comes back to the need to provide excellent models of how to use the revision technique – in this case, explaining in what domain-specific scenarios active highlighting

---

13 Jeffrey D. Karpicke, Andrew C. Butler and Henry L. Roediger III. 'Metacognitive Strategies in Student Learning: Do Students Practice Retrieval When They Study On Their Own?', *Memory*, 17(4) (2009), 471–479.

14 Dunlosky et al., 'Improving Students' Learning with Effective Learning Techniques', p 21.

15 Reinhard W. Lindner, Wayne I. Gordon and Bruce R. Harris, 'Highlighting Text as a Study Strategy: Beyond Attentional Focusing'. Paper presented at the American Educational Research Association Annual Meeting, New York, 8–12 April 1996. Available at: https://files.eric.ed.gov/fulltext/ED401320.pdf, p. 1.

can be used to good enough effect. The authors of the study also suggest using pre-highlighted models of text with students.

Dr Yana Weinstein of the Learning Scientists very helpfully referred me to a more recent study by researchers Carole Yue, Benjamin Storm, Nate Kornell and Elizabeth Bjork.[16] This was designed to compare highlighting as a study strategy versus rereading, with both the highlighting and the rereading taking place across four groups: spaced highlighting, massed highlighting, spaced rereading and massed rereading. Interestingly, some of the findings showed that the massed highlighting group performed better on a test one week later. I struggled to understand this: I thought that when you spaced out studying there was a greater chance of developing more retrieval cues, therefore the spaced condition with both highlighting and rereading should lead to better results in the test.

My cognitive dissonance led me to contact one of the researchers involved in the study, Carole Yue, to ask about why the massed highlighting condition may have resulted in better test performance than the spaced condition. I am very grateful to her that she took the time to respond so helpfully. I have included sections from our email exchange below:

Our thought was that, perhaps, having the opportunity to restudy (and re-highlight) previously highlighted text might cause people to think about why they initially chose to highlight some information instead of other information. If that were the case, then re-highlighting might elicit deeper processing of the material, which would be more important in a massed study condition, when we typically do not see deeper processing on a second study session (in fact, people may process information more shallowly upon a second massed reading due to perceived fluency or familiarity). Therefore, highlighting in a massed condition would cause additional processing to occur that we wouldn't normally see with ordinary (i.e. non-highlighting) massed study. These processes may have led to the slight benefit over the spaced/highlighting condition. There certainly could be other explanations as well, and I invite any thoughts you might have on the matter.

I agree, it's somewhat confusing, and I think there is a lot more work to be done to fully explain (and replicate) our results. We also found that people tended to highlight more in the spaced condition than in the massed condition, but also that there was no benefit to highlighting more (in fact, we found a slight numerical disadvantage). There could be some interaction between spaced

---

16 Carole L. Yue, Benjamin C. Storm, Nate Kornell and Elizabeth L. Bjork, 'Highlighting and Its Relation to Distributed Study and Students' Metacognitive Beliefs', *Educational Psychology Review*, 27(1) (2014), 69–78.

highlighting and number of words highlighted that we can't fully explore with our data.

So it may be that, when compared to rereading and spacing, highlighting in a massed condition *could* potentially lead to deeper processing as more thought goes into what was highlighted in the first highlighting session and why.

All in all, though, highlighting probably doesn't paint quite as fluorescent a picture of happiness when compared to the other highly rated techniques in the Dunlosky review.

Rereading

There are many reasons as to why tropical rainforest environments should be protected in the short and long term. Reasons ranging from biodiversity to water sources and even the human environment all work together in ensuring a sustainable tropical rainforest environment for the future.

Tropical rainforests provide around 50% of all plants and species in the world and are home to many thousands of animals, with some not even discovered yet. Many plants become extinct before they have been discovered and documented, highlighting the significant and delicate nature of this natural environment.

The Amazon rainforest is known as the 'lungs of the Earth' where around 29% of the world's oxygen is produced due to photosynthesis. The Amazon rainforest is also identified as a carbon sink where tonnes of carbon is absorbed through the vegetation and stored in the delicate soil system.

Indigenous people (e.g. tribes) live in balance with the tropical rainforest through sourcing material sustainably and ensuring their way of life does not cause an imbalance (e.g. too much wood taken by their communities). Indigenous communities are currently under threat due to large-scale deforestation for the cattle ranching industry.

The tropical rainforest is an important environment for water supply due to the intense rainfall each day. Estimates show around 20% of the world's fresh water is located in the Amazon rainforest basin alone.

Tropical rainforests also provide many resources such as medicines and hard woods which are mainly sourced for HICs (higher income countries).

A good example of an area that is tackling issues surrounding deforestation is Brazil. They have reduced deforestation from 21,000 km² per year (1987) down to 6,000 km² per year (2015). The Brazilian government have pledged to reduce illegal deforestation, promote conservation and to not allow consumer pressure surrounding products to play a role in the destruction of this natural environment.

Reading the above text (written by geography teacher Jon Haston) and then rereading it a couple more times straight after is an example of massed rereading. If I read the text and then reread it – as compared to someone who read it and then reread it two or three more times than I do, so has more practice (or 'dosage' as it is called in the Dunlosky review[17]) – would it actually make any difference?

I might reread the first paragraph and say to myself that the most important ideas here are the reasons why tropical rainforest environments should be protected – that is, I'm telling myself I must remember this as I'm doing the rereading! Then I put the text down and an hour or so later reread the same passage and tell myself that the same information I read an hour ago is still important and needs to be remembered.

Or how about a little spaced rereading: read the text once, leave it for three or four days (or weeks) then read it again, followed by a test – as compared to another student who reads it once and then writes it out from memory after three or four days (or a week) and then does a test?

Or how about expanding the spacing of the rereading: read it through once, leave it a day, reread it (telling myself how important it is to know how much fresh water there is in the Amazon rainforest basin), leave it five days, reread it, leave it ten days, reread it and so on until a test?

Or how about if I were to have access to this passage during an open-book test, read and reread the text during the test, and then use what was in the passage to write my answer?

In their work on 'desirable difficulties', Robert and Elizabeth Bjork suggest that we regard our memories as rather like a recording device, so we think that rereading information over and over will somehow 'record' it.[18] However, this is not how our memory works. When

17 Dunlosky et al., 'Improving Students' Learning with Effective Learning Techniques', p. 6.
18 Bjork and Bjork, 'Making Things Hard on Yourself', p. 62.

compared with the other study skill techniques referred to in the Dunlosky review, rereading is rated as a low-utility revision skill.

Rereading a chapter can lead to a false sense of fluency – what Benedict Carey refers to as the 'fluency illusion'.[19] We think we know the material because rereading it gives us a sense of familiarity, so retrieval strength could be high during a massed rereading revision session. However, we have simply been presented with the same material again; we have not had to generate an answer or toil over recalling any of the information, which are both key attributes of more durable learning. Revision is a lot less difficult if we choose to focus on rereading.

The Bjorks refer to the greater gains made in learning through generating an answer or solution to a problem (compared to being told or presented with the answer or solution) as 'the generation effect'.[20] In short, looking up an answer or asking someone else, rather than using what you already know to produce an answer, is really cheating yourself of a strong learning opportunity and might just sum up why rereading is not as effective as practice testing.

As Logan Fiorella and Richard Mayer stress in *Learning as a Generative Activity*, a learner may well be able to read and process the words in the presented material but they are often unable to apply it in another context or to solve a new problem.

As with many of the study techniques looked at in this book, the effectiveness depends on the durability of recall and application. The Dunlosky review notes that a number of studies have shown more recall of main ideas than details from rereading. In a nod, perhaps, towards why distributed practice ranked so highly in the review, Dunlosky et al. discuss massed rereading versus spaced rereading, concluding that spaced rereading generally shows greater effects.[21]

Despite its apparent ease of use and applicability by students, rereading does not make the medal table though. Dunlosky et al. raise concerns over its effectiveness in comparison to the other techniques evaluated: on the tests that have showed positive effects of rereading as a study technique, they note that free recall has been the most common way of assessing the outcome.[22]

Can rereading as a learning strategy transfer across different domains and content? It's important to recognise that there is a distinction between reading and rereading, and that

---

19 Carey, *How We Learn*, loc. 1219.
20 Bjork and Bjork, 'Making Things Hard on Yourself', p. 61.
21 Dunlosky et al., 'Improving Students' Learning with Effective Learning Techniques', p. 27.
22 Dunlosky et al., 'Improving Students' Learning with Effective Learning Techniques', p. 28.

reading depends on background knowledge. To treat reading as a transferable skill without considering the issue of background knowledge is wrong in the extreme.

In response to a blog post by Doug Lemov (@Doug_Lemov) (the author of *Teach Like a Champion*) on mistaking knowledge problems for skill problems, Spanish and English teacher Knikki Hernandez (@teacherknikki) tweets: 'A true paradigm shift for Ts. Analysis is not an isolated skill to be taught but rather a result of knowledge and understanding of context.'[23] However, despite some studies in this area, the degree to which rereading outcomes rest on the knowledge of the 'rereader' is an area of research which has not yet been targeted, according to the Dunlosky review.[24]

There is an acknowledgement by Brown et al. in *Make It Stick* that rereading is not a particularly effective strategy. There may be a benefit in rereading something once, the authors suggest, if a good amount of time has gone by since the first time it was read. But there is a problem with massed rereading: doing rereading after rereading and hoping to embed the key points in the passage is unlikely to be effective.

Overall, the effectiveness of rereading in promoting durable learning appears to be doubtful.

Summarisation

Nuclear radiation comes from the nucleus of atoms. There are three types:

■ Alpha (α) particles – These are made up of two protons and two neutrons, identical to a helium nucleus. They have a large mass and travel at about 5–10% of the speed of light. An alpha particle has a charge of +2, therefore they are highly ionising. They can be stopped by a sheet of paper or approximately 6 cm of air.

■ Beta (β) particles – These are very fast-moving electrons, moving at approximately 90% of the speed of light! Because they are electrons they have a small mass and a charge of -1, so they are moderately ionising. They can be stopped by a thin sheet of aluminium.

---

23 Doug Lemov, 'My Favorite No: Mistaking Knowledge Problems for Skill Problems', *Teach Like a Champion* [blog] (12 December 2016). Available at: http://teachlikeachampion.com/blog/favorite-no-mistaking-knowledge-problems-skill-problems/. See also https://twitter.com/teacherknikki/status/888162734973607936.
24 Dunlosky et al., 'Improving Students' Learning with Effective Learning Techniques', p. 28.

■ Gamma (γ) rays – These are a type of electromagnetic wave and therefore have no charge. They have a high frequency and have very high energy – this makes them weakly ionising. They have no mass so travel at the speed of light. Thick concrete or lead can stop most of them, but some will always get through.

All nuclear radiation can cause ionisation (so can also be known as ionising radiation). This means that they can change an atom into an ion by the loss or gain of electrons. This makes them dangerous as this process can damage our cells and DNA, sometimes leading to cancer.

Reading the above section on nuclear radiation (written by physics teacher Mike Browne) and then writing three key sentences to summarise the content from each paragraph, but trying to retain the meaning, could be a way to use summarising as a revision tool away from the classroom.

I might decide to choose a sentence from the text and shorten it. For instance, from the first paragraph I might decide to write (while looking at the text) a sentence like, 'Alpha particles are two protons and two neutrons with large mass.' It's certainly a more concise representation, and when I come back to revise this area of my notes in a few days' time, it will save me having to reread the whole passage again.

I might consider online methods of automatic text summarisation. Abstractive text summarisation software could provide me with a summary of the document in the form of a series of brief sentences. This might be more beneficial than an extractive summary which only identifies the most relevant sentences and presents these word for word as they appear in the original text.[25]

Or how about summarising the whole text in 30 words using an extractive technique, then in the next lesson/revising session only having 20 words to summarise it, then 10? A little gimmicky perhaps, but I might end up with something like 'Alpha two protons/neutrons, Beta charge -1, Gamma rays no charge.'

How about harnessing dual coding (see below) to summarise it? Or combining a summary with some visuals and words?

25 For some useful discussion on this see: Pranay Mathur, Aman Gill and Aayush Yadav, 'Text Summarization in Python: Extractive vs. Abstractive Techniques Revisited', *Rare Technologies* [blog] (5 April 2017). Available at: https://rare-technologies.com/text-summarization-in-python-extractive-vs-abstractive-techniques-revisited/.

What if I sat at home with a copy of this passage on my knee and I copied out word for word, without any paraphrasing, what I believed to be the three most important lines from the piece, all the while having access to the passage?

What if I read the passage out loud once and then turned the page over and then did a verbal 30-second summary? (Is this still a summary or a verbal free recall test?) Finally, what if someone else read the text to me and I had access to the text and read along? Or if I read along out loud and then put into no more than 30 words a summary of everything I have just heard and read out loud? Might the impact of reading the passage out loud benefit my summary of the content?

A number of studies in the Dunlosky review and in *Learning as a Generative Activity* show summarisation to be quite effective when compared with control groups who did not carry out the technique. However, one of the issues noted by Dunlosky et al. is that previous summarising interventions have focused on teaching students how to summarise effectively (i.e. teaching them how to pick out key words and so on) as opposed to discovering its efficacy as a revision tool.[26] As Carl Hendrick and Robin Macpherson observe in *What Does This Look Like in the Classroom?*, if students aren't able to accurately analyse what to include in their summaries, then their summaries won't be very effective.[27]

In *Learning as a Generative Activity*, summarisation is described as being at its optimum when students have been taught how to use the technique. The authors note, however, that it is less effective when used for 'complex spatial relations (such as physics or chemistry concepts)'.[28] Where there are spatial relationships there are usually procedures. If these are part of a process, then it's hard to see how certain steps could be less relevant than others if they all contribute towards the same end point. It may not be possible to simplify a scientific method while still retaining the key points.

In *Efficiency in Learning*, the authors discuss how diagrams can help to support more efficient learning. In a visual, the whole can be viewed simultaneously, whereas in writing information is given sequentially, one sentence at a time. This is particularly helpful when the information contains multiple elements: a diagram can show these spatial relationships, while text demands greater use of inference.[29]

Dunlosky et al. state that it is difficult to measure the effectiveness of summarisation as a study skill because the strategy is applied in a number of different ways across different

---

26 Dunlosky et al., 'Improving Students' Learning with Effective Learning Techniques', p. 15.
27 Carl Hendrick and Robin Macpherson, *What Does This Look Like in the Classroom? Bridging the Gap Between Research and Practice* (Woodbridge: John Catt Educational, 2017), pp. 139–140.
28 Fiorella and Mayer, *Learning as a Generative Activity*, p. 21.
29 Clark et al., *Efficiency in Learning*, loc. 982.

studies.[30] For example, an experiment assessing the efficacy of summarising as a study skill could evaluate summarisation involving participants who are instructed to summarise using one-word summaries, paragraph summaries, sentence summaries and so on.

Furthermore, if the students aren't able to decide what to include in their summaries then their summarisation won't be very helpful. In *Learning as a Generative Activity*, the authors acknowledge that the effectiveness of summarisation may also depend on the level of training the learner has experienced: 'summarizing may be most effective when students are provided with pretraining in how to summarize'.[31] For the study skill to be successful, students need to have seen the strategy modelled, making summarising less practical than some of the other techniques described in the next chapter.

So, the case *could* be made that summarisation works as a way of improving students' performance on future tests, but this will depend on whether the learners can produce constructive summaries in the first place. Ouch, a claim of sorts …

It is not only the quality of the training that learners have had, but also whether or not the summarisation takes place with the to-be-revisited/to-be-revised material present or not. In other words, is summarisation more effective when combined with retrieval practice?

There is an interesting study on the effectiveness of open-book and closed-book tests, and the benefits (or not) of having the notes present while being tested. This helped me to think about the ways in which summarisation might take place: with access to all the notes, some of the notes or none of the notes. Is that a summary or a recall test?

Perhaps there is scope for a two-pronged free recall test for those students well-versed in summarising, which assesses their ability to recall only what they believe to be the most relevant aspects of the material they had been studying. But, again, is this a measurement of the effects of retrieval practice or how well the learner can summarise from memory?

If it's recall from memory, then if the learning materials are not present while the learner is making their summary, this might help to inform them about what they do and don't know. Although this could also come under one of Henry Roediger, Adam Putnam and Megan Smith's ten benefits of testing (i.e. benefit 7: testing improves metacognitive monitoring).[32]

---

30 Dunlosky et al., 'Improving Students' Learning with Effective Learning Techniques', p. 15.
31 Fiorella and Mayer, *Learning as a Generative Activity*, p. 21.
32 Henry L. Roediger III, Adam L. Putnam and Megan A. Smith, 'Ten Benefits of Testing and Their Applications to Educational Practice', *Psychology of Learning and Motivation*, 55 (2011). Available at: http://psych.wustl.edu/memory/Roddy%20article%20PDF%27s/BC_Roediger%20et%20al%20 (2011)_PLM.pdf.

In a customarily belting blog post, Dr Carolina Kuepper-Tetzel (@pimpmymemory) of the Learning Scientists describes how retrieving information can help to support metacognition.[33] She refers to a study by Dunlosky, Rawson and Middleton in which one group was asked to retrieve information before saying how well they thought they would be able to remember it in a later test, and the other group were just asked how well they thought they would remember. The group who had been asked to retrieve the information improved their metacognitive accuracy from 0.57 to 0.73 compared to the other group.

(While we are on the subject of metacognition, head teacher and author John Tomsett wrote a barnstorming blog post on his thinking as he completed a GCSE economics paper. The modelling of the thought processes that he goes through as he takes the exam could be a really powerful tool for your students.[34])

Both *Learning as a Generative Activity* and the Dunlosky review acknowledge that some studies have shown benefits for learners who produce summaries with the material present and not present. Dunlosky et al. also highlight that the benefits of summarising have generally been observed in undergraduate students.[35] This might possibly explain why summarisation may be less suitable than other techniques for GCSE students, unless the students have been well-trained in it by domain experts.

A potential way to adopt summarisation for GCSE content could be to use it for those subjects which involve essay writing in exams (rather than subjects which are assessed with multiple choice questions). As the Dunlosky review points out, because summarising involves the learner in production, this is likely to support the demands of generative testing better than tests relying on knowing the right answer.[36]

However, having to spend time teaching students how to use summarisation effectively contributed to Dunlosky et al. giving this study skill a lower rating than the others reviewed. The researchers also cite a lack of classroom-related research studies involving summarisation as being another reason for its low utility. So, the verdict on summarisation is that the jury is still out. It can be effective following training and is described as being one of the ways to promote generative learning in *Learning as a Generative Activity*.

33 Carolina Kuepper-Tetzel, 'How To Improve Your Metacognition and Why It Matters', *The Learning Scientists* [blog] (28 March 2017). Available at: http://www.learningscientists.org/blog/2017/3/30-1. See also John Dunlosky, Katherine A. Rawson and Erica L. Middleton, 'What Constrains the Accuracy of Metacomprehension Judgments? Testing the Transfer-Appropriate-Monitoring and Accessibility Hypotheses', *Journal of Memory and Language*, 52 (2005), 551–565.

34 John Tomsett, 'This Much I Know About … the Sutton Trust/EEF Toolkit and the Golden Thread from Evidence to Student Outcomes, Via Deliberate Intervention', *johntomsett* [blog] (13 February 2015). Available at: https://johntomsett.com/2015/02/13/this-much-i-know-about-the-golden-thread-from-evidence-to-student-outcomes/.

35 Dunlosky et al., 'Improving Students' Learning with Effective Learning Techniques', p. 16.

36 Dunlosky et al., 'Improving Students' Learning with Effective Learning Techniques', p. 17.

A close friend of summarising, note-taking, is discussed in *Efficiency in Learning*, particularly in the context of lectures. Clark et al. consider note-taking both while listening to a lecture and while reading. A high load is imposed on students' working memory as they listen and make notes (they refer to 'emphasis phrases' which are a way of signalling to learners to take notes at a particular point).[37] Taking notes from a text, on the other hand, may have a lower load on working memory as students can pause, review and revisit at their own pace. [38]

It's also worth noting that producing a word-for-word, typed transcription of what someone says may not involve the essential semantic processing associated with taking notes by hand – that is, pausing, reviewing, paraphrasing and so on. Toby French (@MrHistoire) has written a beautifully straightforward and interesting blog post on note-taking using the Cornell note-taking system.[39]

In *Peak*, K. Anders Ericsson and Robert Pool refer to Benjamin Franklin's wish to write like the journalists in *The Spectator*, and how this led him to adopt an innovative technique which combined summarisation and revisiting.[40] Franklin summarised sentences from the writers whose work he admired, then later wrote his own practice articles based on these prompts. He then went back to the original articles to check and correct his writing.

The idea of harnessing forgetting as a way of enhancing learning was put to good use, even back then! It's tempting to consider how this technique could be applied across subject domains: read something, write a sentence summary or short paragraph (but not copying verbatim), leave a little time for forgetting, then look back at the summary and try to write in the same style. Maybe summarisation should be worthy of a top-rating after all.

Keyword Mnemonic

John Dunlosky has described the usefulness of the keyword mnemonic in an article in *American Educator* as 'Somewhat helpful for learning languages, but benefits are short-lived.'[41]

---

37 Clark et al., *Efficiency in Learning*, loc. 1446.
38 Clark et al., *Efficiency in Learning*, loc. 1463.
39 Toby French, 'Summarising with Y9', *MrHistoire.com* [blog] (1 October 2016). (This post is no longer available.)
40 K. Anders Ericsson and Robert Pool, *Peak: Secrets from the New Science of Expertise*, Kindle edn (London: Bodley Head, 2016), loc. 2656.
41 John Dunlosky, 'Strengthening the Student Toolbox: Study Strategies to Boost Learning', *American Educator*, 37(3) (2013), 12–21 at p. 20.

The example that cognitive scientist Daniel Willingham gives to illustrate how the keyword mnemonic works in an earlier edition of the *American Educator* is: 'The Spanish word for *mushrooms* is *champiñones*, which sounds like the English word *champions*. Create a visual image of a boxing champion in the ring, arms aloft in victory, wearing big mushrooms on his hands instead of gloves.'[42] Being a languages teacher by trade, I have dabbled with this technique, although lately I have been using an adaptation of it by adopting elaborative interrogation with vocabulary (an example of which appears in the next chapter).

In the same article, Willingham raises potential difficulties if a student were to revise French followed by Spanish. The similarities in the material that is to be learned might depend on the same cue (in English) to provoke the retrieval of the target words in both languages. The example used is the cue of 'red' which would act as a cue for *rouge* and *rojo*. This takes us back to the need for students to form distinctive memories. An interleaved revision plan could be devised to avoid confusion over retrieval cues – for example, studying subjects which depend on very different types of retrieval cues in succession to lessen the problem of interference.

In the Dunlosky review, several studies on using the keyword mnemonic to learn vocabulary are mentioned (and not just those which showed positive effects). The authors conclude that it could be extended across other content and domain-specific terminology,[43] so why does it not make it onto the podium?

According to Dunlosky et al., there are three reasons why its effectiveness as a study technique is in question. The first is that finding a suitable keyword based on the sound of the foreign language target item can sometimes prove troublesome. Words don't always lend themselves well to having a keyword (the example given is *revenir* (come back) and how 'revenge' as a potential keyword might be difficult to connect to the foreign language meaning). The second is a lack of studies which have involved learners in developing their own keyword strategies, as opposed to having had the keywords given to them. The final reason concerns whether or not the effects of the keyword method actually last and lead to durable learning.[44]

The authors also highlight the problem of keywords which may have a number of potential targets. For instance, in the earlier example of *champiñones* with the keyword 'champions', and an image of a boxing champion wearing mushrooms as gloves, after a period of disuse the learner might struggle to retrieve the target 'mushrooms', which could lead to interference with other potential targets like 'gloves' or 'boxing' when they attempt to retrieve the word again.

---

42 Willingham, 'Ask the Cognitive Scientist: What Will Improve a Student's Memory?', p. 23.
43 Dunlosky et al., 'Improving Students' Learning with Effective Learning Techniques', p. 21.
44 Dunlosky et al., 'Improving Students' Learning with Effective Learning Techniques', pp. 22–23.

In other words, when the images associated with the keyword mnemonic have decayed over time, can the correct part of the image to give the correct meaning of the word be remembered or will it be another associated part of the mnemonic? A potential solution lies in regular retrieval practice of the link between the keyword and the image. I'll be looking out for it in the next lesson observation that I carry out …

Just as my confirmation bias kicks in, I find this on the Mempowered website, courtesy of Dr Fiona McPherson:

Note that it is not the keyword itself that fails to be remembered. It is the image. The weakness then is in the link between keyword and image. (For example, the Tagalog word araw, meaning sun, is given the keyword arrow; when tested, araw easily recalls the keyword arrow, but the image connecting arrow with sun is gone). This is the link you must strengthen.[45]

Overall, however, the keyword mnemonic doesn't make the cut. Dunlosky et al. accept the fact that it may be useful for material that is 'keyword friendly', so retrieval practice with carefully selected keyword-friendly vocabulary may be the way to go.

Imagery for Text

One way of using imagery for text as a strategy might be to make a mental image while reading. For example, take the passage on tropical rainforests at the start of the section on rereading (see page 55). You could begin by reading it (or listening to someone else read it aloud) and then be prompted to form mental images (e.g. 'Imagine how your textbook might show the Amazon as a carbon sink … Picture the rainfall as well as the indigenous people and how they are living … Visualise the processes of photosynthesis occurring in the Amazon'). In fact, listening to someone else reading the text while making mental images may be a better bet than reading the text yourself and making mental images while you read.

Reading a text and then using your imagination to make mental images of the key points is described in chapter 5 of *Learning as a Generative Activity*.[46] The processes, which are designed to promote generative learning, are also discussed in the Dunlosky review. Both

45 See http://www.mempowered.com/strategies/using-keyword-method-learn-vocabulary.
46 Fiorella and Mayer, *Learning as a Generative Activity*, pp. 79–96 (Learning by Imagining).

sources describe imagining as a way to mentally enhance the organisation of the material and integrate it, and both refer to the same paper to illustrate the potential powerful effects of imagining. The study by Detlev Leutner, Claudia Leopold and Elke Sumfleth involved tenth-grade students making mental images while reading a text on the dipole character of water molecules, with the control group simply reading for comprehension.[47] In the final multiple choice test, the answers needed to be inferred from the text, rather than being explicitly available. The group which had used mental imagery performed better than the control group.

The learner using this technique is forced to transform the text into images, causing an elaboration on the to-be-learned or to-be-revisited material which helps to make it stick. In *Cognition: Theory and Applications*, Stephen Reed describes the effectiveness of images in producing 'a second kind of memory code that is independent of the verbal code'. He goes on to describe dual-coding theory which 'proposes two independent memory codes, either of which can result in recall'.[48]

Ah, dual coding. According to Dr Logan Fiorella (one of the authors of *Learning as a Generative Activity*), 'dual-coding involves processing the same information as both words and images (i.e. verbally and pictorially). Words might be printed or spoken, and images might be provided or mentally imagined. So by this definition, imagining while reading a text is a form of dual-coding. The multimedia principle is also an example of dual-coding.'[49] If we can take advantage of a memory being encoded in two places (and therefore two possible routes to retrieve it) for the price of one, then I'm all for it.

Richard Mayer describes the multimedia principle as reflecting the fact that 'People learn better from words and pictures than from words alone.'[50] For more on this see the excellent guide from Oliver Caviglioli at researchED Rugby 2017.[51] The Learning Scientists also do a great little number on dual-coding theory in one of their blog posts.[52]

However, it's also worth mentioning the following tweet from Gary Davies (@gazbd): 'Do people realise that dual-coding in a classroom setting means image + talking and not

47 Detlev Leutner, Claudia Leopold and Elke Sumfleth, 'Cognitive Load and Science Text Comprehension: Effects of Drawing and Mentally Imagining Text Content', *Computers in Human Behavior*, 25(2) (2009), 284–289.

48 Stephen K. Reed, *Cognition: Theory and Applications* (San Diego, CA: Wadsworth Publishing, 2006), p. 156.

49 I wanted to understand dual coding and imagining a little more, so I contacted Dr Logan Fiorella, who very kindly responded to my email. This is part of our correspondence.

50 Richard E. Mayer and Patricia A. Alexander (eds), *Handbook of Research on Learning and Instruction*, Kindle edn (New York: Routledge, 2017), loc. 14777.

51 See https://teachinghow2s.com/docs/HOW2_ResearchED_Rugby.pdf.

52 See Megan Smith and Yana Weinstein, 'Learn How to Study Using ... Dual Coding', *The Learning Scientists* [blog] (30 August 2016). Available at: http://www.learningscientists.org/blog/2016/9/1-1.

image+reading+talking? #toomanywordsonyourslides'.[53] Furthermore, Fiorella and Mayer remark that learners who are adopting imagining might need to be well motivated as there is nothing observable going on (at least, that is how I put it).[54] This raises a question around whether asking a hall full of Year 11 students to make mental images of random facts during an outsourced revision session is really transferable as a revision skill for them away from the classroom?

However, there might be some use in linking images in this way if they are seen as part of 'covert retrieval practice'. In *Small Teaching*, James Lang mentions covert retrieval practice and just how effective it can be.[55] Covert retrieval practice, as identified in a 2013 study by Megan Smith, Henry Roediger and Jeffrey Karpicke, is about keeping the answer/idea in your head and not communicating it.[56] In contrast, overt retrieval practice would be where there is some sort of observable response – so, short answer questions, multiple choice questions, free recall tests and so on. Even a spoken free recall test or short verbal response to a question could be an example of overt retrieval.

There is an acknowledgement in the study that an overt retrieval practice strategy might lead to memories retrieved in this way being more distinctive. However, it also suggests that if covert retrieval demands that the learner hold information in their mind while continuing to think about other aspects (the example given is a covert free recall test) then this could be an instance of a desirable difficulty, given that there are increased demands on memory when using covert retrieval in this way. In the test, the conclusion was that covert retrieval was as effective as overt retrieval.

Dunlosky et al. concede that they chiefly focused on studies which involved using imagery for longer texts. They also emphasise the importance of how the text is received, so if learners listen to a text being spoken aloud or if they read the text being spoken to them, then this may affect the way the text is translated into mental images.[57]

A point made in *Learning as a Generative Activity*, with reference to the potential usefulness of using mental imagery versus a technique like drawing a representation of what is said/read, is that by not drawing but solely imagining, the effects of cognitive load are reduced.[58] In other words, students' working memories are free to focus on the imagining side of things as opposed to being over-taxed by thinking about the image they are drawing.

53 See https://twitter.com/hashtag/toomanywordsonyourslides?src=hash.
54 Fiorella and Mayer, *Learning as a Generative Activity*, p. 84.
55 Lang, *Small Teaching,* loc. 693.
56 Megan A. Smith, Henry L. Roediger III and Jeffrey D. Karpicke, 'Covert Retrieval Practice Benefits Retention as Much as Overt Retrieval Practice', *Journal of Experimental Psychology: Learning, Memory, and Cognition*, 39(6) (2013), 1712–1725.
57 Dunlosky et al., 'Improving Students' Learning with Effective Learning Techniques', pp. 24–25.
58 Fiorella and Mayer, *Learning as a Generative Activity*, p. 84.

Early on in my career, I asked students to do PowerPoint presentations as projects. I now wonder how much thinking went into the presentations and how much into the learning goal? Where was the cognitive load going?

Conversely, according to Fiorella and Mayer, it may be that using imagining as a study skill versus drawing (in the example they use) could be more taxing on working memory because of the need for a learner to hold the images in their head as opposed to reducing the cognitive load by drawing the visual representation and not having to rely on keeping the various images in their heads.[59]

The reason why imagery for text did not make it into the top-rated techniques in the Dunlosky review is that, as with the keyword mnemonic, the usefulness of the technique is restricted to materials which lend themselves well to being manipulated into an image.[60] However, they acknowledge that it may be that more research on using imagery is needed.

Before moving on to consider what techniques have been shown to work more effectively in Chapter 4, this quote from David Didau is probably a good way of finishing off this chapter:

I've had to integrate everything I do and think to fit with my new understanding – some of what I thought was right has had to be revised, other things have been rejected utterly. My views are still shifting and as they shift so do I.[61]

---

59 Fiorella and Mayer, *Learning as a Generative Activity*, p. 84.
60 Dunlosky et al. 'Improving Students' Learning with Effective Learning Techniques', p. 26.
61 Didau, *What If Everything You Knew About Education Was Wrong?*, p. 166.

Chapter 4
What *Might* Work Better

Having referred to the learning strategies which didn't make the cut in the previous chapter, it's time for a discussion of the learning strategies which did rank highly or show promise.

There are a number of fantastic blog posts out there which refer to how some of the study skills discussed in this chapter are being used and promoted as whole-school initiatives: Shaun Allison's excellent blog Class Teaching, in particular the post 'Supporting Learning Through Effective Revision Techniques';[1] Phil Stock's great summary of the revision strategies that are being employed at his school;[2] Dawn Cox's piece on how to design an effective revision session;[3] and Jamie Davies's post on the Dunlosky review,[4] to name just a few of them. (I feel like I'm doing a leaving speech where there are that many excellent people, you don't really want to name names for fear of leaving someone out …)

A distilled version of the Dunlosky review, which appeared in *Scientific American Mind*, referred to the study skills strategies which have been shown to work more effectively as 'gold star' and the ones which were of use but requiring more research as 'runners-up'.[5] Here is a reminder of the five techniques shown to be most effective:

1. Self-testing (or practice testing) (gold star standard)

2. Distributed practice (gold star standard)

3. Elaborative interrogation (runner-up)

4. Self-explanation (runner-up)

5. Interleaved practice (runner-up)[6]

---

1   Allison, 'Supporting Learning Through Effective Revision Techniques'.
2   Phil Stock, 'Five Strategies for Encouraging More Effective Independent Study', *Must Do Better* [blog] (24 March 2016). Available at: https://joeybagstock.wordpress.com/2016/03/24/five-strategies-for-encouraging-more-effective-independent-study/.
3   Dawn Cox, 'Using Research to Design a Revision Session', *missdcoxblog* [blog] (12 January 2016). Available at: https://missdcoxblog.wordpress.com/2016/01/12/using-research-to-design-a-revision-session/.
4   Jamie Davies, 'No More Highlighting – Improving Learning with Effective Techniques', *Jamie Davies* [blog] (15 March 2014). Available at: http://jamiedavi.es/no-more-highlighting-improving-learning-with-effective-techniques-575.php.
5   Dunlosky et al., 'What Works, What Doesn't',
6   Dunlosky et al., 'What Works, What Doesn't'.

There are no bronze medals here; just two golds and three silvers. As we have already seen, there is a significant overlap from the Dunlosky research with the less successful and more successful strategies referred to in Fiorella and Mayer's *Learning as a Generative Activity* and by the Learning Scientists. Also interspersed in this chapter are some additional strategies, such as knowledge organisers, which have not yet featured explicitly (as far as I know) in any randomised controlled trials. These have been included to give some practical examples of how techniques like practice testing might work in the classroom.

I've hedged my bets on calling this chapter 'What *Might* Work Better'. There are no wild claims here that doing a particular physics problem will create a million extra neurons in your students' brains! But hopefully you will find some useful techniques to use in your classroom.

Learning as a Generative Activity

Before we discuss the techniques identified as being more effective in the Dunlosky review, it is worth just picking up on some of the shared features referred to in *Learning as a Generative Activity* and how these are defined by the authors.

Logan Fiorella and Richard Mayer refer to generative learning happening:

---

when the learner engages in appropriate cognitive processing during learning, including attending to the relevant information (i.e., selecting), mentally organizing incoming information into a coherent cognitive structure (i.e., organizing), and integrating the cognitive structures with each other and with relevant prior knowledge activated from long-term memory (i.e., integrating).[7]

The idea that students need to generate their own understanding of the material they are studying by elaborating on it in some way is arguably a key feature of the more effective study skills covered by the Dunlosky review, *Learning as a Generative Activity* and the six strategies set out by the Learning Scientists. However, it is worth noting that Fiorella and Mayer also describe the high-ranking strategies interleaving and distributed practice as 'practice-scheduling strategies rather than learning strategies'.[8]

7   Fiorella and Mayer, *Learning as a Generative Activity*, p. 1.
8   Fiorella and Mayer, *Learning as a Generative Activity*, p. 198.

In *What If Everything You Knew About Education Was Wrong?*, David Didau discusses 'the generation effect'[9] (one of Robert Bjork's 'desirable difficulties' discussed in Chapter 2). Bjork emphasises 'the long-term benefit of generating an answer, solution, or procedure versus being presented that answer, solution, or procedure'.[10]

Many of the learning strategies which have been shown to be more effective involve an output of some kind. As we saw earlier, rereading material involves an input whereas a free recall test, for example, involves an output. Testing or quizzing involves an output, as does elaborative interrogation and self-explanation. Highlighting involves little output except for creating garishly embellished revision workbooks and perhaps a few notes. Cramming or massing the practice involves a lot of input but a quick evaporation of what has been learned. By keeping the retrieval strength topped up throughout the cramming, there's no forgetting and therefore no gain in terms of storage strength.

I attended Geoff Petty's lecture at the University of Wolverhampton on the nature of high quality teaching and learning, which touched on the need for students to build an understanding of the material.[11] Many of the study skills that have been shown to work are based on students practising, testing and building comprehension through an output which involves them attaching meaning to the content. Even practice testing using flashcards can be adapted to elaborate on the material and not just test recall (see the strategy 'Flashcards' in Part 2 for how this could work). A point stressed by Brown et al. in *Make It Stick* is that repeated contact with the material alone isn't going to help that much. It is retrieval that is the key.

In the same lecture, Petty refers to the following research on SATs:

Research on SATs found that 80% of 12 year olds with calculators could do this:

$225 \div 15 =$

But only 40% can do this:

If a gardener has 225 bulbs to place equally in 15 flower beds, how many would be in each bed?

Most of the failing pupils did not know which mathematical operation to use.[12]

---

9   Didau, *What If Everything You Knew About Education Was Wrong?*, pp. 243–244.
10   Bjork and Bjork, 'Making Things Hard on Yourself', p. 61.
11   Geoff Petty, 'What is High Quality Teaching and Learning?' [video] (9 December 2015). Available at: https://www.youtube.com/watch?v=g-DKu7Q5_wAandfeature=youtu.be.
12   Petty, 'What is High Quality Teaching and Learning?'

According to Petty, the problem is that students can't make the link between division and their prior knowledge. He describes this as going from a concrete example to an abstract concept, and suggests that unless the student has a concept for division linked to their prior knowledge, then the learning cannot take place.

The issue with students not seeing the concrete example hidden behind the surface structure of a problem is raised by Daniel Willingham in *Why Don't Students Like School?* when he poses the following mathematical problems:

Jayne is reseeding her lawn. The lawn is 20 feet wide and 100 feet long. She knows that lawn seed costs $10 per bag, and that each bag will seed 1,000 square feet. How much money does Jayne need to seed her whole lawn?

Jon is varnishing his tabletop, which is 72 inches long and 36 inches wide. The varnish he needs costs $8 per can, and each can will cover 2,300 square inches. How much money does he need to buy the varnish?[13]

Willingham goes on to explain that these problems rely on the same series of steps: first, working out the area of a rectangle and then calculating the amount needed to seed the lawn/varnish the table. The steps are essentially the same, but the surface structure (i.e. the wording of the problems and how they are framed) is different, and learners are drawn towards the surface structure and miss the underlying deep structure needed to solve comparable problems. As a solution, Willingham observes that 'experience helps students to see deep structure, so provide that experience via lots of examples'.[14]

Kris Boulton covers flexible and inflexible knowledge in a blog post.[15] Knowing the answer to 225 ÷ 15 could be an example of inflexible knowledge: knowing the answer to this sum is one thing, but being faced with a similar type of problem in an example which effectively obscures the problem is another. In the second example from Petty's lecture, there are more concepts to understand in how the question is framed (i.e. gardener, bulbs, flower beds).

---

13 Daniel Willingham, *Why Don't Students Like School? A Cognitive Scientist Answers Questions About How the Mind Works and What It Means for the Classroom* (San Francisco, CA: Jossey-Bass, 2009), p. 97.

14 Willingham, *Why Don't Students Like School?*, p. 102.

15 Kris Boulton, 'What Rote Knowledge Isn't – A Short Introduction to Inflexible and Flexible Knowledge', … *To the Real* [blog] (25 April 2015). Available at: https://tothereal.wordpress.com/2015/04/25/what-rote-knowledge-isnt-a-short-introduction-to-inflexible-and-flexible-knowledge/.

All of this has implications for those study skills which have been shown to work more effectively, especially practice testing, in terms of identifying why students struggle with certain types of problems. For example, on the OCR GCSE higher maths sample paper, there is a question about a restaurant menu having a particular number of starters, mains and desserts from which candidates have to show that there are 744 different ways of choosing a meal.[16] Generating a similar problem, but using a different surface structure, could be effective as a revision study skill, provided the practice test is low stakes or no stakes and with feedback on any mistakes made. For instance:

A sweet shop has 3 types of blue sweets, 16 types of red sweets and 10 types of black sweets on offer.

Customers can make up a bag of sweets from the following selection

▮ Blue and red sweets (48)

▮ Blue and black sweets (30)

▮ Blue, red and black sweets (480)

Show that there are 558 different ways that customers could make up a bag of sweets.

This might seem obvious; however, in my first few years of teaching it wasn't apparent to me why the surface structure of a problem might be a potential stumbling block to students' understanding (let alone grasping that by providing additional examples with different surface structures I might help to boost their understanding). I remember mentoring Year 11 students and focusing my conversations around the ubiquitous revision planner (discussing time management strategies and ensuring that they divided up their revision plan into nice, neat half-hour chunks) and tricks or tips to improve performance in summative tests (the culture of working at grades and target grades, using examiner reports, etc.). I never got into the specifics of which questions they found difficult and why.

Of course, it was partly down to the fact that I wasn't a subject expert across the full suite of GCSE options, but I don't think that this necessarily would have stopped me giving it a go in terms of helping them to look at each question and working together to figure out the underlying problem. It was more of my lack of understanding of cognitive psychology and how that knowledge might be used to help me appreciate what was happening in their minds. Had I been better informed, I might have been better able to source other examples with different surface structures.

16 See http://www.ocr.org.uk/Images/169001-higher-tier-sample-assessment-materials.pdf.

It would be tempting, perhaps, to create practice problems around the notion of surface structure – analysing past paper questions, tweaking the surface structure while keeping the basic problem the same, creating a bank of questions which mirror the problem, then mixing up the order of the practice problems to promote a level of transfer. Using this type of strategy as an aid to better understand the subject domain gets my vote, but not if it is focused on a short-term exam performance goal.

Elaborative Interrogation

Elaborative interrogation is another of the silver award winners referred to in 'What Works, What Doesn't' and the Dunlosky review. In other words, it's a promising technique which deserves to be researched further.

The essence and effectiveness of elaborative interrogation has been summed up well by Andy Tharby (@atharby) and colleagues from Durrington High School.[17] The first strategy they describe to help improve a student's memory is 'Asking "why" something is true. If students are compelled to do this form of elaboration while working or revising then they will be compelled to think about meaning.' In short, this means stating a fact and then expanding on why that fact is true. There is a level of output from the student as they are being asked to activate prior knowledge about the material and generate new meanings.

The prompt to get students to elaborate on why a stated fact is true could be something like this for geography:

Warm sea temperatures/sea temperatures in excess of 27°C have the potential to cause a tropical storm. Why is this true?

Migration can lead to an increased number of people in a city. Why is this true?

Another illustration appears in Robert Marzano and John Brown's book, *A Handbook for the Art and Science of Teaching*, where students in a maths lesson are presented with this problem: 'If you change the dimensions of a square but keep it as a rectangle with the same

---

17   Durrington High School, 'What Will Improve a Students' Meomory [sic]?'

unit area, how will its perimeter change?'[18] The students are asked to apply prior knowledge in defence of their answer.

In the Dunlosky review, the rationale behind why elaborative interrogation works is said to be because it integrates new learning with existing knowledge, thus increasing overall learning.[19] The authors refer to a study of elaborative interrogation carried out by Michael Pressley and colleagues in which undergraduate students were prompted to elaborate on the actions of a man when shown a list of sentences describing his actions. On the final cued recall test, the elaborative interrogation group performed much better than the other two groups, who were either presented with an explanation for each sentence or simply instructed to read them.[20]

Fiorella and Mayer raise concerns about elaborative interrogation in *Learning as a Generative Activity*, suggesting that its effectiveness is limited to factual knowledge and so it is less useful for learning about concepts.[21] This is also highlighted as a potential drawback by Dunlosky et al. They suggest that if the material is complex, then knowing which aspect of the content to target with elaborative interrogation becomes more difficult (the example they use is the digestive system). However, as an effective revisiting or revision tool, it still might be worth a shot at using elaborative interrogation with students for less factually based concepts.

I've tried using a form of elaborative interrogation when revisiting key vocabulary and short phrases with students – I've suggested utilising it as an alternative to the keyword method when they are away from the classroom. This (unresearched) application to languages went something like this when I modelled it with a student for the rest of the class:

Me: The word *taller* (*in Spanish*) means 'workshop'. Why is this true?

Student: (*After a pause*) *Taller* means workshop because when Santa works with the elves in his workshop he is taller than everyone else.

I appreciate this may sound ridiculous, but the vocabulary, and most importantly the meaning, stuck. If I had to guess why, I would say it was because the student was able to

18 Robert J. Marzano and John L. Brown, *A Handbook for the Art and Science of Teaching* (Alexandria, VA: Association for Supervision and Curriculum Development, 2009), p. 70.

19 Dunlosky et al., 'Improving Students' Learning with Effective Learning Techniques', p. 8.

20 Michael Pressley, Mark A. McDaniel, James E. Turnure, Eileen Wood and Maheen Ahmad, 'Generation and Precision of Elaboration: Effects on Intentional and Incidental Learning', *Journal of Experimental Psychology: Learning, Memory, and Cognition*, 13 (1987), 291–300.

21 Fiorella and Mayer, *Learning as a Generative Activity*, p. 128.

combine their own prior knowledge of Santa and his elves using the retrieval cue of the English word 'taller' to associate an image with the meaning of the hitherto meaningless Spanish word *taller*. Although, I could be wrong.

As a way of elaborating on content, it's not exactly going to rock the research field of cognitive psychology, but the application seemed to work for this student. And by 'work' I mean that when he saw it in a reading extract some weeks later, he could pick out the meaning. Furthermore, when I presented the cue of *el taller* again, he was able to recall the meaning of it. Transfer success!

The ease of retrieval of the target word here was helped by the student's self-generated cue. In the past I had tried modelling the keyword method in class (as well as my own application of elaborative interrogation with vocabulary and short phrases) using my own cues. I never understood why this didn't work as effectively as I'd hoped, but I now see that the students were simply learning *my* understanding and *my* retrieval cues rather than their own, which would have been more distinctive. Perhaps there is a sort of distinctiveness effect going on here (touched on in the Dunlosky review) – that information which is peculiar can be more easily recollected.

I have trialled providing the students with a list of vocabulary or longer phrases and adopting this strategy with a whole class. For example:

1. *desde hace* + verb in present tense = to have been (and still be) doing something (*vivo aquí desde hace cinco años* = I've been living here for five years)

2. *compartir una habitación/un dormitorio* = to share a room

3. *ruidoso* = noisy, *ruido* = noise

4. *partido* = match (football, tennis, etc.)

5. *equitación* = horse-riding, *montar a caballo* = to go horse-riding

6. *hacer vela* = sailing

7. *piragüismo* = canoeing

8. *primavera* = spring, *verano* = summer, *otoño* = autumn, *invierno* = winter

9. *triste* = sad

10. *país* = country

11. *sensible* = sensitive

12. *tengo que* + infinitive = I have to …

13. *asco* = disgust, *asqueroso* = disgusting

14. *hace* = time phrase – ago (*hace cuatro años* = four years ago)

If we take the first instance from the list above, it might go something like:

---

desde hace + verb in present tense = to have been (and still be) doing something *(vivo aquí desde hace cinco años* = I've been living here for five years)

Why is this true?

Because *Des(de)* and *Hace* have been friends for years and still are.

I am sadly lacking in empirical evidence to show that this is a perfect way of harnessing the distinctiveness effect, but I have successfully presented content like this and got the students to create their own particular reason why the sound or look of a word or phrase could mean what it does.

It is worth noting here the difference between *maintenance rehearsal* of an item (where you just repeat it to yourself over and over again without tying it to anything) versus *elaborative rehearsal* (where you connect the item to be remembered to other items you know). If I'm honest, I never did any sort of elaboration when I was revising at home. As an erstwhile GCSE student, I sat with lots of lists of content from different subjects and repeated words and key terms over and over again, hoping that they would stick. All that staring and repeating of information to myself was sadly lacking in elaboration and depth of processing, and consequently lacking in effectiveness.

In *Cognitive Psychology: Connecting Mind, Research, and Everyday Experience*, Bruce Goldstein discusses the 'self-referencing effect' and suggests that memory is improved through relating a word to oneself.[22] He refers to a study by Timothy Rogers and colleagues in which participants were shown a question, then a word and then had to answer 'yes' or 'no' in response to a question asking if it described themselves. The results showed that those who took part tended to recall better those words that referred to themselves.[23]

---

22 Goldstein, *Cognitive Psychology*, p. 177.
23 Timothy B. Rogers, Nicholas A. Kuiper and William. S. Kirker, 'Self-Reference and the Encoding of Personal Information', *Journal of Personality and Social Psychology*, 35(9) (1977), 677–688.

In language lessons, I have trialled the technique (borrowed from Daniel Willingham's suggestion in *Why Don't Students Like School?*[24]) of asking students to rate words according to how much they like each one, how little they like each one and so on. I have explained this to students in class, and parents at parents' evenings, as a way of revising – for example, 'Read through the list of key vocabulary I have given you and note down your eight favourite words and why. Then leave it a few days while revising another subject, ideally one that is not similar in content, before returning and looking only at the English meanings and writing down as many words as you can from memory.'

Perhaps linking words (or key terminology) across a range of domains and encouraging students to self-reference with this material might be worth a punt as a means of elaborating on it, if we extend the technique to longer phrases and key terms in other domains and not just vocabulary.

Incidentally, a fascinating in-school study involving Year 8 students learning Tier 2 vocabulary focused on students first matching up French cognates with the English Tier 1 equivalents and then matching the English Tier 1 equivalents with the English tier 2 equivalents.[25] I mention this as a potential area of knowledge (Tier 2 vocabulary) which could potentially be targeted with techniques like the self-referencing effect.

Dunlosky and colleagues describe more pronounced effects of using elaborative interrogation where there is already a high level of prior knowledge – that is to say, the more one knows, the more detailed and accurate the explanations will be.[26] Using elaborative interrogation when you have no prior knowledge on the topic you are trying to elaborate is a no-no.

It seems obvious, but students may not elaborate well enough (due to lack of prior knowledge, for instance) if applying this technique away from the classroom and without feedback, so there has to be a system in place whereby they can check on the quality of their work. Clearly, none of the techniques discussed here are likely to be as effective if there is no feedback.

However, there are some potential benefits to the learner having a level of uncertainty when adopting elaborative interrogation and self-explanation (see below). It may be that these techniques, which clearly involve self-questioning, may promote a level of curiosity in the learner and so lead them on to find out more about the subject. (Or not – I may be wrong.)

---

24 Willingham, *Why Don't Students Like School?*, p. 63.
25 Emma Bilbrough and Danielle Walters, 'Teaching Tier 2 Vocabulary', *Class Teaching* [blog] (8 December 2016). Available at: https://classteaching.wordpress.com/2016/12/08/teaching-tier-2-vocabulary/.
26 Dunlosky et al., 'Improving Students' Learning with Effective Learning Techniques', p. 9.

As a former A level geographer, I have a little prior knowledge to model how elaborative interrogation could work with the first key idea on the subject content page of the AQA geography exam specification.[27] In other words, I'm going to revise my GCSE geography using elaborative interrogation. No cheating and no peeking, I'm going to do this as I write (after I've turned off the broadband).

Key idea	Specification content
Natural hazards pose major risks to people and property.	Definition of a natural hazard. Types of natural hazard. Factors affecting hazard risk.

Natural hazards pose major risks to people and property: why is this true?

This is true because natural hazards pose major risks to people and property because natural hazards like flooding, storms, droughts and earthquakes, for example, can lead to settlements being flooded (if populations have settled on a flood plain, for instance) or crops being destroyed and people's houses or land will no longer be habitable. Earthquakes also pose a major risk to people and property. This is true because earthquakes not only do damage to buildings when they occur but they can also have secondary effects. For example, if an earthquake destroys sanitation units, water plants or power plants, people could be left without clean water or electricity. This could then affect their quality of life and standard of living.

That's my understanding of the first key idea using elaborative interrogation as the revision technique. How good is it? My instinct is that it's not a bad effort, and I have to say that my mind certainly didn't wander off as I was doing it (as it may have done had I chosen to read, reread or even make a summary with the text present while I summarised). In terms of an output task, I felt compelled to focus on generating a meaning and bringing an understanding to the statement. Obviously, I need to check to see if I could have written a better answer and if there are any misconceptions in my own elaboration. If revising at home I won't have access to a geography specialist, of course, but I could use my revision notes from the lesson, type it in online or onto the school's website and so on. Artificial

27 See http://filestore.aqa.org.uk/resources/geography/AQA-8035-SP-2016.pdf.

intelligence isn't quite there, so I can't ask the in-house robot yet … There are more examples of this technique in Part 2.

In *Learning as a Generative Activity*, Fiorella and Mayer compare elaborative interrogation to a similar technique which is also mentioned in the Dunlosky review – self-explanation, which we will come on to next. In Part 2, there are some examples (provided by subject teachers) of how elaborative interrogation could work as a learning strategy. There are also hybrid forms of what might be considered self-explanation crossed with elaborative interrogation, which include embedded elaborative interrogation prompts.

Self-Explanation

Before I took my driving test I asked my instructor if he thought the examiner would mind if I talked through aloud what I was about to do during the test. I didn't frame it or expect it to become some sort of thinking aloud protocol, but in any case he didn't think the examiner would mind. I adopted a rudimentary self-explanation technique during the test with the commentary going something like this:

Examiner: If you could take the next left at the roundabout and then drive straight on until the following roundabout where I would like you to take a right, please.

Me: OK, thanks John. What do I need to do first? So, I'm firstly looking in the mirror because I need to change lanes, and looking in the mirror is the first thing to do before I make any manoeuvre. What other information do I have? I can see that there is a car approaching behind me in the other lane and I will wait for it to pass. What is the next procedure I need to adopt? Looking back in my mirror, I am now going to put on my indicator and move into the other lane before then …

I passed! The idea of talking through what each step in a set of procedures or worked example means to you, and explaining how this relates to your prior knowledge of the problem to be solved, has shown to be a promising and effective learning strategy, even if some of my self-explanation teetered towards the monitoring or paraphrasing in the example above.

Self-explanation is touched on in *Small Teaching* in the same context in which I am using it here. The author, James Lang, got his daughter to describe to him what she did while she was driving.[28] Seemingly, neither Lang nor I appeared to be aware that self-explanation was occurring, just that what was happening seemed to be working. In my experience, it helped me to break down an admittedly freshly automated skill into its component parts, even if it did make me sound a little odd.

So, self-explanation is essentially talking through and explaining what each part of a process, for instance, means to you and how it relates to information you have already processed or that you have in your long-term memory. The rationale is based on the idea of integrating new knowledge with prior knowledge.

In the Dunlosky review, the underlying feature of self-explanation is that students talk through their thinking as they are learning something new.[29] Fiorella and Mayer describe self-explanation as being applicable to use with texts, diagrams and worked examples.[30] In *The Content of Physics Self-Explanations*, Michelene Chi and Kurt VanLehn distinguish between self-explanation and elaboration in terms of the difference between something which is created in the context of learning something new (self-explanation) and using existing knowledge to further embed that knowledge but in a new context (elaboration).[31]

Common types of prompts which might encourage self-explanation could be students asking themselves, 'What does this mean to me?' or 'How does this problem relate to what I already know?', and verbalising their thought processes as they work their way through the task. Note that these are generic prompts and not subject-specific prompts. More specific prompts, which would be related to domain-specific content, could be used alongside worked examples. For instance, Chi and VanLehn state that the learner must use self-explanation for each step in a worked out example in order that they can fully understand the ways in which each component develops from the previous one.[32]

Alexander Renkl and Robert Atkinson explore the worked example effect in 'Learning from Worked-Out Examples and Problem Solving'.[33] To paraphrase, a worked-out example is a problem, the steps to solve the problem and the solution to that problem. They suggest

---

28 Lang, *Small Teaching*, loc. 2251.
29 Dunlosky et al., 'Improving Students' Learning with Effective Learning Techniques', p. 11.
30 Fiorella and Mayer, *Learning as a Generative Activity*, p. 124.
31 Michelene T. H. Chi and Kurt A. VanLehn, 'The Content of Physics Self-Explanations', *Journal of the Learning Sciences*, 1(1)(1991), 69–105 at pp. 71–72. Available at: http://www.public.asu.edu/~mtchi/papers/ChiVanLehn.pdf.
32 Chi and VanLehn, 'The Content of Physics Self-Explanations', p. 70.
33 Alexander Renkl and Robert K. Atkinson, 'Learning from Worked-Out Examples and Problem Solving'. In Jan L. Plass, Roxana Moreno and Roland Brünken (eds), *Cognitive Load Theory*, Kindle edn (New York: Cambridge University Press, 2010), ch. 5, loc. 1859–2184.

that using self-explanation during the steps of a worked example would enhance near transfer, but also cite studies showing far transfer.

They also discuss the idea of fading, which is pretty much taking away one part of a worked example and replacing it with a practice problem. For example, there might be a set of worked examples with the first step missing, another set with two steps missing and so on until you are just left with the practice problem. Completion problems might also be an example of fading – for instance, the learner has to complete some of the steps involved to solve an algebra worked example (there is an example of this in Part 2).[34]

An example of a 'backwards-faded worksheet', courtesy of author, speaker and science teacher Kelly Morgan (@kmorgan_sci_ed), is set out below (we will return to this again in Part 2).[35]

---

1. Convert 20.33 cm to m

$$\frac{20.33 \text{ cm} \quad \big| \quad 0.01 \text{ m}}{\big| \quad 1 \text{ cm}} = 20.33 \text{ x } 0.01 \text{ / } 1 = \boxed{0.2033 \text{ m}}$$

2. Convert 12.06 l to cl

$$\frac{12.06 \text{ l} \quad \big| \quad 1 \text{ cl}}{\big| \quad 0.01 \text{ l}} = 12.06 \text{ x } 1 \text{ / } 0.01 = \boxed{1206 \text{ cl}}$$

3. Convert 32.27 kg to g

$$\frac{32.27 \text{ kg} \quad \big| \quad 1000 \text{ g}}{\big| \quad 1 \text{ kg}} = 32.27 \text{ x } 1000 \text{ / } 1 =$$

---

34 There is a whole chapter dedicated to worked examples, completion problems and cognitive load in Sweller et al., *Cognitive Load Theory*, loc. 1524–1680.

35 Kelly Morgan, 'Teaching with Worked Examples – Save Learner Time and Effort While Increasing Performance!', *Kelly Morgan* [blog] (10 February 2011). Available at: http://kellymorganscience.com/teaching-with-worked-examples-save-learner-time-and-effort-while-increasing-performance/.

4. Convert 13.09 m to cm

$$\frac{13.09 \text{ m}}{} \left| \frac{1 \text{ cm}}{0.01 \text{ m}} \right. =$$

5. Convert 3.47 mm to m

$$\frac{3.47 \text{ mm}}{} \left| \frac{\text{m}}{\text{mm}} \right. =$$

6. Convert 33.81 kg to g

$$\frac{33.81 \text{ kg}}{} \left| \frac{}{\text{kg}} \right. =$$

7. Convert 9.92 kl to l

$$\frac{9.92 \text{ kl}}{} \left| \right. =$$

8. Convert 2.61 g to mg

$$\frac{2.61 \text{ g}}{} \left| \right. =$$

9. Convert 24.37 g to mg

10. Convert 28.77 l to cl

Part of the appeal of self-explanation seems to be that it moves learners away from passive learning activities and encourages them to reflect on and fill in potential gaps in knowledge through building inferences.

In the chapter on self-explanation in *Learning as a Generative Activity*, Fiorella and Mayer explore a model of learning proposed by Michelene Chi.[36] In 'Active-Constructive-Interactive: A Conceptual Framework for Differentiating Learning Activities', Chi describes the different activities which would be classed as active, such as copying steps towards a solution (a physical manifestation of something); constructive, where the learner produces something that has additionality beyond the original information; and interactive, which would involve someone or something else (interacting with multimedia and so on might be an example of this).[37] A passive activity would be one in which a learner displays no physical activity.

Because information during self-explanation goes further than the information that is simply presented in a diagram or as part of the solution steps in a worked example, for instance, then it could fall under a constructive activity in Chi's framework.

Greg Ashman helpfully refers to the worked example effect in his blog post on cognitive load theory:

> Reducing load for complex tasks is supported by research demonstrating the worked example effect where providing worked examples for students to study is superior to asking them to solve equivalent problems. Increasing load for simple tasks is supported by research demonstrating 'desirable difficulties'. For instance, if you want a student to learn the capital of Australia then it might be best to first ask them to guess before telling them the correct answer. This will get them thinking about what they know about Australia before you slot in the new information.[38]

Ashman also touches on element interactivity, which Clark and colleagues refer to in *Efficiency in Learning* as the coordination of a number of elements of information in the memory in order to complete a task.[39] Clark et al. describe certain types of vocabulary as being lower in element interactivity because each word is independent of other words. Getting the students to recall the meanings of vocabulary (i.e. with me standing at the front calling out the target word and the students calling out the English) could be

---

36 Fiorella and Mayer, *Learning as a Generative Activity*, p. 128.
37 Michelene T. H. Chi, 'Active-Constructive-Interactive: A Conceptual Framework for Differentiating Learning Activities', *Topics in Cognitive Science*, 1(1) (2009), 73–105.
38 Greg Ashman, 'Cognitive Load Theory – "The Single Most Important Thing for Teachers to Know"', *Filling the Pail* [blog] (27 January 2017). Available at: https://gregashman.wordpress.com/2017/01/27/cognitive-load-theory-the-single-most-important-theory-for-teachers-to-know/.
39 Clark et al., *Efficiency in Learning*, loc. 403–417.

described as an activity with low element interactivity. Previously I referred to retrieval strength success criteria as 'demonstrating' progress in lessons; perhaps it was also a case of demonstrating low element interactivity success criteria.

A task which involves processing a number of different elements in working memory to solve a problem (the example that Ashman uses is an algebraic equation) would have high element interactivity. For languages, a task in which students produce grammatically accurate sentences using an array of time phrases and tenses would be high in element interactivity (as would building sentences, according to Clark et al. in *Efficiency in Learning*). If students are non-experts in their subject domains, as you would imagine students to be, then tasks with high element interactivity will carry a heavy cognitive load, unless that load is managed effectively.

A lot of research into worked examples has taken place in well-structured domains like maths and science. This is a point made by Sweller and colleagues in *Cognitive Load Theory*, where they discuss studies in ill-structured domains like English, for example, where there is no obviously identifiable 'problem' to be solved. The authors cite a study which involved using Shakespeare plays which showed some evidence that the group of participants who had notes combined into the text performed better than the group who had no notes.[40] They suggest that the notes group may have benefitted from a sort of worked example effect. I mention this now as some of the practical examples using self-explanation in Part 2 are based on what might be considered as ill-structured domains like geography, for example; although it has to be said that these examples are not necessarily worked examples as such.

Nick Rose has written about germane load in his blog post on the subject.[41] Germane load refers to processing that is relevant to the construction of a schema in long-term memory, so it would be welcome cognitive load! In a very useful paper by Jeroen van Merriënboer and John Sweller, the authors explain that germane cognitive load can be promoted by adopting the self-explanation technique with worked examples with prompts.[42]

However, beware of the potential for the expertise reversal effect. As novices become more expert and build up schemas, less guidance is needed. As Nick Rose and David Didau note, learners may be processing unnecessary information when you are giving them

---

40 Paul Chandler, Annishka Oksa and Slava Kalyuga, 'Expertise Reversal Effect in Using Explanatory Notes for Readers of Shakespearean Text', *Instructional Science*, 38(3) (2010), 217–236.

41 Rose, 'Germane Load'.

42 Jeroen J. G. van Merriënboer and John Sweller, 'Cognitive Load Theory in Health Professional Education: Design Principles and Strategies', *Medical Education*, 44 (2010), 85–93. Available at: http://sites.uci.edu/medsim/files/2015/03/Cognitive-Load-Theory-in-Health-Professions.pdf.

additional instructions and guidance, thereby increasing their cognitive load as they try to synthesise this with existing information.[43]

There are a number of other studies, in addition to the work by Chi mentioned earlier, which measure the effectiveness of self-explanation. Dunlosky et al. cite a study by Dianne Berry in which one set of participants undertook self-explanation after they had completed a problem, while another group adopted the strategy while they were completing the problem. The outcomes were compared with no self-explaining and showed that there were positive effects from self-explaining afterwards, but not as much as self-explanation carried out while solving the problem. Why not trial doing both with a class![44]

Trialling using self-explanation with a text as a reading aid has, at times, felt a bit like I've been using a sort of reading comprehension strategy. Daniel Willingham and Gail Lovette note that reading comprehension strategies can make use of simple, easily learned, generic questions which, surprisingly, do help students to comprehend what is being read. They compare this to very generalised instructions for assembling a piece of flat-pack furniture, such as: 'Put stuff together. Every so often, stop and look at it, and evaluate how it's going. It may also help to think back on other pieces of furniture you've built before.'[45] Some of my examples may have come across in this way when I've been using content-free prompts. However, I felt that they did help me when I used the generic prompts myself; at the very least, they helped me to connect the ideas to prior knowledge and reminded me what to think about.

Interestingly, in *E-Learning and the Science of Instruction*, Clark and Mayer encourage using self-explanation through active observation. They refer to potential benefits (for 'mature learners') in 'observational learning' which involves 'watching a human tutor explain problems to a student'. They cite a study which involved students watching a recording of a tutor explaining a physics problem to a student, noting that because this presented students with a modelled answer for the given problem, it also ensured that they were actively engaged in the worked example.[46]

As a video can be stopped and started at will, this means that a film of a tutor explaining a physics problem, say, can be self-paced, so that those watching it can take their time to apply the technique. This may help to reduce cognitive load which can lead to the

43 Didau and Rose, *What Every Teacher Needs to Know About … Psychology*, p. 75.
44 Dunlosky et al., 'Improving Students' Learning with Effective Learning Techniques', p. 11. See also: Dianne C. Berry, 'Metacognitive Experience and Transfer of Logical Reasoning', *Quarterly Journal of Experimental Psychology*, 35A (1982), 39–49.
45 Daniel Willingham and Gail Lovette, 'Can Reading Comprehension Be Taught?', *Teachers College Record* (26 September 2014). Available at: http://www.danielwillingham.com/uploads/5/0/0/7/5007325/willingham&lovette_2014_can_reading_comprehension_be_taught_.pdf.
46 Clark and Mayer, *E-Learning and the Science of Instruction*, loc. 5123, 5131.

transient information effect – essentially the disappearance of information before the learner has had an opportunity to sufficiently process it or connect it to something else.

One of the conditions necessary to maximise active observation, according to Clark and Mayer, is to use very able students who will ask searching questions of the teacher throughout the process.[47] This also made me think that using a model student's book from which to draw best practice could also work. Using the study habits of excellent students as a worked example might be a little bit of a stretch, but if it helps …

Finally, in 'Supporting Self-Explanation in the Classroom', Jennifer Chiu and Michelene Chi describe the potential of adopting self-explanation alongside an incorrect example, suggesting that learners may learn more from this than if they use it alongside a correct example.[48] Why might this be the case? Possibly because students are forced to reflect more on any 'gaps in understanding' or 'faulty information'.

For example, the following incorrect worked example might be one to adopt with self-explanation. Thanks again to Dan Frankton for coming up with it.

$$4x + 5 \ = \ 16$$
$$\div\,4 \qquad\quad \div\,4$$
$$x + 5 \ = \ 4$$
$$\quad\ -5 \qquad -5$$
$$x \ = \ \text{-}1$$

You might think that combining self-explanation with this incorrect example and then with the correct worked example would confuse a learner. However, as Craig Barton notes in *How I Wish I'd Taught Maths*, he leads his students towards adopting self-explanation with an incorrect answer after they have done some practice on the correct version first.[49]

---

47 Clark and Mayer, *E-Learning and the Science of Instruction*, loc. 5131.
48 Jennifer Chiu and Michelene Chi, 'Supporting Self-Explanation in the Classroom'. In Victor A. Benassi, Catherine E. Overson and Christopher M. Hakala (eds), *Applying Science of Learning in Education: Infusing Psychological Science into the Curriculum* (2014). Available at: https://scholars.unh.edu/cgi/viewcontent.cgi?article=1286&context=psych_facpub.
49 Barton, *How I Wish I'd Taught* Maths, loc. 3781–3794.

Practice Testing

> While the brain is not a muscle that gets stronger with exercise, the neural pathways that make up a body of learning do get stronger, when the memory is retrieved and the learning is practiced. Periodic practice arrests forgetting, strengthens retrieval routes, and is essential for hanging onto the knowledge you want to gain.[50]

Testing has traditionally been viewed as a summative, end-of-unit/end-of-course assessment which is designed to show that the learner has attained a certain level, grade or proficiency. It is a means of assessing what has been learned, not of boosting learning itself. We have already touched on practice testing (or retrieval practice) a number of times in this book. However, in the context of revisiting and revision, I think it's important to pull some of it together here.

In the edublogosphere, there are lots of blog posts and articles on quizzing as an effective way to enhance learning, not simply as a means to assess learning. Retrieval practice even has its own website courtesy of assistant professor and cognitive scientist, Pooja Agarwal (@poojaagarwal), www.retrievalpractice.org, with a great, free downloadable guide about how retrieval practice works. It has also added its very own YouTube channel.

In *How We Learn*, Benedict Carey describes retrieval practice as a way to enhance learning (it is also known as 'the testing effect'). He suggests that the term retrieval practice was promoted to reduce the level of resistance towards seeing testing purely as a means to measure learning. The act of getting learners to retrieve information from memory as a way to develop more effective learning is discussed by Carey in the context of the Bjorks' 'desirable difficulties'. The idea is that having to retrieve, as opposed to reread/review prior learning, requires the brain to work harder. It is more difficult, and as a result the storage and retrieval strength for this learning is improved.[51]

In a 2011 study called 'Ten Benefits of Testing and Their Applications to Educational Practice', Henry Roediger and colleagues discuss and give evidence for practising retrieval over restudying. Among the ten benefits are that it can help to promote the transfer of knowledge to new areas and improve metacognitive monitoring and knowledge organisation.[52]

---

50 Brown et al., *Make It Stick*, p. 3.
51 Carey, *How We Learn*, loc. 1385.
52 Roediger et al., 'Ten Benefits of Testing'.

Retrieval practice isn't a panacea; even one of its proponents, Henry Roediger, says so.[53] However, there is a lot of research out there which points to it being an extremely effective learning strategy, especially when used alongside spacing. David Didau suggests that if practice testing is combined with two other well-rated strategies, spacing and interleaving, then the effects might be 'extraordinary'.[54] (Spacing and interleaving are covered later in this chapter.)

Some research into retrieval practice has taken place in laboratories, not in classroom settings, with the tested material randomly chosen by the researchers. Nonetheless, given that retrieval practice has been shown to be effective across a range of studies, I think it's a pretty good place to begin planning a revisiting or revision schedule. (Even if, as Didau describes, there have been arguments against practice testing being effective with complex materials[55] – although there are even counter arguments against this.[56])

Practice testing referred to as self-testing is covered by Fiorella and Mayer in *Learning as a Generative Activity* as an effective way of getting learners to make to-be-learned material more accessible later on. They provide an example for readers to complete which involves studying factual information about the sun followed by a practice free recall test.[57] The test is designed to trial the testing effect itself, not to assess how much is known.

The Dunlosky review cites a 2006 paper by Jeffrey Karpicke and Henry Roediger, which describes two effects of practice testing on the learners taking the tests: mediated (indirect) and unmediated (direct) effects. Some of the direct effects of testing mentioned include learners being able to identify the areas they didn't know and learn from this feedback. As for the mediated effects: 'testing promotes learning by making later studying or encoding more effective'.[58]

53 See Francisco, 'Ask the Cognitive Scientist: Retrieval Practice'.
54 David Didau, *What If Everything You Knew About Education Was Wrong?*, p. 240.
55 David Didau, 'The Testing Effect is Dead! Long Live the Testing Effect!', *The Learning Spy* [blog] (20 May 2015). Available at: http://www.learningspy.co.uk/featured/the-testing-effect-is-dead-long-live-the-testing-effect/.
56 Jeffrey D. Karpicke and William R. Aue, 'The Testing Effect Is Alive and Well with Complex Materials', *Educational Psychology Review*, 27(2) (2015), 317–326. Available at: http://link.springer.com/article/10.1007/s10648-015-9309-3/.
57 Fiorella and Mayer, *Learning as a Generative Activity*, pp. 98–100.
58 Henry L. Roediger III and Jeffrey D. Karpicke, 'The Power of Testing Memory: Basic Research and Implications for Educational Practice', *Perspectives on Psychological Science*, 1(3) (2006), 181–210 at pp. 181–182. Available at: http://journals.sagepub.com/doi/10.1111/j.1745-6916.2006.00012.x.

David Didau presents the following patterns with regard to strategies which relate to longer term learning. He defines 'study' as 'the revision of previously studied material':

---

1. Study study study study – test

2. Study study study test – test

3. Study study test test – test

4. Study test test test – test[59]

He observes that while it might seem logical that more studying over spaced intervals would result in better, more durable and longer term learning (as might be expected with study pattern 1), it is actually pattern 4 which is the most powerful. In terms of designing a revision plan, this has implications about what students actually do when they're revising away from the classroom.

David Didau makes the point that 'it doesn't really matter how we test students as long as our emphasis changes. Testing should not be used primarily to assess the efficacy of your teaching and students' learning; it should be used … to *help* them learn.'[60] Having said that, some of the ways that practice testing could be employed include:

1. Free recall tests or 'brain dumps'

2. Exit tickets or sticky notes

3. Multiple choice questions

4. Concept map retrieval (or scaffolded/supported drawing after reading[61])

5. Short answer questions

6. Flashcards (or flashcard apps like Flashcards+[62])

7. Online quizzing (e.g. Moodle, Quizlet, Socrative, Memrise, Quizizz)

---

59 Didau, *What If Everything You Knew About Education Was Wrong?*, p. 234.
60 Didau, *What If Everything You Knew About Education Was Wrong?*, p. 234.
61 For more on this see Clark and Mayer, *E-Learning and the Science of Instruction*, loc. 4693–4701.
62 For suggestions for other apps, see the website of Mark Anderson (@ICTEvangelist), the author of *Perfect ICT Every Lesson*: https://ictevangelist.com, or independent consultant Joe Dale (@joedale): http://joedale.typepad.com.

This list is not intended to be exhaustive but merely indicative of some of the ways that retrieval practice could be used. (There are more examples of how subject-specific content might look with some of these types of tests in Part 2.)

It's worth remembering the power of social media in spreading the retrieval practice word. In January 2017, head teacher Stuart Lock organised a powerful training day involving two of the Learning Scientists, Dr Yana Weinstein and Dr Carolina Kuepper-Tetzel. The researchers delivered effective learning strategy sessions for staff and students including some interesting ways of adopting retrieval practice. Putting my jealousy to one side for a moment that I wasn't there to see it, I have had a look at some of the great stuff that went on via Twitter (see #CVCinset). There are some fantastic looking ways to adopt retrieval practice and an excellent maths example of spacing and testing.

I've been a bit generic with the idea of 'concept map retrieval' here. This could refer to a multitude of concept maps – there are plenty to choose from. However, for the purposes of this section, concept map retrieval refers to any type of concept map where the student fills in the missing information from memory.

Oliver Caviglioli makes some brilliant suggestions about how to construct a concept map in his HOW2s (visuals of teaching approaches) and his website (https://teachinghow2s.com). This tweet in particular shows how the building of a concept map by two students in class could work and how the ideas can be structured so they link effectively to one another.[63] Another excellent book which gives more insight into the organisation of knowledge is Frederick Reif's *Applying Cognitive Science to Education*.[64]

Some of the examples of retrieval practice with subject content in Part 2 are simply questions based on an extract. However, given that even in Pooja Agarwal's guide it is acknowledged that we are probably already using retrieval practice, it's hopefully still worth including them as a way of supporting retrieval 'as a learning strategy, not an assessment tool'.[65]

Both Didau and Carey allude to pre-testing, which could be setting a test for learners at the start of a topic which features content which they will be learning about during the topic.[66] This is, of course, different from retrieval practice in that you are not trying to bring information already covered to mind, as it's not been covered yet!

---

63 See https://twitter.com/olivercavigliol/status/894631641100025857.
64 Frederick Reif, *Applying Cognitive Science to Education*, Kindle edn (London: MIT Press, 2008).
65 See https://www.retrievalpractice.org/overview/.
66 Didau, *What If Everything You Knew About Education Was Wrong?*, pp. 244–246; Carey, *How We Learn*, loc. 1392–1489.

It might take a brave revision planner or progress leader to give a past paper to a group of Year 10 students just as they start their GCSE course, but as Phil Stock says, a past paper is not the same as a quiz. Perhaps a multiple choice quiz on the main features of the course content (or even a wider domain) might be a strategy to trial in making a pre-emptive strike against the forgetting curve.[67]

In *Study Smart*, Nicholas Soderstrom refers to some pre-testing that was trialled in some of Elizabeth Bjork's lectures. In the final exams, student performance on material that had been pre-tested was 10% better than on material that had not been pre-tested. He concludes that pre-testing may alert students to pay closer attention to material when it comes up later on in the course, as they remember how poorly they understood it at the pre-test stage.[68]

It's now time for some hideous self-promotion! I use an activity from my book, *Fun Learning Activities in Modern Foreign Languages,* called 'fast-forwarded learning', which I like to think is pre-test-ish or pre-test-lite (although I knew nothing about pre-testing at the time, so this is not a claim to say 'Look at me! I invented pre-testing all by myself!').[69] I film myself 'teaching' part of the syllabus to an empty room. The students' task is to work out the answers based on the questions I ask and the cues I provide in this 'fast-forwarded' aspect of the course – even though they haven't covered the material yet.

The idea of recording a clip and not just teaching in real time may seem a little gimmicky, although the theory was that it was just another way to vary quizzing and practice as the students and I may otherwise have been plodding through each chapter of a textbook. A more straightforward technique is to look at what was taught last lesson/last week/last term/last year and set a question which targets each part of the course. Alternatively, you could create a hand-out of the scheme of learning after a term's teaching, including the name of each module, chapter and so on, and ask students to brain dump everything they can remember relevant to each module. There are some practical examples of how retrieval practice might look in different subjects in Part 2.

67 Stock, 'Five Strategies for Encouraging More Effective Independent Study'.
68 Soderstrom, *Study Smart*, p. 37.
69 Jake Hunton, *Fun Learning Activities in Modern Foreign Languages: A Complete Toolkit for Ensuring Engagement, Progress and Achievement* (Carmarthen: Crown House Publishing, 2015), pp. 182–185.

Multiple Choice Questions

In a wonderful podcast, Craig Barton asks Dylan Wiliam about what approaches used in the classroom he doesn't think are effective for teaching and learning. Wiliam's response: 'Teachers making decisions about the learning needs of 30 students based on the responses of confident volunteers.'[70] Obviously, the problem is assuming that the rest of the class also know the answer. I have certainly been guilty of this myself.

Barton asks Wiliam what he would advise doing instead. He suggests that a well-planned multiple choice test could be used at some point in the lesson to gain information from the whole class. Quizzing helps us to find out what every student knows (and doesn't know), as well as giving some general feedback to the teacher. Craig Barton has developed a brilliant website, www.diagnosticquestions.com, which helps teachers to design effective multiple choice questions. There is an example in Part 2.

Some interesting conclusions were drawn by the writer Wray Herbert, author of *On Second Thought*, in an article which discusses the findings of some research into multiple choice questions.[71] The participants (undergraduates) studied passages on Yellowstone National Park and the planet Saturn and then took different types of practice tests: some did multiple choice questions which assessed things like the park's oldest geyser, while others had the same question but without the multiple choice options. The final test consisted of questions they had been tested on before, a mix of new questions which were closely connected to the ones they had practised before and questions that were on a passage they had not been tested on previously.

Herbert notes that the final results showed that practising for the multiple choice test 'slightly enhanced recall of these related but novel items' – that is, 'the learning fostered by the multiple-choice tests was broader, including even material that had not been tested'. The researchers believe that the reason the multiple choice practice test helped the participants with the final test was connected with the construction of the questions and answers: 'the wrong answers were plausible enough that the students had to think about why the correct answer was correct – and why the wrong answers were wrong'.

Dr Yana Weinstein of the Learning Scientists discussed multiple choice questions and short answer questions at researchED Maths and Science in 2016. She suggested that if the aim

---

70 Craig Barton, 'Dylan Wiliam – Author, Researcher, Trainer and Assessment for Learning Expert', *Mr Barton Maths* [podcast] (3 November 2017). Available at: http://www.mrbartonmaths.com/blog/dylan-wiliam-author-researcher-trainer-and-assessment-for-learning-expert/.
71 Wray Herbert, 'Two Cheers for Multiple-Choice Tests', *Association for Psychological Science* (29 March 2012). Available at: http://www.psychologicalscience.org/index.php/news/full-frontal-psychology/two-cheers-for-multiple-choice-tests.html.

is long-term retention then we need not worry about the type of test as long-term retention seems to be the same between different types of retrieval practice.[72] Instead, we need
to concern ourselves with the implementation of the questions. In other words, designing
ones which work is difficult.

Fiorella and Mayer touch on the potential issue of multiple choice testing compounding
incorrect knowledge.[73] Clearly, a well-designed multiple choice question wouldn't have
one obvious answer; in fact, it should have several plausible alternatives. The key way to
avoid this is to follow up testing with thorough feedback.

There are a number of edtech tools to help design multiple choice questions, such as
Kahoot! and Quick Key. Daisy Christodoulou also suggests Macmillan Publishing's computer adaptive test site called the Learning Curve.[74] It provides learners with feedback if
they don't get the answer correct and it also provides prompts in the form of hints and an
ebook link to go straight to the source. When they finish, the students receive a study plan
which lets them know what they do and don't understand.

The one thing that everyone agrees on is that multiple choice questions are quicker to
mark!

I have trialled using multiple choice questions to test students on upcoming content, so
they have at least some sort of cue. It's pretty obvious, but probably still worth mentioning,
that using a free recall test when learners don't know anything about the topic is likely to
be less effective than a multiple choice test might be.

Distributed Practice

The other gold medal revision award goes to distributed practice. This is essentially the
technique of spacing out the study, practice and testing of to-be-learned or to-be-
relearned material over time, as opposed to massing the study, practice and testing. It's a
good ally to the silver medal award winner of interleaving: spacing out the topics and
mixing up the practice.

---

72 See https://www.youtube.com/watch?v=bbEezSMGTVY.
73 Fiorella and Mayer, Learning as a Generative Activity, p. 112.
74 Daisy Christodoulou, 'Research on Multiple Choice Questions', *The Wing to Heaven* [blog] (30 October
    2013). Available at: https://thewingtoheaven.wordpress.com/2013/10/30/
    research-on-multiple-choice-questions/.

Phil Stock refers to distributed practice in his blog post on independent study techniques.[75] It could be illustrated in the following way:

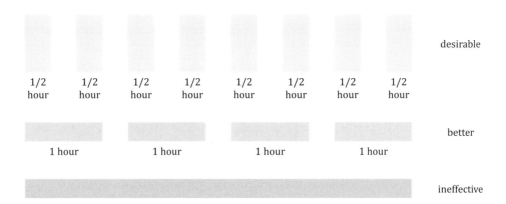

In an article in *American Educator*, Daniel Willingham observes that distributing practice means spacing out the study of material, not devoting additional time to studying.[76] So the same amount of time that would otherwise have been spent in one massed study period is instead spread out over a series of shorter, spaced intervals. As the illustration above shows, instead of dedicating four hours to a solid revision session (or whole day's teaching in school), the schedule is spaced with the same four hours spread across a much longer period of time in 30-minute chunks.

Both Willingham and Dunlosky et al. refer to a study by Harry Bahrick and Elizabeth Phelps which tested the retention of 50 Spanish vocabulary words after an eight-year delay.[77] Three groups each practised producing the list until the words were perfectly recalled on seven or eight sessions, with each session separated by a few minutes, a day or 30 days. Eight years later, the 30-day group recalled the highest percentage of words. However, Willingham suggests that the improved performance of the group with the longer spacing could have been due to the greater amount of practice time they had to write out the list perfectly in each practice session than the other groups.

75 Stock, 'Five Strategies for Encouraging More Effective Independent Study'.
76 Willingham, 'Ask the Cognitive Scientist: What Will Improve a Student's Memory?', pp. 37–39.
77 Daniel Willingham, 'Ask the Cognitive Scientist: Allocating Student Study Time: "Massed" versus "Distributed" Practice', *American Educator*, 26(2) (2002), 37–39. Available at: https://www.aft.org/periodical/american-educator/summer-2002/ask-cognitive-scientist/; Dunlosky et al., 'Improving Students' Learning with Effective Learning Techniques', p. 38. See also: Harry P. Bahrick and Elizabeth Phelps, 'Retention of Spanish Vocabulary Over 8 Years', *Journal of Experimental Psychology: Learning, Memory, and Cognition*, 13(2) (1987), 344–349. Available at: https://www.gwern.net/docs/spacedrepetition/1987-bahrick.pdf.

In a follow-up study, in which the amount of practice and the spacing of the practice was varied, the longest spaced interval of 56 days following testing produced the strongest effect.[78] Didau highlights one of the problems with trying to adopt a spaced practice schedule in schools (which is just as applicable with students who are designing their own revision plan):

Another more serious obstacle is the effort we would need to put into planning a curriculum to ensure content was spaced in the best way possible. Bahrick found that 13 sessions spaced 56 days apart yielded comparable retention to 26 sessions with a 14 day interval. Neither of these lends itself well to the complexity of the subjects we have to teach.[79]

However, he also makes the point that spacing out the time between studying is still beneficial and desirable. He recommends the app SuperMemo which allows learners to discover 'the perfect interval and number of repetitions for users to learn new information at the point of optimum forgetting'.

It seems that by leaving longer lags between study sessions, you discover more about which retrieval cues and associations have worked and which haven't. You also get to root out the triggers that have and haven't helped to make it stick during the last practice revision session.

In the Dunlosky review and in Brian Ross and colleagues' *The Psychology of Learning and Motivation*, the term 'deficient processing' is referred to in the context of the antithesis to distributed practice –massed practice.[80] Deficient processing occurs if only a little time has been left between one spaced interval and the next revisiting of it. As we have already ascertained, if there has been little struggle to recall the material the second time, the learner hasn't had to work hard to retrieve the material from memory and so is drawn into thinking that they know it well.

Discussing a test that he took as part of his research for *How We Learn: The Surprising Truth About When, Where and Why It Happens*, Benedict Carey describes how he was caught by

---

78 Harry P. Bahrick, Lorraine E. Bahrick, Audrey S. Bahrick and Phyllis E. Bahrick, 'Maintenance of Foreign Language Vocabulary and the Spacing Effect', *Psychological Science*, 4(5) (1993), 316–321. Available at: http://www.psych.utoronto.ca/users/shkim/Bahrick%20et%20al.%20(1993)%20spacing%20effect.pdf.

79 Didau, *What If Everything You Knew About Education Was Wrong?*, p. 223–224.

80 Dunlosky et al., 'Improving Students' Learning with Effective Learning Techniques', p. 36; and Brian H. Ross, Peter F. Delaney, Peter P. J. L. Verkoeijen and Arie Spirgel, *The Psychology of Learning and Motivation: Advances in Research and Theory* (Burlington, VT: Academic Press, 2010), pp. 65–66.

the fluency illusion – the trap of not seeing the difference between knowing something deeply and being able to recall some facts or formulae straight away.[81] When designing optimally spaced revision timetables, and to avoid the fluency illusion, Didau suggests an interval of one to two days a week before the test, a one-week interval a month before, a two-week interval two months before, a three-week interval six months before and a four-week interval a year before.[82]

Dunlosky et al. consider the desired length of time that we might want to actually remember something for, beyond simply a test performance. For example, the longer you need to recall something for (e.g. five years), the more the learning would need to be spaced out (e.g. 6 to 12 months apart). For a shorter time (e.g. a week), the learning would need to take place every 12 to 24 hours.[83] There is also evidence to suggest that expanded retrieval practice – where the intervals between each space expand as opposed to being equally spaced – can be more effective.[84]

The idea of spacing out the study of different topics seems to be key to an effective revision plan. We turn next to the content in-between the spaces – that is, interleaving.

Interleaved Practice

Interleaving involves mixing up the learning and not following the order that a traditional textbook, for example, might set out, with the delivery of one discrete unit followed by delivery of the next discrete unit and so on. Elizabeth and Robert Bjork categorise interleaving as one of the 'desirable difficulties' – that is, strategies which change the order, type and content of learning rather than grouping it into topics or blocks.[85]

In *What If Everything You Knew About Education Was Wrong?*, Didau discusses interleaving in detail and presents an extremely useful spaced and interleaved schedule. Mixing up different topics makes for more difficult revision, which he suggests 'helps us to encode new information in a way which makes it easier to retrieve'. In contrast, 'Massed practice allows pupils to get in a groove, which leads to the illusion of knowing.'[86]

---

81 Carey, *How We Learn*, loc. 1214 and 1219.
82 Didau, *What If Everything You Knew About Education Was Wrong?*, p. 224.
83 Dunlosky et al., 'Improving Students' Learning with Effective Learning Techniques', p. 37.
84 David A. Balota, Janet M. Duchek and Jessica M. Logan, 'Is Expanded Retrieval Practice a Superior Form of Spaced Retrieval? A Critical Review of the Extant Literature'. In James S. Nairne (ed.), *The Foundations of Remembering: Essays in Honor of Henry L. Roediger III* (New York: Psychology Press, 2007), pp. 83–105.
85 Bjork and Bjork, 'Making Things Hard on Yourself', p. 58.
86 Didau, *What If Everything You Knew About Education Was Wrong?*, p. 230.

In *Make It Stick*, Brown and colleagues have the following to say on interleaving:

When you *space out* practice at a task and get a little rusty between sessions, or you interleave the practice of two or more subjects, retrieval is harder and feels less productive, but the effort produces longer lasting learning and enables more versatile application of it in later settings.[87]

Of course, there has to be a certain amount of teaching before mixing things up, otherwise you're left with next to no knowledge of either skill.

Shaun Allison makes explicit reference to interleaving as an effective revision strategy, encouraging students to 'alternate their practice of different kinds of items or problems when revising rather than sticking to one single topic'.[88] Instead of revising in 'topic blocks', he advises chunking up areas and interleaving them, as outlined below:

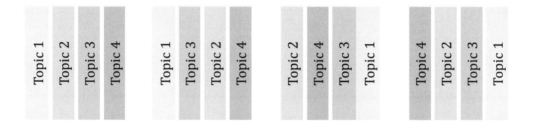

As it's a silver medal winner for revision, we're looking at a promising technique. Dunlosky et al. suggest that it needs further exploration but, according to Doug Rohrer and Kelli Taylor, it is a strategy which has some positive effects.[89]

According to the Dunlosky review, there are a number of theories on why interleaving works. One view is that because students are comparing different types of problems, they draw on both 'organizational processing' and 'item-specific processing'.[90] This view is supported by William Emeny: 'Interleaving is effective because it gives students experience in

87 Brown et al., *Make It Stick*, p. 4.
88 Allison, 'Supporting Learning Through Effective Revision Techniques'.
89 Doug Rohrer and Kelli Taylor, 'The Shuffling of Mathematics Problems Improves Learning', *Instructional Science*, 35(6) (2007), 481–498.
90 Dunlosky et al., 'Improving Students' Learning with Effective Learning Techniques', p. 41.

selecting a strategy to solve a problem as well as executing the strategy. In blocked practice we give students the strategy and they don't gain experience in selecting it.'[91]

In addition to her great guide on retrieval practice, Pooja Agarwal has also created an equally excellent guide to interleaving with fellow researchers Doug Rohrer and Robert Dedrick called *Interleaved Mathematics Practice: Giving Students a Chance to Learn What They Need to Know*.[92] In it, the researchers touch on the issues raised by Emeny: that blocked practice of the same type of problem, particularly when the learner already knows what strategy to use, will not help to combat the illusion of mastery. In other words, if learners complete the same type of problem again and again, they might think they have mastered it. But when faced with a similar task in an exam featuring problems from across the domain, where the strategy needed to solve the problem is not explicitly named, the learner fails to apply the strategy correctly.

Interleaved Mathematics Practice also includes some brilliant examples of how blocked practice in maths might look as opposed to interleaved practice. However, the following set of four blocked maths problems have been kindly supplied by maths teacher Dan Frankton.

The first two sets of examples all deal with the same type of problem, so a similar strategy is required to solve them all. The following involve forming and solving equations:

1. I think of a number, double it and subtract 3. The answer is 7. What was the starting number?

2. I think of a number, multiply by 3 and add 2. The answer is 14. What was the starting number?

3. I think of a number, divide by 4 and subtract 2. The answer is 3. What was the starting number?

4. I think of a number, add 2 and double it. The answer is 16. What was the starting number?

---

91 William Emeny, 'Building Interleaving and Spaced Practice Into Our Pedagogy', *Great Maths Teaching Ideas* [blog] (1 February 2015). Available at: http://www.greatmathsteachingideas.com/2015/02/01/building-interleaving-and-spaced-practice-into-our-pedagogy/.
92 See http://uweb.cas.usf.edu/~drohrer/pdfs/Interleaved_Mathematics_Practice_Guide.pdf.

This set involves expanding single brackets:

---

a) $3(x + 3)$ d) $3(2x + 4)$

b) $2(x - 4)$ e) $5(3x - 7)$

c) $7(x + 2)$ f) $6(4x - 3y)$

In contrast, a set of interleaved problems might look like the example below where a different strategy would be needed to solve each problem from different areas of maths: the first problem is to do with area (converting units of measure and costing); the second involves forming and solving equations; the third involves using the fraction of an amount to solve a worded problem; and the fourth one involves using the mean average.

1. A 2 m by 3 m patio needs relaying with new slabs measuring 60 cm by 30 cm. Each slab costs £6.50. How much will it cost to buy the required number of slabs?

2. Andy is X years old and Bill is 3 years older than Andy. Carl is twice as old as Bill. Their combined ages are 89 years. How old is Andy?

3. A quarter of a class wear glasses and 27 students don't wear glasses. How many students are in the class in total?

4. A farmer owns 5 pigs. The mean weight of the 5 pigs is 325 kg. The farmer buys a new pig at the market. The mean weight of his pigs is now 320 kg. How much did the new pig weigh?

If there are no textbooks, worksheets or other related resources available (and short of crowdfunding your own textbook), then a useful recommendation from Agarwal et al.'s *Interleaved Mathematics Practice* is that you take a handful of problems from blocked end-of-chapter quiz questions from a textbook or revision guide to build your own revision or revisiting guide. There are some examples of how questions across a scheme of learning might look for maths in the section on practice testing in Part 2.

Other suggestions as to why interleaving might be more effective than blocked practice could be that students have the information to complete a problem still lurking somewhere in their working memories, so it is not as cognitively demanding to solve the problem because retrieval strength is still high. However, when interleaved practice is employed, each time the students are faced with a new type of problem to solve they have to retrieve the answer from their long-term memories, which strengthens the memory for the retrieved answer.

Another potential reason for its effectiveness is that when students work on different types of problems, instead of massing all of the practice on one type of problem, they are made aware of the differences between two or more types of problems.

In terms of implementing an interleaved revision plan, the Dunlosky review stresses that where the examination presents learners with a mixture of problems in the same test, then preparation for it should be practised through interleaving. The practice of each new type of problem should be interleaved with problems from previous sessions, so the students are able to distinguish between different types of problems.[93]

Part 2 explores how these medal-taking and effective learner-making study skills might look in practice.

93 Dunlosky et al., 'Improving Students' Learning with Effective Learning Techniques', p. 44.

Part 2

The Strategies

Subject-Specific Examples

In Part 2, we will look at some practical examples of the learning strategies which the Dunlosky review identified as being the most promising. I have also included one or two of the strategies singled out in Fiorella and Mayer's *Learning as a Generative Activity*, and I am grateful to the Learning Scientists for kindly allowing me to refer to their work.

The examples suggest practical ways to use elaborative interrogation, self-explanation, practice testing (retrieval practice), interleaving and distributed practice and how this could work in the classroom or how they might be used away from the classroom as 'revision'.

I offer the caveat that this is only how the subject content provided *could* look. The answers are based on my own understanding and interpretations. For the self-explanations, I have included my own commentary, and as an erstwhile GCSE student of all the techniques trialled in this section I'm clearly not an expert, so someone else trialling them might find what I say obvious. It all depends where a learner (or a relearner?) is on the knowledge acquisition. The content itself has been provided by subject specialists, and my commentaries have been checked to remove any egregious errors.

The first set of examples are for elaborative interrogation.

Elaborative Interrogation

As we saw in Chapter 4, at its simplest elaborative interrogation uses 'why' questions. Some potential questions to tag on to the end of a factual statement could be: Why is this true? Why is this a fact? Why does this make sense? Why is this important? These are generic prompts, of course, so there are some examples below of how elaborative interrogation might look alongside different subjects and how a possible answer could look using this technique.

Business Studies

The first two examples have been adapted from content from the AQA GCSE business studies specimen paper.[1] I worked alongside business studies teacher Lucy Maclachlan to design these questions, and I am equally grateful for Lucy's input into the business studies retrieval practice examples later on.

Factual statement	Potential ways to adopt elaborative interrogation	How an answer *could* look ...
1. Communicating in a company could be said to be less difficult with a flat organisational structure as opposed to a tall organisational structure.	Why could a tall organisational structure potentially lead to more communication problems than a flat structure? Communicating could be said to be less difficult with a flat organisational structure as opposed to a tall organisational structure. Why is this true?	Because a taller organisational structure involves more people through whom to communicate which, in turn, could lead to missed or mixed messages.

---

1   See http://filestore.aqa.org.uk/resources/business/AQA-81321-SQP.PDF.

Factual statement	Potential ways to adopt elaborative interrogation	How an answer *could* look ...
2. Stakeholders (like the local community) who are connected to a business can be affected when a new business opens.	Why could a stakeholder like the local community be affected when a new business opens? Stakeholders (like the local community) who are connected to a business can be affected when a new business opens. Why is this true?	Because a new business will bring more traffic to the area and cause traffic problems. It could also create more jobs for the people in the local community.

PE

The first two examples have been adapted from some of the content from the AQA GCSE PE specimen papers.[2] I am grateful to PE teacher Joe Newton for his help with these.

Factual statement	Potential ways to adopt elaborative interrogation	How an answer *could* look ...
1. Flat bones can help to provide protection for the body during sports activities.	Why would it make sense to say that flat bones can help to provide protection for the body during sports activities like football or rugby?	Flat bones like the cranium or pelvis can help to protect the body during sports activities like football or rugby because the cranium helps to protect the

Factual statement	Potential ways to adopt elaborative interrogation	How an answer *could* look ...
	Flat bones can help to provide protection for the body during sports activities. Why is this true?	brain when heading the ball and the pelvis helps to protect the reproductive organs when you are tackled in rugby.
2. Faking an injury in football, for example, so that the ball is kicked out of play could be an example of gamesmanship.	Why would feigning an injury in a football match so that the ball is kicked out of play be an example of gamesmanship?	Because if you feign an injury in a match so that the ball is kicked out then you are wasting the opposition's time and you are gaining an unfair advantage by doing so, or you could be preventing the opposition from continuing playing for a moment and this could lead to breaking up the play. This would also not be in the spirit of the game and wouldn't be demonstrating good sportsmanship.

These examples have shown how elaborative interrogation might work with separate factual statements with just one elaboration prompted by one or two questions. However, examples of elaborative interrogation provided by the Learning Scientists include multiple elaborations on the same theme or throughout the text.[3] Psychology professor Mark McDaniel and Dr Carol Donnelly, in their paper 'Learning with Analogy and Elaborative Interrogation', make the point that we want learning to go further than merely knowing or remembering facts. The learner should be able to use information/knowledge in new

3   See Megan Smith and Yana Weinstein, 'Learn How to Study Using … Elaboration', *The Learning Scientists* [blog] (5 July 2016). Available at: http://www.learningscientists.org/blog/2016/7/7-1.

contexts and in new ways, and therefore teachers should teach in such a way as to enable learners to use inferential thinking.[4]

One of the examples that the Learning Scientists include is based on history and includes questions (*in italics*) other than 'why'.

Imagine you're studying World War II, and specifically the attack on Pearl Harbor. You could ask yourself, *how did this attack happen?* On December 7, 1941, the Imperial Japanese Navy attacked the United States Naval Base at Pearl Harbor. The attack included Japanese fighter planes, bombers, and torpedo planes. *Why did this happen?* The Japanese intended to destroy the United States' Pacific Fleet so that it could not interfere with Japanese operations. Here you could also ask another type of question: *What was the result of this historic event?* Well, Japanese casualties were light, while they damaged eight U.S. Navy battleships. The *Arizona* was among those that the Japanese sunk, and was not raised from the shallow water. U.S. aircraft were also destroyed, and 2,403 Americans were killed (1,178 were injured). *Why is this event important?* The day after the attack, Roosevelt delivered his Infamy Speech, the United States formally declared war on Japan, and Japanese-Americans were then relocated to internment camps. You could then go on: *How did the U.S. enter the war? How did the Pearl Harbor attack lead up to the release of the atomic bomb? How did the war end?* And so on. There are so many ways to explain the idea and add details![5]

History

The next example is based on the AQA GCSE history topic on Edward the Confessor and features several prompts which lead on from one another.[6] I am grateful to history teacher Anna Hunt for helping with these examples and for the practice questions later on.

---

4   Mark A. McDaniel and Carol M. Donnelly, 'Learning with Analogy and Elaborative Interrogation', *Journal of Educational Psychology*, 88(3) (1996), 508–519. Available at: http://ldt.stanford.edu/~educ39105/paul/articles_2006/Learning%20with%20analogy%20and%20elaborative%20interrogation.pdf.

5   Smith and Weinstein, 'Learn How to Study Using … Elaboration'.

6   See http://filestore.aqa.org.uk/resources/history/AQA-81451-NORMANS-SOW.PDF.

Factual statement	Potential ways to adopt elaborative interrogation	How an answer *could* look ...
Edward the Confessor helped to steady the government of England after the rule of Cnut's sons.	Why did Edward the Confessor's relationship with Godwine help to steady the government of England after the rule of Cnut's sons?	Edward's favouritism towards his Norman followers caused resentment among the houses of Wessex and Mercia. As these two houses had considerable power, seeking an alliance with Godwine through marriage to his daughter ensured greater stability in England. Edward allowed Godwine to have a lot of power in England, even to the point where Godwine ran the country for 11 years.
	Why did the relationship lead to instability?	Edward's continued favouritism towards his Norman followers, and the argument over who should be Archbishop of Canterbury led to the threat of possible civil war in 1052. However, Godwine's men were unwilling to support him against the king so Godwine ended up fleeing to Flanders.

Factual statement	Potential ways to adopt elaborative interrogation	How an answer *could* look ...
	Why did Godwine return?	Godwine came back with an army commanded by Harold and Tostig, Godwine's two sons. Reluctant to start a civil war and leave the country vulnerable to foreign invasion, Edward restored Godwine to his earldom. However, they continued to disagree over the appointment of the Archbishop.
	Why did Edward's attempt to prevent the House of Wessex from becoming too dominant fail?	After Godwine's return, Edward attempted to prevent them becoming too dominant in England. He tried to make sure that even when Harold succeeded to the earldom of Wessex, none of his brothers were given earldoms. The Wessex house was now weaker than it had been when Edward became king. However, due to the deaths of key noblemen in England by 1057, Harold and his brothers controlled all of England except Mercia. In 1066,

Factual statement	Potential ways to adopt elaborative interrogation	How an answer *could* look ...
		it is believed that Edward named Harold as his successor.

I worked with history teacher Ben Curtis to come up with the next example on the English Civil War. I am also grateful to Ben for the questions on testing later on. Each statement here uses the question, 'Why is this true?' No-frills elaborative interrogation time!

Factual statement	Potential ways to adopt elaborative interrogation	How an answer *could* look ...
1. Oliver Cromwell ruled in a similar way to Charles I.	Oliver Cromwell ruled in a similar way to Charles I. Why is this true?	He ruled without a proper parliament, as did Charles I.
2. Economics caused both the English Civil War and the French Revolution.	Economics caused both the English Civil War and the French Revolution. Why is this true?	Both monarchs raised taxes beyond the point at which people could pay.
3. Popular understanding of the conditions of the First World War is often led by culture rather than by facts.	Popular understanding of the conditions of the First World War is often led by culture rather than by facts. Why is this true?	The lions led by donkeys myth appears in films and poems about trench conditions.
4. There was no progress in medicine during the medieval period.	There was no progress in medicine during the medieval period. Why is this true?	Because the Church promoted Galen as an authority.

Factual statement	Potential ways to adopt elaborative interrogation	How an answer *could* look ...
5. The Nazis came to power because of the Great Depression.	The Nazis came to power because of the Great Depression. Why is this true?	The people of Germany turned to extremist parties in desperation because of their situation.

PE and Biology

This is an example of elaborative interrogation which follows on from a previous answer using aerobic and anaerobic respiration. This example is thanks to teachers Joe Newton (PE) and Anne Clay (biology).

Factual statement	Potential ways to adopt elaborative interrogation	How an answer *could* look ...
Glucose is produced through the process of photosynthesis.	Why is glucose produced during photosynthesis?	Glucose is produced during photosynthesis to release energy as it's then used for respiration and to help plant cells grow. The glucose is released by photosynthesis and some is used in respiration. There are two types of respiration.
	Why are there two types of respiration?	There are two types of respiration: aerobic respiration and anaerobic respiration. These make energy.

Factual statement	Potential ways to adopt elaborative interrogation	How an answer *could* look ...
		Aerobic respiration uses oxygen to make it work, whereas anaerobic respiration does not use oxygen. More energy is released through aerobic respiration than anaerobic respiration.
	Why is more energy released during aerobic respiration than anaerobic respiration?	More energy is released through aerobic respiration than through anaerobic respiration because during aerobic respiration oxygen combines with glucose to break down the glucose to give a lot of energy. Anaerobic respiration releases much less energy as there is not enough oxygen taken in to break down the glucose. So, if glucose is not broken down fully then a lot of energy cannot be released. A product of anaerobic respiration is lactic acid. Aerobic and anaerobic respiration take place during different levels of intensity in sports, for example.

Factual statement	Potential ways to adopt elaborative interrogation	How an answer *could* look ...
	Why do different activities use either aerobic or anaerobic respiration?	Because aerobic respiration might take place when doing sports which require moderate exercise – in other words, exercise and sports which use oxygen to release enough energy to sustain an endurance-type activity like distance running or jogging. Anaerobic respiration is when not enough oxygen can be taken in during high intensity workouts, for example, sprinting.

Maths

Two questions which could be applied to elaborative interrogation as a technique to revise maths were suggested by Dan Williams. They are: 'Why is this the process for calculating … ?' and 'Why are the brackets the first thing we calculate?'[7] This example adapts these questions to revise some simple order of operations tasks with the acronym BIDMAS (brackets, indices, division and multiplication, addition and subtraction). With thanks to maths teacher Dan Frankton for checking this.

7   See Dan Williams, 'Making Maths Work', *furtheredagogy* [blog] (4 April 2016). Available at: https://furtheredagogy.wordpress.com/2016/04/04/making-maths-work/.

Factual statement	Potential ways to adopt elaborative interrogation	How an answer *could* look ...
4 x (8 – 4) = 4 x 4 = 16	Why are the brackets the first thing we calculate?	Because when there is more than one operation to be made, the order has to take the form of BIDMAS. BIDMAS means brackets, indices, division and multiplication, addition and subtraction, and is applied from left to right.
	Why does BIDMAS matter to the order of the operations in the answer?	The sum in the bracket is what has to be calculated first according to BIDMAS, as this calculation is in the bracket, so that is 4.
	Why does BIDMAS matter with the rest of the calculation?	Because the 4 at the beginning is multiplied, this must be calculated next according to the order of BIDMAS with what I did first in the brackets (8 – 4) so that makes 4 x 4 and gives 16.

Design and Technology

This example is based on a section from a CGP GCSE design and technology revision guide. The passage without elaborative interrogation is followed by the adapted passage with elaborative interrogation (without answers this time). The questions were designed by myself and head of design and technology Debbie Barwell.

Packaging has an *environmental impact*

1. Producing packaging for products uses up *materials*. For example, packaging is often made of *plastic*. Most plastic is made using *crude oil*, which is a *finite resource* (it'll run out eventually).

2. It's not just materials – the *processes* used to make packaging also have an impact. For example, moulding plastic uses *energy*. Most of this energy comes from burning fossil fuels – which causes air pollution and emits carbon dioxide, which contributes to *global warming*.

3. Packaging also produces *waste* – and it's mostly disposed of in landfill once it's removed from the product. If the packaging is made from non-biodegradable materials it'll be there for centuries.

Adapted passage with elaborative interrogation **[in bold]** embedded into the text:

Packaging has an *environmental impact*

1. Producing packaging for products uses up *materials*. For example, packaging is often made of *plastic*. **[Why is packaging often made out of plastic?]** Most plastic is made using *crude oil*, which is a *finite resource* (it'll run out eventually). **[Why would this have an environmental impact?]**

2. It's not just materials – the *processes* used to make packaging also have an impact. **[Why might processes like making plastic have an environmental impact?]** For example, moulding plastic uses *energy*. Most of this energy comes from burning fossil fuels **[Why would burning fossil fuels have an environmental impact?]** – which causes air pollution and emits carbon dioxide, which contributes to *global warming*.

3. Packaging also produces *waste* – and it's mostly disposed of in landfill once it's removed from the product. **[Why is packaging mainly disposed of in**

landfill?] If the packaging is made from non-biodegradable materials it'll be there for centuries.

For this and the following example I have given suggested revision routines which can be adapted for all examples.

Perhaps combining elaborative interrogation with retrieval practice could be a way to go with this one – for instance, reading the text and asking/answering the elaborative interrogation questions, followed by some time for some forgetting to kick in, followed by a brain dump of all that can be remembered from the text with a single prompt of 'Write down all you can about why packaging has an environmental impact.'

Alternatively, perhaps reading through the text while using elaborative interrogation, then leaving some time for forgetting, followed by some short written responses to the same or similar questions that were used as part of the elaborative interrogation might be worth trialling.

Another suggestion could be to read through the text while using elaborative interrogation, followed by someone else who was listening writing a set of practice questions (which may or may not differ from the elaborative interrogation questions) to test retrieval later on after a period of forgetting.

In summary, perhaps a revision routine like the following might be worth a try:

1. Students read the text using embedded elaborative interrogation.

2. The teacher designs a set of practice questions on the material. Questions could include some of the following:

   - Why would making packaging out of plastic have an environmental impact?

   - What process is used to make plastic?

   - How might processes used to make plastic affect the environment?

   - How might disposing of plastic packaging affect the environment?

3. Revise another topic or subject and leave some time for forgetting (for retrieval strength of the material to fall) before coming back to the questions and answering them.

Physics

This example is based on an 'Efficiency' section from a CGP GCSE physics revision guide. The elaborative interrogation questions are again embedded into the passage that would be revised. The passage without the elaborative interrogation is followed by the adapted passage. I have worked alongside physics teacher Mike Browne for all the physics examples, although he has expressed his doubts about using elaborative interrogation in physics. He thinks it might be tricky for students to answer in sufficient depth on certain topics, so mechanics might be a better example than this one on machine efficiency.

---

1. For any given example you can talk about the types of energy being input and output, but remember: *NO* device is *100% efficient* and the wasted energy is usually transferred to useless *thermal energy stores*.

2. *Electric heaters* are the *exception* to this. They're usually *100% efficient* because *all* the energy in the electrostatic energy store is transferred to 'useful' thermal energy stores.

3. Ultimately, *all* energy ends up transferred to *thermal energy stores*. For example, if you use an *electric drill*, its energy transfers to lots of different energy stores, but quickly ends up all in thermal energy stores.

Here is the same passage with the suggested examples of elaborative interrogation included **[in bold]**:

---

1. For any given example you can talk about the types of energy being input and output, but remember: *NO* device is *100% efficient* **[Why is this true?]** and the wasted energy is usually transferred to useless *thermal energy stores*. **[Why does this happen?]**

2. *Electric heaters* are the *exception* to this. They're usually *100% efficient* because *all* the energy in the electrostatic energy store is transferred to 'useful' thermal energy stores. **[Why is this energy 'useful'?]**

3. Ultimately, *all* energy ends up transferred to *thermal energy stores*. For example, if you use an *electric drill*, its energy transfers to lots of different energy stores, but quickly ends up all in thermal energy stores. **[Why would this be true? What are the energy transfers?]**

Adopting the steps in the previous example to use retrieval practice could go something like this:

1. Students read the text using embedded elaborative interrogation.

2. The teacher designs a set of practice questions/tasks to do with the material. Questions could include some of the following:

   ● What does energy efficiency mean?

   ● Explain how energy can be useful and wasted.

   ● What are the energy transfers that take place in: (a) an electric heater, (b) an electric drill, (c) an electric light bulb and (d) a car engine?

   ● Identify the useful and wasted energy in each of the examples above.

   ● What makes a machine more efficient?

Revise another topic or subject and leave some time for forgetting before coming back to the questions and answering them without reading the text again.

Self-Explanation

I will be using many of the following content-free prompts in the examples in this section, some of which have been suggested by author Robert Harris.[1]

1. What information do I need to know in order to solve this problem?

2. Where can I find this needed information?

3. Has this already been solved or answered?

4. Do I have all the parts or information I need?

5. What should I do next?

6. What would be another example of this?

7. Does that sound right?

8. Do I understand the ideas used in that line?

9. Do I understand why those/these ideas have been used?

10. How do those ideas link to other ideas in the proof, other theorems or prior knowledge that I may have?

11. Does the self-explanation I have generated help to answer the questions that I am asking?

12. What conclusions can I draw from this?

13. What does this mean to me so far?

14. How does this information relate to what I already know?

15. What parts of this page are new to me?

16. What does the statement mean?

17. Is there anything I still don't understand?

18. What new information does each sentence provide for me?

---

1   Questions 1–7 are from Robert Harris's 'Learning Strategy 5: Self Explanation', *VirtualSalt* (27 February 2014). Available at: http://www.virtualsalt.com/learn5.html.

19. How does it relate to what I've already read?

20. Does it give me a new insight into my understanding of what a particular concept means and how this works?

21. Does it raise any questions for me?

Ensuring that self-explanations are indeed self-explanations, and not paraphrasing or monitoring, might not be as easy as we think. Lara Alcock offers some helpful hints in *How to Think About Analysis* on self-explanation versus monitoring and paraphrasing in maths.[2] Broadly, in self-explanation inferences are made and developed, whereas monitoring might involve saying something like, 'I understand that X means Y'. This is another reason to ensure that students learn self-explanation techniques via domain-specific modelling. For this reason, my self-explanation examples and consequent commentary have been checked out by subject teachers to ensure that what I'm saying is correct. Only a subject expert will do!

Kelly Morgan's Backwards-Faded Worksheet

A potential prompt that Kelly Morgan mentions in her blog post on worked examples is: 'Where did that number come from?'[3] This is the only content-specific prompt I'm going to allow myself for any of the examples with self-explanation, albeit with a tiny tweak. Every other prompt will be a variation of one of the content-free prompts listed above.

Incidentally, I am actually adopting this technique with this worksheet while scrolling back and forth between my previous comments, what I want to type, the prompts and checking the worked example step, which may be an example of the split-attention effect where the example, prompts and my commentary are physically separated, leading to extraneous load.

Extraneous load can also occur when a problem to be solved involves working out the area of a triangle, for example, where the information needed to calculate the area is substantially separated from the information in the triangle and thus imposes an unnecessary load (one such example is presented shortly). In order to integrate self-explanation comments and reduce unnecessary load, a potential solution could be for the teacher to write the notes on the worksheet next to the worked example and provide this to the learner. There is a similar risk of the split-attention effect if self-explanation prompts are physically separated from the worked example or text.

---

2   Lara Alcock, *How to Think About Analysis* (Oxford: Oxford University Press, 2014), pp. 39–43.
3   Morgan, 'Teaching with Worked Examples'.

I decided to contact Professor John Sweller about the split-attention effect, and I am very grateful to him for having responded so quickly. I have included part of our email exchange below:

Your interpretation of the problem seems valid to me but so is the potential solution you provide: 'In order to integrate self-explanation comments and reduce unnecessary load, a potential solution could be for the teacher to write the notes on the worksheet next to the worked example.' That seems exactly what should be done. Alternatively, if the instruction is being presented via a computer, the prompts might be presented in spoken rather than written form, assuming that the prompts are simple and brief.

A caveat to this is that if, when faced with worked examples, an expert or someone with a relatively high level of domain expertise might experience extraneous load because they are processing material that is redundant. They don't really need the worked example to support them. The expertise reversal effect is mentioned in the Craig Barton and Kris Boulton podcast referred to earlier.[4] Barton asks Boulton what he would do with a student in class who has already been taught how to solve simultaneous equations by a private tutor, while the rest of the class are being taught about simultaneous equations. Barton wonders if the student who already has a level of knowledge might be better off working through problems instead of examples.

Here is my commentary on the backwards-faded worksheet that we first met in Chapter 4 (see page 82). Ideally, as the fading out of the worked example occurs, my relative expertise in completing the task should increase:

1. In this first task I have to convert a figure in centimetres into metres. Where did the 1 cm come from in the worked example? Well, I know that there are 100 cm in a metre and so 1 cm would mean that is basically 1/100 of a metre. I know that 1/100 could be expressed as a decimal as 0.01. How does this information relate to what I already know? Well, if I'm expressing this as a decimal, as 0.01, then I will need to ensure that the units change to show that this is now in metres. What does the completion step 20.33 x 0.01 say to me? Well, I know that to convert a smaller measurement into a bigger measurement I will have to multiply the smaller measurement by how that measurement is converted in the bigger measurement terms. So, to convert 20.33 cm into metres, I would have to multiply it by what 1 cm is in metres which is 0.01. So, I would multiply 20.33 by 0.01 to find out what 20.33 is in metres.

---

2. How does the information in the second worked example relate to what I already know? This seems like it is the same principle as in the first example as 1 cl is basically 1/100 of a litre. What other information do I have in the worked example? Well, the answer is provided as 1206 cl. What does that mean to me? I can see that to find this the worked example shows 12.06 multiplied by 1 and then divided by 0.01, so I know that I would have to divide the 12.06 l by 0.01 which would now give 1206 cl.

3. What information is missing in this example? The solution is not there. What information do I need in order to solve this problem? I know that there are 1000 g in a kilogram, so if I am converting 32.27 kg into grams, what should I do next? I can multiply 32.27 by 1000 to convert this figure into grams. This would give 32,270. This would be expressed as 32,270 g.

4. Has this example already been solved or answered? No. What other information is missing? There is no information to tell me what to multiply now. What should I do next? I need to look at what needs to be converted. This is 13.09 m to cm. What information do I know already? I know that there are 100 cm in a metre and I will need to multiply 13.09 by 100 if I want the new figure to be in centimetres. This would give me 1309. So, there are 1309 cm in 13.09 m.

5. How does what I have already read relate to what I already know with this next example? Well, I am lacking the information for the metre conversion for 3.47 mm, so what should I do next? If I know that in 1 m there are 100 cm and that in 1 cm there are 10 mm then 100 x 10 is 1000, so that means there are 1000 mm in 1 m. How does this information help me? If I have to convert 3.47 mm to metres then this will effectively be a thousandth of a metre which comes to 0.00347.

6. What information do I have to help with this example? I only have one of the units given – kilograms. Also, 33.81 kg is the only information that I have to help work out what it would be in grams. I know from a previous example that there are 1000 g in a kilogram and that in order to work out a conversion from kilograms into grams I would have to multiply the kilogram figure by 1000 which gives the amount that it would be in grams, which would be 33,810 grams.

7. I have to convert 9.92 kl to litres in this next example. What information is provided for me? I only have the figure to convert given here – 9.92 kl. How does this relate to what I've already completed or read? Well, I have already completed an example involving litre conversion and that was to do with converting litres into centilitres. What information do I need to know in order to solve this problem? I need to know what a kilolitre unit stands for. Well, what do I know about kilograms? What would be another example to help with this? A kilogram is a multiplication of 1000 g, with kilo essentially meaning a multiplication of 1000, so then a kilolitre must be 1000 litres. How does this

knowledge help me to solve the problem? If I want to convert 9.92 kl into litres, I would therefore have to multiply it by 1000 which gives 9920 l.

8.   What information do I have for this example? The information given is to convert 2.61 grams into milligrams (mg). How does this information relate to what I already know about what a milligram is? I know that the prefix 'milli' means a thousandth and that the previous example of millimetre was, of course, a thousandth of a metre. Given this information, what should I do next? If I want to convert 2.61 g into milligrams then I need to multiply the grams by 1000 as this will convert to the number of milligrams found in 2.61 g. This is based on 1000 mg per gram. How would this relate to showing working on the 'faded' sections of this worked example? If I were to show the working on this, then on the top row this would be 1000 mg with the section underneath as 1 g or 1 gram. What should I do next? I need to show on my working out that I would multiply both numbers across the top dividing by 1 to give 2610 milligrams.

9.   What parts of this problem are new to me? Well, the layout of the problem is slightly different as there is no table as in all of the previous examples. Although there are no workings out, how does the information in the problem relate to what I already know? Has this already been solved or answered? Well, I have just completed a problem where I converted grams into milligrams, so let's take advantage of that high retrieval strength to put the previous knowledge to good use! If I want to convert grams to milligrams then I know that 1 g is equivalent to 1000 mg, so if I want to convert 24.37 g into milligrams then it's straightforward enough to multiply 24.37 by 1000, giving me 24,370 mg.

10. How does this final problem relate to what I have already done? Well, in an earlier example I converted litres into centilitres. What do I know about the previous example which can help me to complete this one? I know that there are 100 cl in 1 litre so if I want to know what 28.77 l would be in centilitres, this would be 28.77 multiplied by 100 (cl). This would give 2877 cl.

Maths

As an erstwhile lover of maths, but a victim of the effects of forgetting, this example will take me back a bit. Before we get to that, though, let's suppose that a maths revision guide or hand-out included the following worked example:

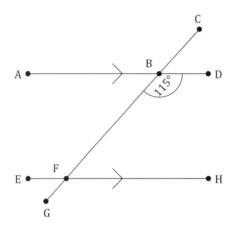

Imagine that the rest of the worked example (below) is separated from it – for example, on a separate page.

Find the value of $\stackrel{\frown}{EFG}$

$\stackrel{\frown}{FBD} = \stackrel{\frown}{EFB} = 115°$

Because of 'alternate angles'

$\stackrel{\frown}{EFG} = 180° - 115° = 65°$

Because 'angles on a straight line add up to 180°'.

This might lead to an undesirable cognitive load on my working memory because I am spending limited resources trying to make sense of two separate sources of information which depend on each other in order to be intelligible. The potential for this split-attention effect to lead to inefficient learning might be resolved by adopting a more integrated approach, as in the following example:

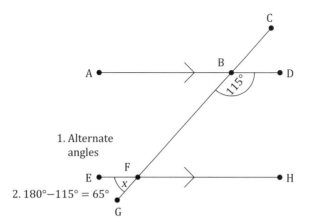

Here the information is integrated so that I am no longer having to expend precious working memory resources looking back and forth between each set of information. This spatial contiguity is touched on in a chapter by Paul A. Kirschner and Yana Weinstein in *What Does This Look Like in the Classroom?*, where they describe how integrating explanatory information and a diagram can help to reduce the potential extraneous load imposed through the split-attention effect.[5]

With this in mind, I'm going to try self-explanation with a partially completed integrated worked example. Thanks to maths teacher Dan Frankton for designing these worked examples, and to Professor John Sweller who has kindly checked for the potential of the split-attention effect.

On Professor Sweller's advice, in future examples of the self-explanation effect I have integrated the prompts and presented the self-explanation as speech below it. He observed that if the commentary is split from the problem it 'can't be understood without mental integration'. The implication is that the prompts would work better as part of the diagram: 'In other words, the diagram, its associated worked example statements, and the self-explanations should all be physically integrated.' In the examples below, therefore, I have integrated the prompts into the visuals and followed up with the self-explanation commentary, which represents speech and is not intended as written instruction.

5   Paul A. Kirschner and Yana Weinstein, 'Memory and Recall'. In Carl Hendrick and Robin Macpherson (eds), *What Does This Look Like in the Classroom? Bridging the Gap Between Research and Practice* (Woodbridge: John Catt Educational, 2017), pp. 122–142 at p. 128.

Find the value of *x*

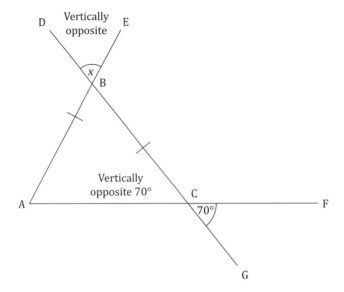

1. What is the problem? I need to find the value of *x*, so what information do I have so far in order to solve this problem? I know that the angle GCF is 70° as this is the given information. I also know that vertically opposite angles are equal and so the given information also tells me that this opposite angle is 70°.

2. What further information do I need to know in order to solve the problem? Well, I know that in order to find *x* I need to know angle DBE. What should I do next? I know that two sides of an isosceles triangle are equal and so angle BAC must be equal to BCA. How does this information relate to what I already know? I know that this angle is 70° because of the two vertically opposite angles – BAC is also 70°.

3. How does this information relate to what I already know? Well, if angle BAC is 70° then I already know (as a maths fact!) that since I have a triangle, all of the angles should add up to 180°.

4. How does this information help me to solve the problem of 'Find the value of *x*'? Now I know that the two angles added up together make 140° and that with an isosceles triangle all of the angles add up to 180°, so all I need to do is to subtract 140° from 180° which will give me the angle for angle ABC. So, the angle for ABC is 40°.

5. How does this information help me to find the value of x? Well, I know that vertically opposite angles are equal and the angle for ABC is 40°, so therefore x must be 40° because it is vertically opposite.

Before we move on to applying self-explanation to domains unrelated to maths, it is worth mentioning that there are a number of excellent examples showing how to reduce extraneous load in maths worked examples in Craig Barton's *How I Wish I'd Taught Maths*, which he relates to the importance of working memory.[6] Both Kirschner in the same chapter referred to earlier in *What Does This Look Like in the Classroom?* and Barton also refer to temporal contiguity; that is that combining graphics and narration at the same time as opposed to one after the other can lead to more efficient learning. Since graphics are a visual and narration audio then they are processed in different channels in working memory and so separating these sources of information does not make learning more efficient. Just as *The Unified Learning Model* places working memory as an effective cornerstone around which learning occurs, so too does Barton's book.

Geography

This example is based on how self-explanation could look for the hydrological cycle. Thanks to geography teacher Jon Haston for sketching a hydrological cycle (see page 130) and checking my commentary.

1. OK, the first thing is that as it's a cycle there doesn't seem to be a real start or end, so I'll start with the ocean/sea/lake. What do the three arrows moving up towards 'evaporation' mean to me here? Well, water evaporates from the ocean and rises up into the air. Why does this happen? What does evaporation mean to me? Well, when the sun heats the ocean the water changes state. Evaporation is the change from liquid state to a gas. So, this is water vapour.

2. What information do the three arrows pointing from condensation tell me? What do I know about warm air and cool air? Well, when water vapour rises it cools and forms condensation because the air temperature is decreasing. So, the water vapour turns back into a liquid. What does this mean to me so far? Well, condensation is what happens on windows and mirrors and this is also what leads to clouds. What happens with the clouds in the diagram? What do I know about clouds? Water droplets in the clouds become too heavy and then fall as rain. In the diagram there are two arrows showing transportation before the clouds on the right. What does this tell me? This is carrying the moisture across towards the top of the mountain before it then falls as precipitation.

---

6   Barton, *How I Wish I'd Taught Maths*, loc. 3200–3225.

Water/hydrological cycle

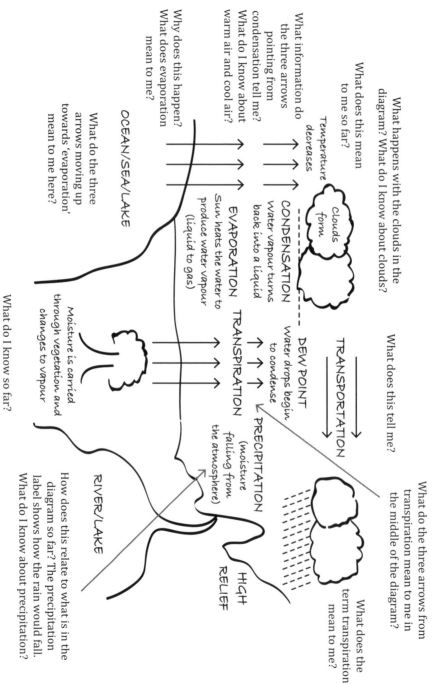

What happens with the clouds in the diagram? What do I know about clouds?

What does this mean to me so far?

What information do the three arrows pointing from condensation tell me?

What do I know about warm air and cool air?

Why does this happen? What does evaporation mean to me?

What do the three arrows moving up towards 'evaporation' mean to me here?

Temperature decreases

Clouds form

OCEAN/SEA/LAKE

CONDENSATION
water vapour turns back into a liquid

EVAPORATION
Sun heats the water to produce water vapour (liquid to gas)

Moisture is carried through vegetation and changes to vapour

TRANSPIRATION

DEW POINT
Water drops begin to condense

TRANSPORTATION

What does this tell me?

What do the three arrows from transpiration mean to me in the middle of the diagram?

What does the term transpiration mean to me?

PRECIPITATION
(moisture falling from the atmosphere)

HIGH RELIEF

RIVER/LAKE

What do I know so far?

How does this relate to what is in the diagram so far? The precipitation label shows how the rain would fall. What do I know about precipitation?

3. What do the three arrows from 'transpiration' mean to me in the middle of the diagram? Well, water is lost from plants through transpiration and this water rises. On the diagram it is added to the water which has evaporated from the ocean into the air. What does the term transpiration mean to me, though? Transpiration means that the water would be moving up through the roots of the plants until it evaporates at the end of the leaves; a bit like sweating in humans, the leaves have things like pores to allow this to evaporate. This vapour from transpiration would be added to the water that has evaporated from the oceans.

4. How does this relate to what is on the diagram so far? The precipitation label on the diagram shows how the rain would fall. What do I know about precipitation? Precipitation is not just rain but could be snow or hail. There could be snow at the top of the mountain and this could be there because of the lower temperature towards the top of these mountains.

5. What do I know so far? Water has evaporated from oceans and condensed and formed clouds. Once the water vapour in the clouds has become too heavy it falls as precipitation.

Biology

This example is based on how self-explanation might look when used to support revision of the carbon cycle in GCSE biology. Thanks to biology teacher Anne Clay for having checked the commentary and sketched a carbon cycle for me. Again, the prompts are integrated into the diagram and the commentary below is based on what was said while carrying out the self-explanation.

Carbon cycle

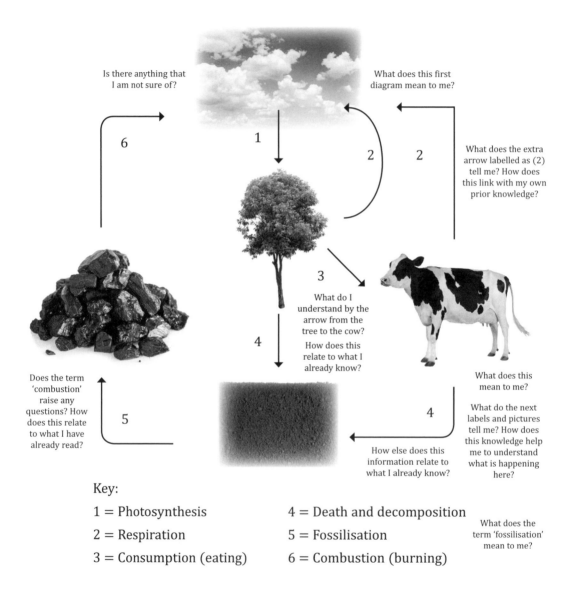

Key:

1 = Photosynthesis   4 = Death and decomposition

2 = Respiration   5 = Fossilisation

3 = Consumption (eating)   6 = Combustion (burning)

1. What does this first diagram mean to me? The arrow going towards the tree means that carbon dioxide is being absorbed by the tree. I know that this diagram must be of the daytime and I know that photosynthesis takes place during the day because

water, sunlight and, of course, carbon dioxide are needed for it to happen, so this must obviously mean that carbon dioxide is almost brought back by photosynthesis.

2. Looking to the right of the diagram, I can see that the second step is an arrow pointing back up to the sky. What does this mean to me? Well, this must mean that this is what happens at night, as shown on the diagram, as I know that carbon dioxide is released from plants and trees.

3. What does the extra arrow labelled as (2) tell me? Obviously it is coming from an animal, which means that carbon dioxide is being released from an animal. How does this link with my own prior knowledge? Well, I know that during respiration living things are using oxygen and producing carbon dioxide. So if they're using oxygen and producing carbon dioxide then the carbon dioxide is released into the atmosphere, as I know already that carbon dioxide is released as a product of aerobic respiration.

4. What do I understand by the arrow from the tree to the cow? Well, I think that there are carbon compounds in grass, trees and plants, so if animals feed on this then carbon will be consumed by them. How else does this information relate to what I already know? Well, I know that there is a food chain so I would imagine that animals eat plants that contain carbon, and if they are eaten by other animals then this carbon would be passed on as well.

5. What do the next labels and pictures tell me? Well, respiration helps with decomposition, which kind of dissembles things that have died, through decomposers which take them apart. How does this knowledge help me to understand what is happening here? Well, if the cow (or any living thing) dies then I think that this would also release carbon dioxide (as well as consuming carbon when other animals feed on dead plants and animals). How does this relate to what I already know? Well, I know that carbon dioxide is released during respiration and living things respire, so I would imagine that when they respire carbon dioxide is released back into the atmosphere.

6. What does the term 'fossilisation' mean to me? Well, I know that a fossil is obviously something that might have been dug up! So, I imagine that the dead plants, animals and so on have accumulated sediment over millions of years and become fossils.

7. The final label that I haven't yet referred to is combustion. Does the term 'combustion' raise any questions? How does this relate to what I have already read? I know the term 'fossil fuels' and how burning these must release carbon dioxide back into the atmosphere.

8. Is there anything that I am not sure of? I understand that the whole process of the carbon cycle is that everything is contained and through different processes (respiration, combustion, photosynthesis) carbon is transferred throughout the cycle.

Computer Science

This time I have used self-explanation alongside a text which has been written by head of computer science Joan Fuller. I'll start the self-explanation commentary from the second paragraph.

In *Learning as a Generative Activity*, Fiorella and Mayer provide an example of self-explanation from a chapter on the human circulatory system.[7] I'm going to use some of the same question prompts they suggest, but adapt them to self-explain this passage on binary, bits and bytes. I'm going to read each sentence out loud and explain what it means to me using some of the self-explanation prompts.

Binary, Bits and Bytes

There's a (very old, somewhat rubbish) joke about binary: 'There are only 10 types of people: those that understand binary and those that don't.' In fact, there's a whole article about binary jokes; it contains only four jokes! So, a subject that can only produce a grand total of four jokes cannot be very complicated. However, this topic links to lots of other parts of computer science, so I've put in some suggestions for you to extend your knowledge and make important topical links.

What does the term 'binary' mean to me?

The binary system uses only two numbers: 1 and 0. I'm not going into the maths of binary or how to convert denary to binary here (or binary to hexadecimal for that matter); go and learn about binary number systems for that. All you need to know here is that 1 is on and 0 is off. If you look at your kettle, or at some other vintage electronic equipment (washing machine, dishwasher) you can see how that applies to real life.

What does the statement 'Originally computers were made up of big transistors. In an iPhone 6 there can be 2 billion transistors' mean to me?

Originally computers were made up of big transistors. In an iPhone 6 there can be 2 billion transistors. Moore's law says that the number of transistors in an integrated circuit board will double every two years. This was true for a very long time, but now there are signs that it is speeding up.

How does this information relate to what I already know about transistors?

What new information do the ideas in the fourth paragraph tell me? What does the term 'CPU' mean to me? What does the term 'Python' mean to me?

7   Fiorella and Mayer, *Learning as a Generative Activity*, p. 126.

Effectively, a computer uses a transistor as a switch which can be turned on or off by the instructions in a program. When you write a program in, for example, Python, the computer cannot understand it and it has to be converted to machine code (read up on compilation or translation to understand more about that). Machine code is just 1s and 0s which the computer's CPU does understand. The CPU then uses the instructions to change the status of a transistor.

How does this knowledge help me with the rest of the paragraph?

What new ideas are presented in this next paragraph?

Each single digit of machine code will contain either a 1 or a 0. This is stored in the main memory (the RAM) of the computer when it is being executed and in the secondary storage (the HDD or hard disk drive) when it is not being used.

Does this knowledge give me any new insight into my own understanding?

What do the ideas in the following paragraph tell me?

Each digit takes up space and the amount of space is called a bit, just like a small unit of length measurement is called a millimetre. So, a 1 will take up 1 bit, and so will a 0. If you had an instruction in machine code of 10101 that would take up 5 bits.

How does this relate to my prior knowledge of bits?

What do the ideas in this next paragraph mean to me?

When we have 8 bits we call that a byte. When we have 4 bits we call that a nibble or a nybble (no, that's not another bad joke, and no that's not bad spelling either).

How do the ideas in the next paragraph relate to my prior knowledge?

Every program on a computer is stored in machine code as 1s and 0s. So is every piece of data: that means all your music, all your photos, all your texts, all your bank account details, every email, every website – everything is stored as 1s and 0s.

What parts of this next paragraph are new to me?

This means we have to find a way to turn our letters (like the ones I am writing now) into numbers so that the numbers can be converted into binary and stored as 1s and 0s. Two of the most common methods of doing that are ASCII or UNICODE, and you will need to find out more about these too.

Why is this knowledge important to me?

What do the ideas in the last two paragraphs mean to me?

Computer programs are sets of instructions. Each instruction is translated into machine code – simple binary codes that activate the CPU. Programmers write computer code and this is converted by a translator into binary instructions that the processor can execute.

All software, music, documents, and any other information that is processed by a computer, is also stored using binary.

What does this mean to me?

---

1. What does the term 'binary' mean to me? Well, I know that the prefix 'bi' is related to two, so obviously a binary system involves two numbers. If there are two numbers involved, what are the two numbers? In the binary system there is 1 and 0.

2. What does the statement 'Originally computers were made up of big transistors. In an iPhone 6 there can be 2 billion transistors' mean to me? Well, I know that transistors must have clearly got smaller over the years otherwise 2 billion of them wouldn't fit in an iPhone! How does this information relate to what I already know about transistors? Well, I think a transistor is a tiny switch which turns on and off according to the instructions given by the computer code. So, I would imagine that a 1 means on and a 0 means off.

3. What new information do the ideas in the fourth paragraph tell me? What does the term 'CPU' mean to me? I know that CPU stands for central processing unit and I think it is a bit like a sort of executive function which makes all of the decisions. What does the term 'Python' mean to me? I have heard of this term and it is a programming language. How does this knowledge help me with the rest of the paragraph? The coding language in Python must be converted into binary code, which is the machine code. The CPU uses this binary coding to 'tell' the transistors to change to on or off.

4. What new ideas are presented in the next paragraph? When the computer is telling the transistors using the machine code to turn on and off, this will be in the main memory and that main memory is known as the RAM (random access memory). Does this knowledge give me any new insight into my own understanding? I wonder if the computer's RAM is like a human's working memory as the machine code is effectively being stored there when it is being used. I'm not sure if that would make the HDD (this secondary storage) a sort of long-term memory store.

5. What do the ideas in the following paragraph tell me? I understand that 1 bit is equivalent to 1 digit in a binary code. Therefore, if you have a machine code of 101 that

would be 3 bits. How does this relate to my prior knowledge of bits? I seem to remember having an 8-bit computer many years ago. I presume that this would have been to do with the 8-digit binary code which would have taken up that space as 8 bits.

6. What do the ideas in the next paragraph mean to me? OK, so I have heard of processors, I think, as 32 bit and 64 bit. Obviously a byte is bigger than a bit then. Bits are the smaller units that make up a byte.

7. How do the ideas in the next paragraph relate to my prior knowledge? I already know that machine code is binary code, and this tells me that not only are the programs stored as machine code but also the data – some of the examples given are music and photos. What else is there that is data which is stored as machine code? If anything that is there is stored as machine code then this also makes me think that any spreadsheets and typed documents will also be stored as 1s and 0s.

8. What parts of this next paragraph are new to me? Well, I didn't know the names ASCII or UNICODE. Why is this information important to me? Well, I now know that there are a few processes to go through in order to convert what is being typed into numbers so that then it can be converted into binary. Why is this knowledge important to me? It makes me think that the data I have typed out from the commentary is also something that will have to be converted. It has to be converted to binary but in order to be converted to binary the typed letters must be converted to numbers.

9. What do the ideas in the last two paragraphs mean to me? Well, I know that a computer programmer is someone who writes in computer code. What does this mean to me? I already know that computer code is like Python or another programming language. This makes me think of an interpreter or translator from Spanish to English and vice versa. It has to be translated by the programmer into binary before it can effectively be understood by the computer.

Biology

I am grateful to head of biology Anne Clay again for having written the passage and checked my self-explanation commentary.

What do the statements 'The different food groups are all polymers' and these are 'chains of lots of smaller units put together' mean to me?

Digestion

Do I under-stand the ideas in the next line?

The different food groups are all polymers – chains of lots of smaller units put together. Digestion is the breakdown of these large polymers into those smaller pieces called monomers. This breakdown is carried out by enzymes, otherwise it would take too long.

What parts of this are new to me?

The food type (group), the enzyme type which breaks it down and the monomers which they're broken into are summarised in the table below.

What new information does the table provide for me?   *How does this information relate to what I already know?*

Food type	Enzyme type	Monomer
Carbohydrate	Carbohydrases (e.g. amylase)	Sugars (e.g. glucose)
Protein	Proteases (e.g. pepsin)	Amino acids
Fats (lipids)	Lipase	Glycerol and fatty acids

How does the information in the next line relate to what I already know?   *What new information does the next section provide for me?*

Where each of the different food groups are digested depends on which enzymes are present in which organ. This is because different organs produce different enzymes.

What do the next few lines mean to me?

The mouth produces amylase, a specific carbohydrate to digest starch, while the food is still being chewed and swallowed. However, this is prevented from working as soon as the food reaches the stomach, due to the hydrochloric acid which is present in the stomach. The acid is necessary to kill any bacteria which may be in the food, and also because the proteases in the stomach need those acidic conditions in order to digest the proteins properly. *What do I know already about the term 'proteases'?*

What does the next line mean to me: 'As the food leaves the stomach it needs to be neutralised so the liver releases bile to do this'?

As the food leaves the stomach it needs to be neutralised so the liver releases bile to do this. As well as this the bile emulsifies the fats, which doesn't mean that they digest the fats but more that it takes large clumps of fats and breaks them into smaller parts – it increases the surface area so that when the lipases are released they can work more quickly.

What does the line 'it increases the surface area so that when the lipases are released they can work more quickly' mean to me? How does this relate to what I already know?

The pancreas then releases nearly every enzyme back into the already chewed, churned, acidified, neutralised, emulsified and partly digested food.

What other new information does the text tell me?

What do I understand about the term 'emulsified'?

What does the information regarding the pancreas tell me? Does this raise any questions?

What do I understand by the ideas in the next statement: 'As this mixture passes into the small intestine, some of the small monomers will already have been formed, and they can be absorbed straight away through the surface of the small intestine into the surrounding blood supply'?

This ensures that the digestion of all of the food types can continue to occur. As this mixture passes into the small intestine, some of the small monomers will already have been formed, and they can be absorbed straight away through the surface of the small intestine into the surrounding blood supply.

What do I know already about enzymes?

For those pieces of food which are still to be digested, the enzymes are able to work on breaking them down as they pass through the small intestine. Anything which has not been digested by the end of the small intestine will not be absorbed and will be passed through the remaining digestive organs as fibre and released as faeces.

What does the information in the last few lines of the text tell me?

1. What do the statements 'The different food groups are all polymers' and these are 'chains of lots of smaller units put together' mean to me? Well, it makes me think of a link in a chain which would connect to another link and build a much longer chain, and that the process of digestion would break up the links in the chain. Do I understand the ideas in the next line? Yes: the fact that digestion breaks down these polymers (bigger chains) into smaller links. What parts of this are new to me? Well, I think that once digestion has broken down the polymers then the monomers must be like the links in the chain.

2. How does the information in the next line relate to what I already know? I have heard of the term 'enzyme', but now I know that it is the enzymes which help to break down these big polymers. So, an enzyme is like a way of speeding things up to help break up the chain.

3. What new information does the table provide for me? The table tells me the food type, the enzyme type which would be used in order to break down that food type and then in the final column the 'link' or the monomer that the enzyme would break it down into. How does this information relate to what I already know? I know that I like potatoes! I also know that potatoes are heavy on carbohydrates, and so looking at the table I now know that the enzymes used to break down potato would be carbohydrases, and once this has been broken down this would lead to polymers, which are sugars.

4. What new information does the next section provide for me? I didn't know that where each of the different food groups are digested depends on which enzymes are present in each organ, and this is because different organs produce different enzymes. I imagine then that wherever the food group is in the body, there will be a specific enzyme used to break down a specific part of that food group. The text tells me that the mouth produces amylase which is used to break down starch.

5. What do the next few lines mean to me? Well, I know already that different enzymes operate in different organs of the body, so when the food makes its way to the stomach it encounters a different enzyme. I know that stomach acid (or hydrochloric acid) is strong stuff! The text talks about proteases. What do I know already about this term? I know that proteases are enzymes and that in the table they are the enzyme used to break down proteins. However, according to the text they need acidic conditions in order to break down the proteins. Does that sound right? I know that simply put protein is needed for growth, so the acidic conditions in the stomach must work with the proteases to break down the protein.

6. What does the next line mean to me: 'As the food leaves the stomach it needs to be neutralised so the liver releases bile to do this'? Well, if I remember back to the pH scale from my chemistry lessons a long time ago, then I think that anything from 0 to 7 on

this scale is acidic and anything above 7 is alkaline. So the stomach, with the acid which I know is needed to break down the proteases, must be low on the pH scale. Therefore, bile must be alkaline if the text says that it is used to neutralise. What other new information does the text tell me? That the bile not only neutralises the acidity of food from the stomach but it also acts as a way of emulsifying fats. What do I understand about the term 'emulsified'? If you have an emulsion of something then that is effectively two liquids which don't mix together, but they don't dissolve, so I think the bile and the fats don't mix together.

7. What does the line 'it increases the surface area so that when the lipases are released they can work more quickly' mean to me? Well, I know that lipases are a type of enzyme. How does this relate to what I already know? The lipases, being a type of enzyme, break down the fats.

8. What does the information regarding the pancreas tell me? Does this raise any questions? I know that the pancreas is associated with insulin and keeping the right balance of blood sugars in the body, so in terms of digestion the text tells me that its function at this point is to release many different enzymes into the food to break it down. What do I know already about enzymes? Well, I know that each enzyme is assigned to a specific food group to break that food group down, so if several enzymes are being released by the pancreas then what it is doing is breaking down a number of different food groups together. Does that sound right? Reading the text it says: 'This ensures that the digestion of all of the food types can continue to occur.'

9. What do I understand by the ideas in the next statement: 'As this mixture passes into the small intestine, some of the small monomers will already have been formed, and they can be absorbed straight away through the surface of the small intestine into the surrounding blood supply'? Well, thinking back to what a monomer is, it is like a small link in a chain as a result of polymers having been broken down. So, at this point these 'links' must be at a stage where they have been broken down so well that they are now small enough to be absorbed into the blood supply.

10. What does the information in the last few lines of the text tell me? Well, the enzymes will continue to break down pieces of food and that the small intestine acts as what I like to think of as a type of cut-off point, in that anything that has not been broken down by the end of the small intestine will pass as faeces.

In 'Instruction Based on Visualizations', Richard Mayer suggests that the potential for learning is increased if it is accompanied by a visualisation.[8] He cites a study into retention and

8   Richard E. Mayer, 'Instruction Based on Visualizations'. In Richard E. Mayer and Patricia A. Alexander (eds), *Handbook of Research on Learning and Instruction*, Kindle edn (New York: Routledge), ch. 22 at loc. 14962.

transfer tests which did not yield great results when those involved in the study only read an explanation. To corroborate this view, Anne observed that this example on the digestive system would be better if it was accompanied by a diagram.

But how detailed should a diagram be? Is too much detail counterproductive? In *Organizing Instruction and Study to Improve Student Learning*, Harold Pashler and colleagues note that simple illustrations are more effective in demonstrating key concepts than those which include irrelevant information.[9] So, perhaps one like the following might work?

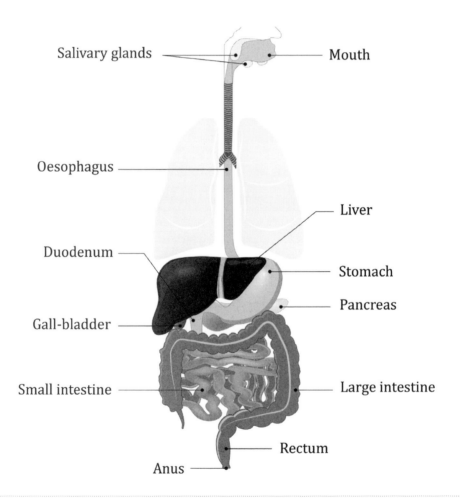

Salivary glands — Mouth
Oesophagus —
Liver —
Duodenum —
Stomach
Pancreas
Gall-bladder —
Small intestine —
Large intestine
Rectum
Anus —

9   Harold Pashler, Patrice Bain, Brian Bottge, Arthur Graesser, Kenneth Koedinger, Mark McDaniel and Janet Metcalfe, *Organizing Instruction and Study to Improve Student Learning* (NCER 2007–2004) (Washington, DC: National Center for Education Research, Institute of Education Sciences, US Department of Education, 2007). Available at: https://ies.ed.gov/ncee/wwc/PracticeGuide/1, p. 25.

Before finishing up this section on self-explanation, it's worth considering the question of whether worked examples result in a more passive level of learning, a point advanced by John Sweller and colleagues in *Cognitive Load Theory*.[10] Self-explanation may be one way to help learners focus on the worked example, of course, but Sweller et al. also raise the concern that someone studying a worked example needs to see how this relates to an immediate problem to be solved if they are to fully engage with the worked example.

Two strategies which can help to focus the learner's attention on the processing of a worked example are the paired alternation strategy (a worked example followed by a similar problem) and the completion problem (a worked example with one or more steps missing). Both techniques can help to reduce extraneous load. Here are two examples (with thanks again to maths teacher Dan Frankton) – one using the paired alternation strategy and the other a completion problem.

Paired alternation strategy

Solve this equation to find x

$$5x - 7 = 2x + 23$$
$$-2x \qquad -2x$$
$$3x - 7 = 23$$
$$+7 \qquad +7$$
$$3x = 30$$
$$\div 3 \qquad \div 3$$
$$x = 10$$

Solve this equation to find x

$$7x + 4 = 3x + 28$$

Completion problem

Find $\frac{5}{6}$ of 48

$$\frac{5}{6} \times 48$$
$$5 \times (48 \div 6)$$
$$5 \times 8 = ?$$

---

10 Sweller et al., *Cognitive Load Theory*, loc. 1603–1610.

Practice Testing/Retrieval Practice

It is important to begin this section on practice testing with a reminder from David Didau: 'Testing should not be used primarily to assess the efficacy of your teaching and students' learning; it should be used as a powerful tool in your pedagogical armoury to *help* them learn.'[1]

Retrieval practice might also be referred to as self-testing or quizzing. In terms of the boundary conditions for self-testing, Fiorella and Mayer say: 'In general, free-recall, cued-recall, or otherwise open-response practice tests appear to be more effective than practice recognition tests, such as a multiple-choice test.'[2] The reason for this could be because of the generation effect which occurs when a learner is forced to generate an answer. This is more powerful than the learner simply having to recognise the correct answer from a set of options.

Before looking at some types of practice testing in detail, I'm going to briefly describe some of my own experiences with practice testing and how I have used it in place of dedicated improvement and reflection time (DIRT), which often focuses on correcting and redrafting recent work and not necessarily promoting generative learning outcomes.

I started by setting output tasks in class (and encouraging the students to do these at home as part of their revision before grammar tests). So, after handing their books back, I would give them 10–15 minutes to do a free recall test on, for example, the formation of the present tense without looking back at their notes or the textbook (although I would sometimes provide prompts like formation, irregulars and meanings in English). This enabled me to identify any common misconceptions and see how each student had interpreted the tense and developed a meaning of it in their own words, as well as (hopefully) making the retrieval of everything to do with the tense more accessible in the future.

The students responded fantastically well to the output tasks (in my clearly unbiased opinion!), and I have since adopted free recall tests as an extension task in class – for example, students writing down all they can remember about a tense covered last week/last term/last year.

Initially, the tasks I used bore a strong resemblance to the type of written task the students would find in their GCSE exam. However, I have since removed many of the prompts which appear on the practice paper because I am trying to find out what the students can recall from a single prompt – for example, 'Write about your interests and your activities'

---

1   Didau, *What If Everything You Knew About Education Was Wrong?*, p. 234.
2   Fiorella and Mayer, *Learning as a Generative Activity*, p. 119.

(as opposed to 'Write about your interests and your activities – mention music and sport'). I like to think that it's a wildly crude attempt at developing a goal-free effect in the 'ill-structured' domain of language writing, where students are not narrowed by the constraints of writing an answer to one particular topic title but are free to express themselves about any interests.

Prompt-free tasks force students to think harder about the material, but hopefully in such a way that they can adopt an approach to free recall which does not have an overly narrow goal. It's not revolutionary, but I'm shifting from using tests to measure what the students can (and can't) do under restrictive exam conditions to using them to free up their working memories and think more widely about other language they could use.

Some other ways that I have trialled using retrieval practice include the following.

Lag Homework/Classwork Feedback

When marking the students' books, I make a note of what they couldn't do so well earlier on in the term (or year) and write a memory task (MT) in their book.

Depending on how well the students have grasped previous learning, this is a task designed to get them to redo or re-explain something. For example, if we covered how to write a short paragraph in the present and perfect tense in French last term, I might write, 'MT: Write as much as you can about what you do in your free time and what you did last weekend.' Or I might simply walk around the class while the students are working and deliver an impromptu free recall test based on material covered the previous week, term and so on, if I spot they have finished and not started an extension task (e.g. 'Write all you can about how the imperfect tense works').

As basic as it sounds, I'm also getting students to use a piece of card to simply cover up explanations, previous exercises or written pieces and asking them to add to them or redo them on a blank page, and then compare the new version with what they did before.

Finally, I provide a task in the following lesson which involves the students applying the material which had its retrieval strength topped up in the previous lesson. It's a no-frills approach to bringing previously noted down information back to mind, with the spin-off of seeing whether the students can do in the here-and-now what they could do in the there-and-then.

I have also tried syllabus and scheme of learning retrieval practice with a Year 11 student I was mentoring. Having downloaded the exam specifications, past papers, mark schemes, specimen papers and examiner reports for all of his subjects, I called up some specimen papers and scrolled down to the 'subject content' section. I then simply used elaborative interrogation with him by reading out the key idea and then adding, 'Why is this true?' I also used a series of fairly generic, content-free prompts. For example, from the AQA GCSE geography spec, I might ask something relatively straightforward like, 'How does the vegetation in temperate deciduous forest adapt to the climate and soils?'

Free Recall Tests

I have also experimented with takeaway free recall extension tasks. I use a store of common pedagogical errors that previous students have made to help inform the tasks. At the start of a term or with a new class, I project the list of potential extension tasks which must be written on a blank page in the students' books from memory if they finish a task before others do. The students make a list of these ten or so retrieval-based extension tasks at the back of their books, and then practise using them throughout the term when they've finished working on a task in class.

Magic Whiteboards and Free Recall Tests

Mini-whiteboards and exit tickets are straightforward, low-tech ways of adopting retrieval practice. I have tried sticking up Magic Whiteboard paper around the room, projecting a list of the takeaway retrieval practice tasks and then asking the students to go 'To the walls', choose a task from the list and write an answer to the task on the paper.

A brain dump with an imaginary Year 11 group in one of the first lessons back after Christmas might go like this:

1. I project four questions or prompts on the board – for example:

    a. Write all you can remember about the conditional tense (covered last lesson).

    b. Write as much language as you can recall from the free time topic (covered last half-term).

    c. Write all you can remember about the imperfect tense (covered in the first half-term this year).

   d. Write as much language as you can recall from the holidays topic (covered in the last half-term of Year 10).

2.   Students come into class and hear 'Go to the walls! You have ten minutes in pairs to complete as much as possible from memory.' As they are familiar with the name of the task they grab a board pen and get to work as soon as they come in.

I'm not making any claim that Magic Whiteboard paper is guaranteed to improve the students' memories more efficiently than any other technique, but the fact that the paper is large helps them to brain dump more freely than they could on a mini-whiteboard, for example. And it adds variety to the retrieval practice repertoire.

In *Memorable Teaching*, Peps Mccrea (@pepsmccrea) writes about outsourcing.[3] This is essentially a strategy designed to lower cognitive load by 'storing live information on *working surfaces*'. By putting up Magic Whiteboard paper around the room and leaving it up all year, you not only create a place for information from any retrieval practice to be written throughout the course, but you also create somewhere for the students to manage content which is high in element interactivity by writing it down.

Of course, outsourcing could also be done in a book or on an A4 sheet, but it can help to increase the number of places where students can work, particularly when they are working in pairs to solve a problem. It also enables you to see immediately what students are doing from across the classroom, as well as the students seeing what other groups are doing. Immediate feedback can be given by the teacher and other students, and immediate corrections and amendments to the task can be made. It's like using a low-tech visualiser!

Overt and Covert Retrieval Practice

We touched on overt and covert retrieval practice in Chapter 3 when discussing imagery for text. In *Small Teaching*, James Lang mentions a college chemistry teacher who adopted retrieval practice in his lectures and enjoyed much success with it. However, the teacher observed that the written assessments he used required all students to give a response (overt response), not just the individuals who tended to dominate the class.[4] In other words, if the same students are always providing answers, then these are the only students

---

3   Peps Mccrea, *Memorable Teaching: Leveraging Memory to Build Deep and Durable Learning in the Classroom* (n.p.: Peps Mccrea, 2017), pp. 54–55.

4   Lang, *Small Teaching*, loc. 620, 690.

whose answers are (a) being sampled and (b) adopting retrieval practice – unless, of course, those who are not answering are answering silently to themselves.

I have used the Magic Whiteboard technique for the revision of key vocabulary. This works by having a list of vocabulary and phrases up on the walls as soon as the students come into the class, with the English meanings covered up (like the example later on in Part 2). I tell the students that they have five minutes to write down as many meanings as possible in pairs before uncovering the meanings on the board and letting them tot up the scores (which I don't take in). There's no magic to it, other than the whiteboard itself. It's all about bringing information to mind. Once they've all finished, it allows me (presentation clicker in hand) to refer to what each pair have retrieved on the boards during the lesson or a previous lesson if I leave the information up on the paper.

Paired retrieval aims to lessen the stakes; however, one of the issues I found at first was that I wasn't sure I was surveying the knowledge of the whole class. Was one student in each pair doing the majority of the work? Was one of the students in the pair taking a back seat? Does making a testing activity for two people lower the stakes? If so, is this to the detriment of the benefits gained from the retrieval? One of the final messages from the study into overt versus covert retrieval by Smith et al. is the need to ensure that learners have indeed engaged in the covert retrieval task; if this is ensured then covert retrieval is just as effective as overt retrieval.[5] Allowing time for students to think and reflect after a question is James Lang's suggestion to promote covert retrieval.[6]

Of course, there are other ways for retrieval practice to occur at the start of lessons, such as a simple question to recap what was learned in a previous learning episode, or at the end of lessons to recap that lesson's content or link it to a prior learning episode. Some of these have been discussed already.

Vocabulary Revisited

When revisiting language vocabulary and short phrases in class, I have adopted some no-frills approaches to testing students' retrieval – for example, knowledge practice using some basic elaboration and reference to it in different contexts, followed by some forgetting time and then retrieval of it.

Robert Peal (@RobertPeal), the author of *Progressively Worse*, has written an outstanding blog post on writing a paragraph, which is applicable to practising and retrieving

5   Smith et al., 'Covert Retrieval Practice'.
6   Lang, *Small Teaching*, loc. 699.

knowledge in a languages lesson[7] – that is, knowledge practice and knowledge retrieval lessons mixed up with paragraph writing lessons, reading lessons and so on across the course. While a far cry from the restrictive aim of satisfying an observer who wants to see a three-part lesson, I think there is a place for spending a whole lesson practising language and testing previous language.

Would I devote a whole lesson to knowledge practice and retrieval practice when being observed by an Ofsted inspector? I wouldn't have done so a few years ago; I might do so now. Would I have done this as an NQT or a new teacher starting at a new school? I'd like to think so, *if* I knew that it was geared towards learning over time. It might also depend on whether the school had the type of culture in which you could feel comfortable being observed teaching a lesson that didn't go that well, or a culture where gamification and fun in the classroom are an unfortunate by-product of a poor whole-school behaviour management strategy – making things entertaining so that things won't kick off.

I use various methods to practise vocabulary or phrases, including mnemonic-type activities like the keyword technique (which we discussed in Chapter 3) and projecting a slide of words/phrases and meanings. I then simply cover up the meanings and call out the French/Spanish/German words and wait for the students to respond with the English, or vice versa. It's a low-tech approach to knowledge practice and retrieval which aims to not over-complicate the teaching too much.

One of the mistakes I made when I first used this technique was that I covered up the meanings pretty much straight away after practising the language knowledge with the students. At the time, I didn't realise that I hadn't left enough time for much forgetting to have kicked in so retrieval strength was high.[8] There was therefore an element of the fluency illusion: the students (and I) believed they had learned the meanings more comprehensively than they had done. The students' retrieval strength was still high – good enough perhaps to promote self-efficacy, but not quite good enough to promote the conditions necessary for embedding knowledge over the longer term.

I also noticed a primacy and recency effect in operation when testing the students' retrieval, at least according to my own (non-researcher but wannabe-teacher-researcher) understanding. This issue is discussed by Jonathan Solity in *The Learning Revolution*, where he explores the Michel Thomas Method to learning languages. In a chapter discussing mixing old spellings with new spellings, Solity notes that typically primary school spelling tests are given weekly: 20 words given on Monday and tested on Friday is usual. After six weeks, when all the spellings are retested, most children will remember

---

7   Robert Peal, 'The Art of the Paragraph', *Robert Peal* [blog] (14 October 2017). Available at: https://robertpealhistory.wordpress.com/2017/10/14/the-art-of-the-paragraph/.

8   See https://twitter.com/learningspy/status/535101853835743232.

the first 20 spellings (primacy effect) and the last 20 spellings (recency effect) but little from those in-between.[9]

As a consequence, I have since adapted retrieval practice when revisiting by testing only the middle part of the list of questions, speaking tasks and so on, so that context is key and the phrases are transferred across different skills. It is not only the order of the words on the list or slide that matters but also the order in which slides, textbook pages and so on are presented. The aim is to mitigate the problems associated with remembering the word or phrase just because you have memorised the sequence and not necessarily the actual meaning. Oh, and leaving time for forgetting to kick in before testing retrieval.

I was fortunate enough to present a session at researchED Rugby in 2016 on 'Knowledge Practice, Retrieval Practice, Generative Learning and Linear Exams'. In the session, I discussed strategies I had used to practise vocabulary and short phrases in language lessons. I also identified the language structures that, if taught and tested over time, would promote better long-term recall of essential content. The vocabulary and phrases were all packed onto a PowerPoint slide with the meanings obscured. (It doesn't have to be PowerPoint, of course; it could be a textbook, a textbook under a visualiser, a hand-out or even an overhead projector.)

I also talked about how some of these activities might transfer to other domains. My reasoning was that many domains have a 'language', in that there is a bank of knowledge which it is essential to acquire in order to be able to analyse and do all of the wonderfully creative things that we would want to do.

For example, strategies like 'penalty shoot-out' might work across other domains as part of spaced retrieval practice. (Doug Lemov, Erica Woolway and Katie Yezzi in *Practice Perfect* relate the names of strategies to what they call the 'transaction cost'.[10] Using several named activities to practise knowledge, and referring to them by name in future lessons, can help to save time – as with 'To the walls'.)

---

9   Jonathan Solity, *Michel Thomas: The Learning Revolution* (Abingdon: Hodder Education, 2008), p. 112.

10 Doug Lemov, Erica Woolway and Katie Yezzi, *Practice Perfect: 42 Rules for Getting Better at Getting Better* (San Francisco, CA: Jossey-Bass, 2012).

Penalty Shoot-Out

The penalty shoot-out activity begins by dividing the class into two sides and then presenting some content to be revisited after a little forgetting time. Ask one side of the class to turn away from the board while the other side face the board. The students facing the board have ten seconds to choose an item of vocabulary or grammar phrase which they call out in the target language. The other side have a few seconds to decide who is best to answer and call out the translation or grammar explanation. I accept the answer from the first person on the side with their backs to the board. This allows for these students, albeit briefly, to discuss with their team who might know the meaning and how sure they are. It also allows me to observe if what I've been teaching has stuck as I can listen in to the discussion and ultimately find out how secure their understanding is and any shared misconceptions.

If the translation or explanation by the side with their backs to the board is correct, then they have 'saved the penalty'. If the first answer is incorrect, then the side looking at the board have 'scored'. I would mark this on the board in the same way that a penalty shoot-out might look:

Left	Right
1. X	✓
2. ✓	X
3.	

The process continues with each side taking turns in calling out a word or phrase that they think no one on the other side will be able to retrieve. Numbering the knowledge presented helps the students looking at the content to refer to the language they think will be the trickiest to get right without actually saying it: 'They'll never get 14' and so on. ('Number the knowledge' is a phrase that I hope will catch on one day!) With each side having five opportunities to try to catch out the opposing students, this should hopefully help to make the knowledge stick for all involved.

Now for the point-scoring (although I have been trying to wean myself off from doing this). I used to regard points as a way to create engagement in class, without fully understanding the term (certainly not the psychological and behavioural elements). At times, the lessons could end up in pandemonium, with the students arguing about the number of points they had been awarded and not focusing their attention on selecting troublesome questions for the other side to answer. These are the times to abandon points and just stick to one side quizzing the other side. If the focus of the activity isn't on the content, it's time to ditch it. Head teacher Clare Sealy (@ClareSealy) has written a hugely impressive blog post called 'Memory Not Memories – Teaching for Long Term Learning'. Among many of the excellent points she makes is that the context of when the memory was formed becomes part of the learning, and consequently there is a danger that the students remember the context but not the content of the learning.

Shell et al.'s *The Unified Learning Model* does a brilliant job of explaining episodic memory.[11] The authors also link the Unified Learning Model to cognitive load theory, although a key difference between the two is motivation. They explain that just because we have working memory capacity at our disposal this does not always mean that it is being focused on the learning goal. Therefore, even if an individual's working memory capacity is fully available, it is what motivates them to concentrate and apply themselves to the task that is key.

I love head of humanities Ben Newmark's (@bennewmark) blog post on starters, in which he describes the effectiveness of a straightforward quizzing routine and how much the students actually enjoyed the feeling of being successful on his low-stakes quizzes. He now starts every lesson with a short 'test' on prior learning, the format of which the students are now completely used to: five questions on last lesson, five on the current topic and five from any previous lesson. The impact of this has been real improvement in the quality and content of students' writing as they have more knowledge and therefore more confidence. What he notes as particularly pleasing was that students really enjoyed and looked forward to the tests: 'They hissed "yesss" and even fist-pumped when I read out answers and they got it right. They groaned when they got answers wrong that they just knew they should have known. One boy even exploded out of his chair and shouted "GET IN!" the first time he got full marks.'[12]

I have always disliked the baggage associated with the idea of games, which seem to imply that some sort of treat or reward will be given to the students if they work hard enough. It's like someone saying that if you eat your greens then you can have dessert. Games might also be considered a poor excuse for behaviour management – creating a superficial sense of fun at the expense of psychological engagement is certainly something to bear in mind.

The engagement matrix in *E-Learning and the Science of Instruction* provides a brilliant way of illustrating how a behavioural activity (e.g. underlining five key points in a text) might not necessarily lead to processing the material in a way that is conducive to the learning

---

11 Shell et al., *The Unified Learning Model*, p. 36.
12 Ben Newmark, 'Nothing New, It's a Review – On Why I Killed My Starters', *Learning History* [blog] (13 November 2017). Available at: https://bennewmark.wordpress.com/2017/11/13/nothing-new-its-a-review-on-why-i-killed-my-starters/.

goal.[13] I fear that, back in Chapter 2, the teacher who was having to show progress to an observer through what the students could recall in a lesson would also have been expected to demonstrate perceived engagement, but which was actually a form of behavioural engagement; just because the students are busy doesn't mean they are psychologically engaging with the content. This is also relevant to the idea of games and gamification; just because there is lots of overt physical activity and running about doesn't always mean efficient processing.

The game tag also seems unhelpful in terms of the rationale behind an activity. Many of these activities are designed to practise knowledge, which in turn might spark off a discussion about related knowledge that might help to embed it. This is not a game! I even go so far as to correct students who use the word game – for example, when asking to *play* 'Random'.

Discussions at my researchED session in Rugby led me to consider ways in which techniques for practising and then discussing knowledge could be applied across other subjects – for example, geography content from a geography knowledge organiser. The following table, written by geography teacher Jon Haston, is an example.

1.	**V-shaped valley**	Steep-sided, V-shaped due to vertical erosion. River is narrow, shallow and turbulent.
2.	**Floodplain**	A wider valley with a flat floor. The river is wider and deeper (lateral erosion) due to an increase in velocity.
3.	**Abrasion**	Rocks carried along a river wear down the river bed and banks.
4.	**Attrition**	Rocks being carried by the river hit together and break into smaller, smoother and less angular particles.
5.	**Cross profile**	The side-by-side cross section of a river channel and/or valley.
6.	**Discharge**	Quantity of water that passes a given point on a stream or river bank within a given time period using an impeller.
7.	**Erosion**	Wearing away and removal of material by a moving force, such as hydraulic action.

13 Clark and Mayer, *E-Learning and the Science of Instruction*, loc. 5429.

8. Gorge	A narrow, steep-sided valley often formed as a waterfall retreats upstream over many years.
9. Hydraulic action	Power of the water being forced into cracks and the pressure eroding the bed and banks of a river.
10. Hydrograph	A graph which shows the discharge of a river, related to rainfall, over a period of time and shows lag time.

Admittedly, a number of potential issues did stand out when I thought about how the activities used for languages might transfer to practising this knowledge, which led to a discussion with a number of geography teachers. The idea of rote learning, where students can retrieve the definition exactly as presented but consequently do not understand it and cannot apply it, was discussed. But we also acknowledged that any knowledge practice in class (i.e. verbalising the term and definition) should be followed up by a quick whole-class discussion of some of the underlying concepts. The idea is that something tested during a revisiting activity should always lead to further elaboration and discussion, and not just the isolated shovelling in and testing of these terms.

Commenting on a belting blog post by maths teacher Kris Boulton, discussing flexible and inflexible knowledge, Anthony Radice (@AnthonyRadice1) observes the following, which made me think about how the situation in any classroom might go:

In my experience, when you require pupils to memorise something, discussions naturally emerge which clarify concepts. Understandably, if there is anything in a fact which they are memorising which they do not grasp, they want to know about it. For example, I recently set pupils to memorise that Shakespeare's *Julius Caesar* is set during the era of the Roman Republic, and it led to an interesting discussion of what exactly a republic is, and how the ancient ones differed from modern versions. The memory point is a kind of peg on which a deeper conceptual understanding hangs.[14]

So, retrieval practice could lead to a more in-depth discussion about further aspects of knowledge and understanding in any subject.

---

14 Boulton, 'What Rote Knowledge Isn't'.

In 2017, author Michael Fordham (@mfordhamhistory) gave a talk to new trainees on the Future Academies SCITT during which he said:

> To be clear, this is absolutely not about learning lists of definitions. If I were to say the word 'working-class' to you, I am confident that you would not immediately think of a definition, but rather of examples of the many contexts in which you have heard that word used. This is not to say that learning definitions might not serve as a useful proxy, but rather that it is not sufficient. The key to cracking an idea such as 'working class' is to encounter it in lots of contexts.[15]

The practising of this knowledge in different ways would then be followed by the retrieval of it in different ways. Covering up meanings (as in the example below) and then getting the students to note down (or verbally express) the definitions in their own words at spaced intervals across the course would be one way (somewhat akin to using a flashcard) for the students to bring this information to mind. This might save time, both in lessons and in terms of preparation. For example, students come in and immediately note down (under a strict time limit) as many definitions as they can from a list on a hand-out or projected onto the board.

1. V-shaped valley	
2. Floodplain	
3. Abrasion	
4. Attrition	
5. Cross profile	

---

15 Michael Fordham, 'Resisting the Pull of the Generic: Knowledge, Specificity and Teaching', *Clio et cetera* [blog] (20 October 2017). Available at: https://clioetcetera.com/2017/10/20/resisting-the-pull-of-the-generic-knowledge-specificity-and-teaching/.

6.	Discharge	
7.	Erosion	
8.	Gorge	
9.	Hydraulic action	
10.	Hydrograph	

When I presented this at researchED, someone commented that I was talking about isolated bits of knowledge or knowledge out of context. My answer at the time was a moderately panicked pseudo-politician's answer which alluded to how all these fragmented bits of knowledge were essential chunks to be transferred into long-term memory in order to free up space in the working memory, so the learner could focus their limited working memory more effectively on solving the problem. I may also have mentioned that I thought you needed knowledge like this in your long-term memory in order to be able to think with it. I didn't refer to the idea of not being able to think critically about something without foundational knowledge, but I would definitely do so now. Perhaps it would have been better if I had referred to this strategy simply as a way of promoting further discussion and exploring the concepts behind the definition.

Retrieval Practice and Retrieval Cues

Let's suppose that the terms have been learned and applied to another context. I've then moved on to another topic, but I want to test the retrieval of these terms to see if I can relate them to another area.

When I first started learning about retrieval practice, I used to think that a good cue to aid students' retrieval would be something along the lines of providing the initial letters of the target term – for example, 'You can see how the water has worn away the banks of the river here – what is the two-word term that we give to this?' Then, if necessary, 'The first word begins with "H" and the second word with "A".'

The students might successfully retrieve the term 'hydraulic action', but a cue like this wouldn't necessarily be in keeping with the elaborative retrieval hypothesis. This means that when you retrieve the answer to something, you also trigger elaborative information related to what you have recalled, and it is this elaborative information which will aid you in retrieving the answer in the future.

In 2011, Professor Shana Carpenter published a study entitled 'Semantic Information Activated During Retrieval Contributes to Later Retention', in which she discusses the potential for testing to be more effective than restudying because of the mediator effectiveness hypothesis.[16] She has found that there is a greater chance of strengthening the link between the cue and the information to be recalled because of mediating information.

An easy cue like 'H' and 'A' doesn't allow for much (if any) activation of elaborative information. There is not a lot of mediating information here in the sense that retrieval from the initial letters alone does not allow for the generation of anything other than the word. It is not tied to any other area of the course and is retrieved in isolation. There is a wonderful science blog post by Pritesh Raichura (@Mr_Raichura) in which he discusses how initial letter cues may be doing more harm than good if they are not central to the understanding of key scientific concepts.[17]

(I should add here that one of the retrieval practice examples later on for English is simply a quotation with missing letters. There is no elaborative retrieval associated with this example, but I have referenced an excellent blog post by Paul Moss (@EDmerger) which refers to the power of storytelling as a way to adopt elaborative retrieval with a quotation (see page 190).)

So, what might be a more effective cue for elaboration than initial letters? I'm not a geography teacher, so I asked head of geography Marc Enser and he very kindly provided the following suggestion: 'If I was going to prompt for the retrieval of the answer "hydraulic action", I would ask "What happens when air is forced into gaps in the rock?" or "Why do cracks in the rock open up further every time a wave crashes into them?"'

16   Shana K. Carpenter, 'Semantic Information Activated During Retrieval Contributes to Later Retention: Support for the Mediator Effectiveness Hypothesis of the Testing Effect', *Journal of Experimental Psychology: Learning, Memory, and Cognition*, 37(6) (2011), 1547–1552.
17   Pritesh Raichura, 'Retrieval Cues: Do Your Questions Help or Hinder?', *Bunsen Blue* [blog] (19 March 2018). Available at: https://bunsenblue.wordpress.com/2018/03/19/retrieval-cues-do-your-questions-help-or-hinder/.

Facts and Element Interactivity

Returning to the idea of element interactivity which we encountered earlier, John Sweller and colleagues explain in *Cognitive Load Theory* how a task such as learning vocabulary could be a hard task in itself but low in element interactivity.[18] This type of task, an example of which might be learning the periodic table, can only be effectively learned by rote. However, in high element interactivity, full understanding is generated when all the interacting elements can be synthesised within working memory.

So, in the interest of having to start somewhere, packing a slide or hand-out with low element interactivity knowledge might be helpful as an introduction before the students can move on to high element interactivity content. It might seem a little incongruous to refer to 'packing a slide' in the context of 'less is more', but I wouldn't advocate including a superfluous diagram alongside some self-explanatory text. Just the facts.

Richard Mayer gives details about how pre-training in the features of important concepts can help to support essential processing.[19] Where images and verbal explanations are presented together, learners make better connections between the key elements of each one. So, practising knowledge followed by a discussion of key facts and concepts might be a useful strategy to employ before adopting a multimedia strategy combining words with pictures.

I have recently started to use bigger 'chunks' of language to test the students, as opposed to individual words or short phrases. Gianfranco Conti has written a blog post on ditching word lists in which he observes: 'Working Memory can only accommodate 4 items at any given time for only a handful of seconds. By learning 4 chunks made up of 4 words each instead of 4 single words, the brain is still processing 4 items but working with 16 words at the same time.'[20]

The idea of presenting longer chunks of content in any subject goes back to what (I think) I was trying to say in my researchED session on identifying which chunks are the most important in a subject no matter what topic is being taught. Shell et al. discuss the role of an 'element' in memory storage in *The Unified Learning Model*.[21] If temporary memory can hold four or five elements at a time, these could be separate words or separate letters – and words obviously contain many more than five letters in total.

---

18 Sweller et al., *Cognitive Load Theory*, loc. 1010, 1027.
19 Mayer, 'Instruction Based on Visualizations', loc. 14962.
20 Gianfranco Conti, 'Patterns First – Why You Should "Ditch" Word Lists, Traditional Grammar Rules and … Your Textbook', *The Language Gym* [blog] (21 May 2017). Available at: https://gianfrancoconti. wordpress.com/2017/05/21/why-you-should-ditch-word-lists-and-traditional-grammar-rules/.
21 Shell et al., *The Unified Learning Model*, p. 27.

Retrieval Roulette

A brilliant example of adopting retrieval practice comes from chemistry teacher Adam Boxer (@adamboxer1), who writes about using an Excel program to promote 'retrieval roulette'. I am grateful to Adam for letting me share the following from his blog.[22]

What it is

A simple Excel program that uses a list of questions and answers to generate a random 10 question quiz. You can set it to ask 5 questions from any point in the course and 5 questions from the current topic (this is what I do).

How I use it

For each topic I write flashcards on Quizlet in question and answer form. The cards are lean and focussed to only have the material necessary and nothing extraneous (occasionally I include practice questions for improving procedural technique). I print off a PDF with all the questions and answers and give it to students at the beginning of a unit. I tell them that all my verbal questions will be based on them and they are expected to begin learning them off by heart and referring to them in their verbal and written answers.

Every three lessons, the class receives a mini quiz generated by the Roulette. I display the questions on the board, give them ten minutes to answer in the back of their books and then peer assess. Students collate their score /5 for the first five questions a score /5 for the second five. Each student receives a small piece of paper which they fold in half. On the outside they write their name, and on the inside they write the two numbers /5. I take these in and record them.

(At the beginning of the year there are only a few questions and a high likelihood of repeated questions. You can hit F9 to refresh the questions. As time goes on the likelihood decreases massively.)

Vocab Piler

Another activity which aims to incorporate knowledge practice and retrieval practice is 'vocab piler'. This activity has a number of steps but the basic idea is as follows:

1. Students look at the key terms and definitions on the board/hand-out/screen.

2. They choose five or six of the terms and definitions and write them down.

3. They rate the ones they have chosen from 1 to 6, with 1 being their favourite and 6 being their least favourite. The criteria for deciding could be to do with the sound of the words or anything else you would like them to focus on.

4. Then it's survey time! In languages, this would involve the students speaking the words or phrases to a partner. As the students verbalise the terms/definitions to each other, they also add to their own list whenever they hear a term/definition they had not written down originally.

5. After a set time limit, they rate all of the remaining terms and definitions. If they've got ten extra ones, for example, then they rate these from 1 to 10.

6. They then pass their books to a partner who states just the term to them and the student being quizzed has to recall the definition. This stage could be left until the following lesson if you wanted to wait until retrieval strength had lessened. They then swap roles.

7. A follow-up lesson could be that they encounter these terms in another context or that they have to apply the terms to another context.

The purpose of the activity is to practise bringing information to mind. Of course, terms and definitions might not be the knowledge you want to practise, but the general idea is that it helps knowledge to stick over time so the students can actually begin to get a little creative with it.

Random

Another way of practising knowledge which might transfer to domain-specific language terms is a simple approach called 'random'. The setting up and running of it goes like this:

1. Present the knowledge to be revisited as a numbered list on a slide (in languages this would be the French, German, Spanish, etc. with the English next to it).

2. Divide the class into two sides.

3. Call out a number and whoever identifies it first stands up and calls out the language and the English translation next to it – they 'say what they see'.

They don't have to stand up, of course, and nor do they have to win a point. (The allusion to the line 'Say what you see', from the game show *Catchphrase*, has always been lost on everyone, including, frighteningly, fellow teachers who are somewhat younger than me.)

I've used the same activity but with the meanings covered up, calling out the English for a phrase or an item of vocabulary, or the students calling it out. See it, say it, retrieve it; it's a simple way of getting the students to bring meanings to mind. The intention is that those who retrieve the meaning correctly and call it out in class are reminding those who didn't.

Try doing this over spaced intervals, while also mixing in other essential content from other areas of the course. In the languages example, there is also the option to discuss with the students which phrases are the most interesting, the most difficult to say and so on in an attempt to promote a debate about meaning.

These strategies can add variety to the ways you undertake knowledge practice and knowledge retrieval with your students. In *Why Don't Students Like School?*, Daniel Willingham emphasises how a change in activity can help to promote attention.[23] The important thing is that the students are engaged and thinking about the content, not distracted by a silly sombrero.

Another strategy that gets straight to the recall of previously taught content would be to give the students three questions testing content from the previous lesson, three from the lesson before that, three from the lesson before that and so on. Or how about towards the end of Year 10, projecting the scheme of learning and pointing to a heading here or a subheading there and asking the students to do a free recall test with a ten minute limit for each one. I'm reminded here of Andrew Old's tweet which beautifully sums things up

---

23 Willingham, *Why Don't Students Like School?*, p. 22.

for me: 'Here's my teaching advice: (1) Just teach them. (2) Make them practise. (3) That's it.'[24]

While we're on the subject of facts and stuff you want students to know, I'm going to make a tenuous link to another belting blog by former head teacher and author of *The Learning Rainforest: Great Teaching in Real Classrooms*, Tom Sherrington (@teacherhead), who refers to a great acronym to use with revision for exams.[25] This was devised by Deborah O'Connor, deputy head at Parliament Hill School in Camden:

- **Facts:** Identify the key facts that need to be known and learn them. Memorise them. Test yourself. You can't explain something if you can't remember the key facts.

- **Apply in context:** Use recall of facts to solve problems in new contexts; it's not enough to learn isolated facts. Test that knowledge in different scenarios using questions in books and past papers.

- **Connect to other ideas:** Increasingly you need to make links between topics – e.g. energy and forces in science from different areas (e.g. mechanics and magnetism); comparing the use of techniques between different texts; seeing common patterns in historical events or geographical processes.

- **Exam practice:** Use past exam questions to rehearse the process of responding under time pressure, demonstrating your knowledge and understanding, taking account of the marks available.

Tom Sherrington gives a brilliant example of how this could look with biology:

- **Facts:** The equation for photosynthesis; the role of chlorophyll; the starch test; the concept of limiting conditions; the concept of gas concentration.

- **Apply in context:** Learn how a graph of crop yields versus CO_2 concentration relates to the equation; learn how results of covered leaf or variegated leaf experiments can be explained.

- **Connect to other ideas:** Link work on crop yields to nitrogen cycle, nitrogen-fixing bacteria and use of nitrate-providing fertilisers.

---

24 See https://twitter.com/oldandrewuk/status/538367068236951552.
25 Tom Sherrington, 'FACE It. A Formula for Learning', *teacherhead* [blog] (19 September 2015). Available at: https://teacherhead.com/2015/09/19/face-it-a-formula-for-learning/.

■ **Exam practice:** Complete exam questions – e.g. a CO_2 graph needs to be analysed for 4 marks; leaf starch test results need to be explained for 3 marks.[26]

A caveat to all of this discussion about facts is that I think it might be quite reductionist to simply say that more facts equals more understanding. I'm simply suggesting some potential ways of practising knowledge and facts as an inchoate step towards connecting these facts and building understanding.

Knowledge practice and retrieval practice activities are certainly not a panacea, but they are ways of practising and retrieving that knowledge with the view to strengthening it over time. Hopefully, these activities will help to add a little variety to your repertoire. There are variations within each activity too – for example, with the penalty shoot-out, one day it might be a whole-class activity with one side being quizzed by the other on key language, another day it might be small groups or pairs quizzing each other and another day it could be a different sort of retrieval practice quiz.

Concept Maps and Retrieval Practice

Certainly the claims that creating visually organised representations of information leads to superior learning, appears unsupported by the evidence.[27]

I ummed and ahhed about putting in this section on concept maps. As it featured in *Learning as a Generative Activity*, I have included a few examples of how mapping might look alongside GCSE content with retrieval practice.

Technically speaking, concept mapping is not explicitly referred to in the Dunlosky review as a separate strategy, although Nick Rose alludes to Dunlosky et al.'s concerns with regard to summarisation being a difficult skill to teach in the same context as mapping being a difficult skill to teach.[28] I am including it because while it might be considered trickier than

26 Sherrington, 'FACE It'.
27 Nick Rose, 'Does Visual Mapping Help Revision?', *Evidence Into Practice* [blog] (25 August 2014). Available at: https://evidenceintopractice.wordpress.com/2014/08/25/does-visual-mapping-help-revision/.
28 Rose, 'Does Visual Mapping Help Revision?'

designing some practice questions, it is still a useful way to employ retrieval practice. In other words, this means reading a text on aerobic and anaerobic respiration (like the one below), letting retrieval strength fade and then creating a concept map – but doing it from memory. Rose adds:

> Recent research appears to suggest that [visual mapping] can effectively be used as a form of retrieval practice (i.e. recall in the absence of the material to be learnt rather than a summarisation technique). However, given that other methods of retrieval practice (e.g. practice questions) may require less training, it could be argued that teachers would be better off encouraging a wider range of retrieval practice strategies (e.g. self-testing using flashcards) in order to help children revise material more effectively.[29]

In the examples below it is imagined that the material would not be there to refer to during the retrieval process. This could involve a partially completed map or one with prompts to make it easier for the learners. This made me think of Clark and Mayer's description of 'supported drawing' in which some elements of a diagram are provided, allowing the learner to focus on the relationships between elements.[30]

A partially completed map has been provided by psychology teacher Grace Theay in which some of the key terms are obscured (see page 166).

It shows how a partially completed concept map might help to provide just enough support (or scaffolding), while also getting the learner to recall some of the key concepts.

In her blog post on retrieval practice activities, Megan Smith describes scaffolding as a way of making retrieval practice more successful for younger students who may not be able to retrieve much information, as they haven't yet learned much about a subject. She also includes some excellent examples of how scaffolded retrieval practice might look.[31]

What follows are some subject-specific examples of how using a graphic organiser with retrieval might look. The first passage on respiration was written by head of biology Anne Clay.

29 Rose, 'Does Visual Mapping Help Revision?'
30 Clark and Mayer, *E-Learning and the Science of Instruction*, loc. 4801.
31 Megan Smith, 'How to Create Retrieval Practice Activities for Elementary Students', *The Learning Scientists* [blog] (6 April 2017). Available at: http://www.learningscientists.org/blog/2017/4/6-1.

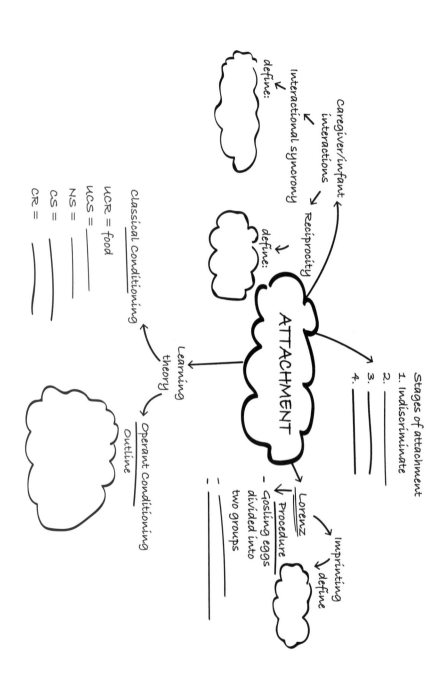

define:

Interactional synchrony

Caregiver/infant interactions

Reciprocity

define:

Classical Conditioning

UCR = food
UCS =
NS =
CS =
CR =

Learning theory

Operant Conditioning
Outline

ATTACHMENT

Stages of attachment
1. Indiscriminate
2.
3.
4.

Lorenz
Procedure
- Gosling eggs
  divided into
  two groups

Imprinting
define

Biology

Respiration, whether aerobic or anaerobic, is a chemical reaction. It is the process which produces energy which is essential for all cells to survive. No energy means the cell dies. All cells require energy all of the time, it's just that if a cell requires more energy than the norm (e.g. a muscle cell), then it will have to do more respiration to make the extra energy required. This energy is stored in the bonds of a molecule called ATP. This molecule is permanently in the cell, but when respiration occurs, the energy released from the reaction becomes stored in the ATP. When the ATP breaks down, it releases the energy to the cell.

Aerobic Respiration

The use of oxygen breathed in from the air, to react within cells with glucose collected from the digestive system. This can be summarised below in both word and formula equations:

Glucose + oxygen → carbon dioxide and water

$C_6H_{12}O_6 + 6O_2 → 6CO_2 + 6H_2O$

This process happens predominantly in the mitochondria of cells and produces lots of energy (38 ATP molecules) for every one glucose molecule.

Anaerobic Respiration

This is respiration but without oxygen. Respiration can go through the first steps whether there is oxygen present or not. However, if there isn't any oxygen then it gets to a certain stage and stops. This means that it can still make a little (2 ATP) energy for every one glucose. Better something than nothing. This process also doesn't occur in the mitochondria.

This can be summarised in the word and formula equations below:

Glucose → lactic acid

$C_6H_{12}O_6 → 2C_3H_6O_3$

The common error when writing about anaerobic respiration, is to put carbon dioxide into the equation. Carbon dioxide is *not* produced during anaerobic respiration.

Also, remember that aerobic respiration will still be proceeding at its maximum rate; however, anaerobic respiration will be providing a top-up of energy.

The issue with your body producing lactic acid after anaerobic respiration is that the acidic conditions produced can be toxic to the body, as it can cause enzymes carrying out reactions to denature and prevent them from working. It is also what leads to the characteristic 'stitch' after high intensity exercise.

Let's suppose I had read the above passage at home, then turned it over, completed a free recall test on a business studies passage I had read half an hour before this one, and then decided to recall everything that I could from memory about aerobic and anaerobic respiration in the table below. If I had anticipated seriously struggling to recall anything, I might have created a partially completed form of this table beforehand.

Category or feature	Aspect 1: Aerobic respiration	Aspect 2: Anaerobic respiration
Oxygen	Needed	Not needed
Energy	A lot of energy released	Small amount of energy released
Lactic acid	Not released	Released

Business Studies

This example is based on content from a CGP GCSE business studies revision guide. I've shown how a concept map might work when contrasting the differences between limited companies and sole traders/partnerships.

The section from the revision guide reads:

There are *two types* of limited company – private and public. But *both kinds* have these five important differences compared to sole traders and partnerships.

1. The business is *incorporated* – it has a *separate legal identity* from the owner.

2. It has *limited liability* so the owners only risk losing the money they invest in the business – no matter how big its debts are.

3. It must have a *Memorandum of Association*. This tells the world *who* the business is and *where* it is based.

4. It must also have an *Article of Association*. This sets out *how* the business will be run.

5. It is owned by *shareholders*. The *more shares* you own, the *more control* you get.

As before, I've noted down everything that I could recall in the table below.

Category or feature	Aspect 1: Limited companies	Aspect 2: Sole traders/partnerships
Legal ownership	Separate legal identity	Sole trader/partners legal owners
Liability	Limited liability	Unlimited liability
Set-up costs	More expensive to set up	Less expensive to set up
Owner characteristics	Shareholders	No shareholders

History

In *Learning as a Generative Activity*, Fiorella and Mayer suggest that 'when students learn from more meaningful learning materials, such as prose passages, self-testing may serve to prime the cognitive processes of selecting, organizing, and integrating'.[32] The following examples aim to show the merits of self-testing using free recall tests to promote generative learning.

What follows are some materials written by history teacher Ben Curtis for A level.

---

32 Fiorella and Mayer, *Learning as a Generative Activity*, p. 102.

Problems in 1450: Timeline of Key Events

November 1449: Parliament is recalled in November 1449 to discuss the attack on Fougères (by a mercenary and his English forces in the pay of Suffolk and Somerset).

Early January 1450: Adam Moleyns, Bishop of Chichester (and keeper of the king's privy seal), a member of the king's inner circle, is sent to Portsmouth to pay demoralised English soldiers returned from France. Due to the fact that parliament has refused to grant extra taxation and the king has little other income, so cannot afford to pay the men from his own funds, the Bishop of Chichester cannot pay them in full. The men kill the Bishop of Chichester. Shortly before his death, the bishop announces that Suffolk had been conspiring to surrender the territory of Maine to the French and to place the French king on the throne of England.

Late January 1450: Suffolk is arrested on charges of treason.

February 1450: English soldiers continue to return from France, hungry, poor and demoralised. The majority of them land in Kent where they resort to stealing food from the local population who are already suffering as a result of economic depression and the ban on exporting wool to Burgundy. This creates great resentment in Kent and other south-eastern counties of England, such as Sussex, Surrey and Essex.

9 March 1450: Suffolk's trial begins. He is accused of plotting to marry his ward Margaret Beaufort (then a young girl) to the son of Charles VII, King of France. He is accused of plotting to place Charles VII on the throne of England and also of stealing approximately £60,000 from the treasury and distributing it amongst his supporters and allies. In particular, Lord Saye comes in for criticism as he had taken over as treasurer in 1449 (appointed by Suffolk), at which point the money started to disappear. The House of Commons argues that this money could have been used to help defend France or pay soldiers. Suffolk is also called Jackanapes, a reference to his livery which is a wooden clog tied to a monkey. A 'Jack of Naples' was a common slang term for a monkey at the time. He is accused of having enriched himself at the expense of the king who had been forced to sell his crown jewels in 1448 and of manipulating the king into giving away all of his lands so that he could not afford to run the government.

17 March 1450: In spite of overwhelming support for the execution of Suffolk on charges of treason, Henry instead decides to banish Suffolk for five years.

30 March 1450: Suffolk sets sail for Calais and exile.

6 May 1450: News reaches the court that pirates had boarded the *Nicholas of the Tower* ship carrying Suffolk, executed him and dumped his body overboard 'for the good of the realm'.

May 1450: Parliament passes an Act of Resumption. This means that any patronage of crown lands granted by the king now return to royal possession. It is hoped that the king's finances would improve as a result of this.

May 1450: Reports begin to spread that Lord Saye had been overheard to remark that revenge should be taken against the people of Kent for the execution of Suffolk. The rumour evolves into the idea that the queen is also pregnant with Suffolk's child and so people in Kent fully expect a revenge attack with the backing of royal forces.

Late May 1450: Members of the higher ranks of peasantry and lower ranks of the gentry (husbandmen, yeoman and freehold farmers) join a rebellion with many men gathered at Ashford in Kent and marching towards Blackheath where they camp. Their leader is Jack Cade. His identity is uncertain. The government claims he is Irish and he calls himself John Mortimer (leading to rumours that he is a relative of Richard, Duke of York). They issue a petition calling for the 'evil councillors' about the king to be removed and for 'true lords' such as York, Buckingham and Exeter to be given roles in the king's council.

Mid June 1450: Henry sends a divided royal army to find the rebels and attack them. One section of the army, led by Humphrey Stafford of Grafton pursues the rebels to Sevenoaks where his forces are ambushed and he is killed. Upon learning of this, Henry commands his section of the forces to march on the rebels at once. However, his forces mutiny and refuse to obey the command. Many of the men share the same grievances as Jack Cade. Henry travels to Greenwich to reunite with his wife Margaret of Anjou. She encourages him to flee to Kenilworth.

Late June 1450: Henry orders that Lord Saye and his son-in-law William Crowmer (the sheriff of Kent) be imprisoned in the Tower of London and Fleet Prison respectively. This impresses no one as many believe Henry has only done this to protect them rather than punish them. Henry then travels to Kenilworth.

Early July 1450: The Kentish commoners march unopposed to the gates of London where the citizens demand they be granted access to the city. The mob enters the city, and despite the best efforts of Cade to control them, the mob runs riot and begins to steal from wealthy men by ransacking their homes. Lord Saye and William Crowmer are dragged from their prisons. They are both accused of corruption in Kent and are thought to have helped Suffolk to cause the loss of Normandy and all that Kent had suffered as a result of it. Both men are executed.

July 1450: Unrest spreads elsewhere and another adviser to the king, Bishop Ainscough, the Bishop of Salisbury, is beheaded in Wiltshire. Threats are also made against the Bishops of Lichfield and Norwich.

Late July 1450: Londoners manage to drive the now unwelcome mob out of the city. They meet Margaret of Anjou who grants them all pardons if they disperse, which they do. Cade breaks the pardon by further acts of looting and is then killed while resisting arrest.

If students read the passage first and are then asked to write down all they can remember (free recall) in an immediate or delayed test, this 'may serve to prime the cognitive processes of selecting, organizing, and integrating' and therefore promote positive generative learning outcomes.[33] On the basis of 'recall, review, repeat',[34] if the students are struggling to retrieve information, then it may be beneficial for them to note down what they can remember and then read the passage back, comparing the original with what they could retrieve, perhaps using a coloured pen to add any bits they missed.

Alternatively, I could scaffold my retrieval of this content. I could read the passage through once and, while looking at the text, note down eight key sentences which will help to trigger my retrieval of the content when I am recalling it after I have put the passage away.

On the theme of scaffolding retrieval practice, I once tutored a highly capable Year 11 student for French. He found a technique that I had been using with GCSE language students to help make their learning stick very useful. It was essentially a rote learning task which he successfully adopted for other subjects too. The steps were as follows:

1. Copy down the original piece five times.

2. On a notes sheet, write down the first three words of every paragraph from the original, three words from the middle and three from the end.

3. Put the original copy and the five extra copies away so you only have your notes sheet available.

4. On a blank sheet, write down everything you can from memory, looking at your notes sheet if you get stuck. If this doesn't act as a retrieval cue then look at the original for five seconds then put it away again before you start writing.

---

33 Fiorella and Mayer, *Learning as a Generative Activity*, p. 102.
34 Smith, 'How to Create Retrieval Practice Activities for Elementary Students'.

5. Repeat this process until you have written as much as you can.

6. Pick up a different coloured pen and, checking against the original, add in anything you missed and correct anything you got wrong.

7. Repeat steps 4–7 on a new sheet of paper.

This could be adapted to work alongside the nuclear radiation text which we first encountered in Chapter 3 (see page 58). The author of the passage, physics teacher Mike Browne, has kindly suggested some useful prompts that could be used to elicit a response following some forgetting time:

- The properties of alpha particles are …

- The properties of beta particles are …

- The properties of gamma rays are …

- Ionisation means …

- All nuclear radiation …

Science teacher Ben Rogers (@BenRogersEdu) has written about a great way to adopt retrieval practice and sentence practice together.[35] 'Expand-a-sentence' has some similarities with the previous example by Mike Browne.

Expand-a-sentence

Give your students a very simple sentence, e.g. 'Magnesium is an element,' or 'The Weimar Republic was unsuccessful.'

The retrieval practice comes in the next stage. Students have to give short answers to as many of the following as possible:

Who _____

What _____

35 Ben Rogers, 'Retrieval Practice and Sentence Practice All in One!', *Reading for Learning* [blog] (7 October 2017). Available at: https://readingforlearning.org/2017/10/07/retrieval-practice-donows-are-great-but-lets-not-forget-sentence-practice/. Expand-a-sentence was adapted from an idea in Judith Hochman and Natalie Wexler's *The Writing Revolution: A Guide to Advancing Thinking Through Writing in All Subjects and Grades* (San Francisco, CA: Jossey-Bass, 2017), ch. 2.

Where _____

When _____

Why _____

How _____

The final step is to expand the original sentence, e.g.

Magnesium is an element

Who: first isolated by Humphry Davy

What: a reactive metal

Where: in Group 2

When: in 1808

Why: _____

How: using a large voltaic cell

Magnesium, a reactive Group 2 metal discovered in 1808 by Sir Humphry Davy using a large voltaic cell, is an element.

I asked history teacher Ben Curtis if this technique could be applied to his subject and he suggested the following examples:

First World War (Germany)

They blamed the November Criminals.

- Who: The Freikorps and right-wing terror groups
- What: The politicians who signed the Armistice
- Where: Weimar Germany
- When: Winter 1918–1919
- Why: 'Stab-in-the-back' myth
- How: Political assassinations

The *Freikorps* and right-wing terror groups carried out political assassinations in Weimar Germany in the winter of 1918, because they blamed the politicians who had signed the Armistice – the *November Criminals* – because of the stab-in-the-back myth.

Cold War

The Potsdam Conference caused tension.

- Who: The United States, the Soviet Union and the UK

- What: The division of Germany

- Where: Berlin

- When: August 1945

- Why: Stalin wanted reparations

- How: Truman adopted a 'get tough' approach

The *Potsdam Conference*, involving the United States, the Soviet Union and the UK, held in Berlin in August 1945, *caused tension* over the division of Germany because Stalin wanted reparations and Truman adopted a 'get tough' approach.

Here is one final and fantastically practical example of a retrieval practice grid by head of history and author Kate Jones (@87History). The grid contains a series of questions for the students to answer based on previous subject content. She says:

The aim of this task is to encourage students to continually revisit content. The students can select which questions they answer but this should also highlight what students know and don't know. Retrieval practice is a scientifically proven effective strategy – the act of retrieving information from long-term memory. It is also more effective when there is no multiple choice as learners have to retrieve that information from memory. The grid contains questions that vary in regards to when the content was taught but also focusing on key terminology, facts and information and chronology. This works very well at the start of a lesson or as a revision strategy.

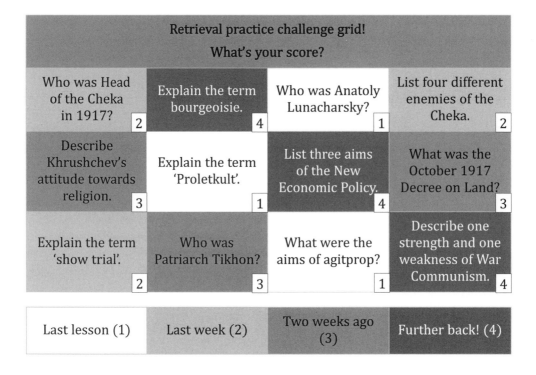

Retrieval practice challenge grid! What's your score?			
Who was Head of the Cheka in 1917? **2**	Explain the term bourgeoisie. **4**	Who was Anatoly Lunacharsky? **1**	List four different enemies of the Cheka. **2**
Describe Khrushchev's attitude towards religion. **3**	Explain the term 'Proletkult'. **1**	List three aims of the New Economic Policy. **4**	What was the October 1917 Decree on Land? **3**
Explain the term 'show trial'. **2**	Who was Patriarch Tikhon? **3**	What were the aims of agitprop? **1**	Describe one strength and one weakness of War Communism. **4**
Last lesson (1)	Last week (2)	Two weeks ago (3)	Further back! (4)

Kate uses colour to differentiate between each type of question, but in this version I have added a number to denote the questions which target subject knowledge from last lesson (1 point), last week (2 points), two weeks ago (3 points) and further back (4 points).

Another way to incorporate this as part of revision towards the end of the course might be to give students a copy with no content other than the numbers denoting how far back the question should test, and then provide a copy of the scheme of learning for them to devise their own questions based on what the course has covered.

Flashcards

In a post on the Learning Scientists blog, Rachel Adragna (@racheladragna) states that one of the frequently reported concerns with flashcards is that 'they encourage students to "just memorize" information, instead of really understanding it'.[36]

36 Rachel Adragna, 'Be Your Own Teacher: How to Study with Flashcards', *The Learning Scientists* [blog] (18 February 2016). Available at: http://www.learningscientists.org/blog/2016/2/20-1.

One of the strategies Adragna advocates is to elaborate on the material on the flashcards. She recommends making two sets of flashcards: one set containing the key terms and another set with instructions on ways to elaborate on the material. Her suggestions include:

- Describe a movie/television scene that depicts this concept
- Describe how an animal might portray this concept
- Describe this concept without using any key words written on the flashcard
- Draw this concept
- Give a real life example of this concept
- How would you explain this to a child/someone who has never heard of it before?
- What is the opposite of this concept?
- What situation in your life has depicted this concept?
- Why is knowledge of this concept useful to you?

In *How Learning Works*, Susan Ambrose and colleagues suggest that research confirms the view that when learners are asked to bring prior knowledge or previous experience to bear on new knowledge, this helps to integrate the knowledge more easily.[37] This would help to support the second to last bullet on how a personal situation in your life may have depicted the concept.

A flashcard app like StudyBlue might be an effective way of preparing the key terms and definitions.[38] William Emeny has also developed an excellent looking set of flashcards based on spaced retrieval practice in maths which can be downloaded from his website.[39]

---

37 Susan A. Ambrose, Michael W. Bridges, Michele DiPietro, Marsha C. Lovett and Marie K. Norman, *How Learning Works: Seven Research-Based Principles for Smart Teaching* (San Francisco, CA: Jossey-Bass, 2010), p. 17.
38 See www.studyblue.com.
39 William Emeny, 'Spaced and Interleaved Retrieval Practice Using Flashcards', *Great Maths Teaching Ideas* [blog] (13 April 2017). Available at: http://www.greatmathsteachingideas.com/2017/04/13/spaced-and-interleaved-retrieval-practice-using-flashcards/.

How many times should you practise retrieval with a flashcard? Here's an imaginary flash-card devised by chemistry teacher Gavin Tilstone.

SIDE 1: Hydrocarbon	SIDE 2: Compound made of hydrogen and carbon atoms only.

Let's suppose I had the flashcard turned to the first side, 'Hydrocarbon', making an attempt to retrieve the short definition and then moving on to doing the same with another flash-card. One time retrieval isn't really going to cut the mustard.

It's the same as we've seen before with the projected geography knowledge organiser with the definitions covered up or the language projected onto a slide with the meanings covered up. Throughout the two years of their GCSE teaching, the students might have their retrieval of key words and phrases tested in this way perhaps 30 times, no matter what topic they are studying. Clearly, for the student retrieving the definition of a hydro-carbon away from the classroom, it is not going to stick at once, so they may need to employ the magic power of three instances of 'perfect retrieval' spaced over time. In other words, the definition has to be retrieved perfectly on three occasions. There may be more than three attempts but they don't count – it only counts if the retrieval is perfect!

In fact, successive relearning was shown to be the most powerful condition when tested as part of a study carried out by John Dunlosky and colleagues involving college students on a psychology course.[40] I mention this study now as one of the three groups, the succes-sive relearning group, had to retrieve information correctly three times spaced across the semester using a computerised flashcard programme. The second group adopted spaced restudying with no retrieval and the final group did not use the programme and contin-ued with their usual study habits. The successive relearning group improved their grades from a C to a B compared to the other two conditions. The findings suggest that succes-sive relearning until a definition on a flashcard, for example, is perfect rely on a spaced schedule of (a minimum of?) three times retrieving the correct answer.

40 Katherine A. Rawson, John Dunlosky and Sharon M. Sciartelli, 'The Power of Successive Relearning: Improving Performance on Course Exams and Long-Term Retention', *Educational Psychology Review*, 25(4) (2013), 523–548. I am grateful to Pooja Agarwal for bringing this study to my attention.

The Leitner System

No section on flashcards could fail to reference the Leitner system, and nor could this language teacher not refer to it. You take a set of flashcards and find three receptacles – boxes, envelopes or the like. You label one of them with 'Every day', one of them with 'Tuesday and Thursday' and one of them with 'Friday' like these below.

BOX 1: Every day	BOX 2: Tuesday and Thursday	BOX 3: Friday

Next you look at the term on side 1 of the flashcard and start using the technique on a Monday of a revision schedule. Business studies teacher Hannah Mutchell has kindly provided the following imaginary set of flashcards to help model this.

SIDE 1: Sole trader	SIDE 2: A business that is set up and run by a single (sole) owner. The business can employ staff. It will have unlimited liability.

SIDE 1: Gross profit	SIDE 2: The profit received from selling the product or service. Calculated by selling price minus variable costs (also known as cost of sales). It does not factor in fixed costs such as rent.

When you read the term 'Sole trader', you try to retrieve as much of the definition as possible on a Monday. If you know it, and check that you know it by turning it round after speaking it out loud, then it goes into the Tuesday and Thursday box. If you read the term and are either patchy on the retrieval or worse, then the flashcard goes in the Every day box. This keeps going until all of the flashcards have been covered and placed in either the Every day box or the Tuesday and Thursday box. Then that's Monday done.

On Tuesday, as well as testing retrieval of the flashcards in the Tuesday and Thursday box, you also test the retrieval of the cards you didn't get perfectly on Monday (which were put in the Every day box). You start with the Every day flashcards first. If you know the definition this time then it goes into the Tuesday and Thursday box. If you try but find that you still don't know a definition, then the card goes in the Every day box again.

Then you test retrieval of the flashcards in the Tuesday and Thursday box. If you retrieve the definition perfectly then it goes into the Friday box. As the definition has been retrieved perfectly twice now then it only needs one more retrieval (in line with the three instances of perfect retrieval mentioned earlier). However, if you can't retrieve a meaning then the flashcard has to be put back into the Every day box.

It's a great no-frills approach to spaced retrieval practice which is demonstrated very well by primary school teacher Jon Brunskill (@jon_brunskill) on YouTube.[41]

Multiple Choice Questions

Multiple choice questions were discussed in Chapter 4, where I referred to Craig Barton's website as an excellent resource, so here is one that he created:[42]

$$\frac{x + 2}{5} = x - 3$$

Which of the following is a correct next step in solving this equation?

A $x + 2 = 5x - 3$ **B** $5x + 10 = 5x - 15$

C $x + 2 = 5x - 15$ **D** $x + 2 = x + 2$

41 See https://www.youtube.com/watch?v=d9u3KxGCio8.
42 See https://diagnosticquestions.com/Questions/Go#/17316.

Daisy Christodoulou discusses multiple choice testing in a blog post on closed questions. She uses the British Columbia High School leaving exam to demonstrate that closed answer questions can help to promote hard thinking about a topic. She observes that the questions made her 'think hard' about complex issues, adding, 'I couldn't have rote learned or memorised the answers to any of them.'[43] She also suggests that one of the advantages of the British Columbia test is that it allows possible misconceptions to be identified.

Chris Peirce (@peirce_chris) and Jude Hunton's (@judehunton) presentation at researchED Rugby in June 2016 on 'Meeting the Challenge of Linear Learning at English GCSE' included a discussion on the use of multiple choice questions. They used two questions from another of Daisy Christodoulou's blog posts:

Which of the following words can be used as a verb?

a.   run

b.   tree

c.   car

d.   person

e.   apple

In which sentences is 'cook' a verb?

a.   I cook a meal.

b.   He is a good cook.

c.   The cook prepared a nice meal.

d.   Every morning, they cook breakfast.

e.   That restaurant has a great cook.[44]

A useful subcategory of the closed question is the hinge question, which can be used when you need to check if the students are ready to move on from a key concept.

---

43   Daisy Christodoulou, 'Closed Questions and Higher Order Thinking', *The Wing to Heaven* [blog] (6 October 2013). Available at: https://thewingtoheaven.wordpress.com/2013/10/06/closed-questions-and-higher-order-thinking/.

44   Daisy Christodoulou, 'Assessment Alternatives 1: Using Questions Instead of Criteria', *The Wing to Heaven* [blog] (7 June 2015). Available at: https://thewingtoheaven.wordpress.com/2015/06/07/assessment-alternatives-1-using-questions-instead-of-criteria/.

According to Dylan Wiliam, a hinge question should 'Relate to important learning outcomes necessary for progression in learning'.[45]

Further Examples of Retrieval Practice

Below are some examples of how retrieval practice might be applied across a range of subjects. One of the caveats is that these examples are only *suggested* ways of adopting retrieval practice, and in some cases they could just be questions. This should at least help to reinforce the fact that knowledge is strengthened through quizzing.

Business Studies

This first example is a set of questions which have been designed by business studies teacher Lucy Maclachlan.

1. Explain the benefits of a small business using no intermediaries as part of its distribution channel.

2. Why might a business choose to use a wholesaler as part of its distribution channel?

3. Explain why a small business might choose direct selling as their method of distribution.

4. What effect might a distribution channel have on the selling price of the product?

5. Explain the potential benefits of a new business using e-commerce to sell their products.

6. What are the potential risks to a business of using telesales to sell their products?

7. Recommend an appropriate distribution channel for a business which manufactures premium products (e.g. designer handbags). Explain your choice.

45 See https://www.dylanwiliam.org/Dylan_Wiliams...files/EARLI%28A%29%2008.ppt.

Let's suppose that I came to 'revise' these following study leave. Let's also suppose that this topic area was covered midway through my own time as an erstwhile Year 10, Oasis-singing, Internet-less student of the summer of 1996 … Without a text to refer to or read through first, I'm faced with some tough recall, and even tougher if this material hasn't been revisited at all.

In *E-Learning and the Science of Instruction*, Clark and Mayer refer to 'calibration accuracy', by which they mean how learners try to judge for themselves how much they know about material they have studied. If a learner thinks they know a lot (or very little), and their test score matches this, then their calibration (or measurement) of their own learning is accurate.[46]

Knowing what you know and what you don't know is clearly important in terms of inform-ing your revision. High calibration accuracy should lead to more efficient revision for a learner.[47]

Another point to consider is a psychological phenomenon called the 'hypercorrection effect', which Wiliam and Daisy Christodoulou describe in 'Assessment, Marking and Feedback'.[48] If you are very confident that you are right about something, and you find out that you are wrong, then there will be a bigger change in your thinking.

---

46 Clark and Mayer, *E-Learning and the Science of Instruction*, loc. 6466.

47 For more information on calibration see Mccrea, *Memorable Teaching*, pp. 104–105.

48 Dylan Wiliam and Daisy Christodoulou, 'Assessment, Marking and Feedback'. In Carl Hendrick and Robin Macpherson (eds), *What Does This Look Like in the Classroom? Bridging the Gap Between Research and Practice* (Woodbridge: John Catt Educational, 2017), pp. 35–40.

Maths

The example below tests material from across the AQA 8300 GCSE maths syllabus rather than just one particular topic. With thanks to maths teacher Dan Frankton for his help with this.

1	Angle properties *(Topic 1)*	
	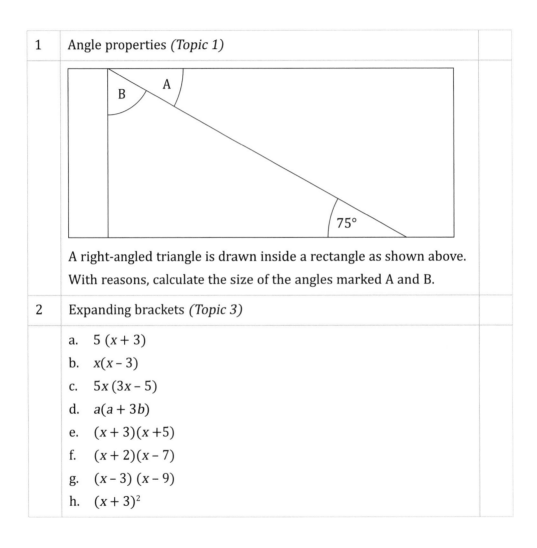 A right-angled triangle is drawn inside a rectangle as shown above. With reasons, calculate the size of the angles marked A and B.	
2	Expanding brackets *(Topic 3)*	
	a. $5(x+3)$ b. $x(x-3)$ c. $5x(3x-5)$ d. $a(a+3b)$ e. $(x+3)(x+5)$ f. $(x+2)(x-7)$ g. $(x-3)(x-9)$ h. $(x+3)^2$	

3	Equations of straight line graphs *(Topic 5)*	
	a.	The gradient of a straight line is 4, and it passes through the point (3,4). What is the equation of this line?	
	b.	A straight line passes through the points (2,7) and (5,13). What is the equation of this line?	
4	Sequences – finding and using the nth term *(Topic 8)*	
	7, 16, 25, 34, 43 ...	
	a.	What is the nth term of the above sequence?	
	b.	Using the nth term, what is the 15th term in the above sequence?	
	c.	Using the nth term, prove whether 106 is or is not in this sequence.	
5	Basic percentages *(Topic 9)*	
	a.	Find 10% of £65.	
	b.	Find 5% of $30.	
	c.	Find 35% of €90.	
6	Area and circumference of a circle *(Topic 11)*	
	a.	A circle has a diameter of 10 cm. Calculate the area and circumference of this circle.	
	b.	A different circle has a radius of 7 cm. Calculate the area and circumference of this circle.	
7	Ratio *(Topic 13)*	
	a.	Share £64 in the ratio 9:7.	
	b.	The ratio of boys to girls at a party is 3:5. There are 12 boys. How many girls were at the party?	

8	Solving equations *(Topic 15)*	
	a. $5x - 8 = 12$ b. $\frac{x}{7} + 4 = 6$ c. $9x - 8 = 7x + 22$	
9	Factorising and solving quadratics *(Topic 18)*	
	Factorise to solve the following quadratic equations: a. $x^2 + 7x + 12 = 0$ b. $x^2 - 7x - 30 = 0$ c. $x^2 - x = 12$	
10	Solving linear simultaneous equations *(Topic 19)*	
	Without using trial and improvement, solve the following simultaneous equations: $3x + 4y = 22$ $2x + 2y = 12$	

English

I called in a little family help for this one. My brother, Jude Hunton, had been working on similar ideas with a colleague, Chris Peirce. They were interpreting the Bjorks' work on 'varying the conditions of practice'[49] by looking to follow some simple principles: first, to identify core knowledge in English and literature, possibly in a departmental shared knowledge organiser and, second, to test this in varied ways.

They looked to many other influential teachers too. They adopted Andy Tharby's work on memory platforms and the following ways of using retrieval practice in English:

1. Retrieve key knowledge from last lesson.
2. Retrieve key knowledge from last lesson.
3. Retrieve key knowledge from last lesson.

49 See https://bjorklab.psych.ucla.edu/research/.

4. Retrieve key knowledge from last week.

5. Retrieve key knowledge from last term.

6. Retrieve key knowledge from last lesson and connect it to knowledge from last term.[50]

They were also impressed by @team_english1 on Twitter whose contributors have developed and made popular many helpful resources. One that really caught people's imagination was a set of worked example sentences (see page 188) created by Grainne Hallahan (@heymrshallahan) in collaboration with Freya O'Dell (@fod3), referred to in glowing terms by Carl Hendrick at researchED English and MFL Oxford 2017.

In the examples below, Jude and Chris use a varied practice model. They try to be consistent in the knowledge recalled; however, the retrieval method is varied – for example, multiple choice, clozes, questions, cued recall, paired recall, individual retrieval, delayed or immediate feedback from teacher to student.

1. What city did Stevenson grow up in and what links it to *The Strange Case of Dr Jekyll and Mr Hyde*?

    Edinburgh, split in two: wealthy new town and corrupt, criminal old town.

2. What phrase is used to describe Victorian morals?

    The Victorian Compromise: in public very Christian and well behaved; in secret quite corrupt.

3. What did Stevenson begin studying at university and what did he switch to?

    Science then law.

4. What did Boxer in *Animal Farm* symbolise?

    The proletariat [you only get one mark for this word!].

5. What does propaganda mean and which character in *Animal Farm* represents it?

    Biased information from a government – Squealer.

50 Andy Tharby, 'Memory Platforms', *Reflecting English* [blog] (12 June 2014). Available at: https://reflectingenglish.wordpress.com/2014/06/12/memory-platforms/.

Upgrade Your Sentence!

The statue stood feeling sad.

Not only but also

Not only did the statue feel sad, but also exposed and vulnerable.

So, so

Its sadness was so strong, so overwhelming, the statue began to tremble, and the dust about him began to shake.

Double adjective start

Furious and helpless, the statue began to curse the diggers.

Less less less

The less the statue saw of the ground, the less sure he was that he would ever be returned to his earthy throne, and the less sure he felt that he was going to like his new exposed position.

Fortunately/ unfortunately

Fortunately, the diggers had no intention of moving the statue, unfortunately, the statue didn't know this important fact.

Whoever/ whenever

Whoever looked upon the statue, whenever anyone spoke his name, his sadness deepened a little more.

More more more

The more of the dirt that was shifted away, the more of the statue's belly that was exposed, and the more indignant the sacred relic became.

Brackets although

The statue felt sad (although, he was too proud to admit it) and wished he could be returned to his previous position.

Verb beginning

Contemplating his situation, the statue's two eyes gazed solemnly across the land.

Adverb beginning

Tragically, no one had asked the statue how he felt about being dug out of the ground.

Triple noun colon

Fury, anger, dismay: the statue felt his sadness slip away and be replaced with more damaging emotions.

6. What is similar about Napoleon and Mr Hyde?

They are both killers.

1. What did Stevenson suffer from during most of his life?

Ill health.

2. Why were Victorians interested in duality?

Because they were learning about evolution and that humans descended from apes, so they were fascinated about our behaviour.

3. What did Stevenson do that shocked people (hint – to do with marriage)?

He had an affair and then married an American woman.

4. What happened to Snowball in *Animal Farm*?

He was expelled by Napoleon and his dogs (secret police).

5. Who does Snowball symbolise?

Trotsky.

6. List four words for 'this shows'.

Suggests, portrays, reveals, implies.

1. List as many positive feelings for the reader linked to the gothic elements of *Jekyll and Hyde* that you can:

Thrilled, excited, in suspense, amazed, scared, frightened, thrilled.

2. List as many negative feelings for the reader linked to the gothic elements of *Jekyll and Hyde* that you can:

Scared, frightened, terrified, shocked.

3. List as many positive feelings for the reader that refer to the detective elements of *Jekyll and Hyde* that you can:

Fascinated, intrigued, fulfilled, astonished.

4. List as many negative feelings for the reader that refer to the detective elements of *Jekyll and Hyde* that you can:

Frustrated, annoyed, perplexed, confused.

The last example is based on testing the retrieval of quotations from *Macbeth*.[51]

1. This s_____l s_____g / C____t be ill, c____t be good.

2. … that s_____n whose horrid image doth u___x my h__r.

3. Thou c___t n_t say I d_d it – never shake / Thy g__y l___s at me.

Here are the missing letters along with some analysis:

1. This supernatural soliciting / Cannot be ill, cannot be good.

    Sibilance: 's' sounds spooky; repetition 'cannot' emphasises Macbeth's uncertainty and confusion; he wants to know why the witches have given him a prophecy.

2. … that suggestion whose horrid image doth unfix my hair.

    Noun: 'suggestion' doesn't want to say murder; metaphor 'unfix my hair' means Macbeth is frightened at the thought of killing Duncan.

3. Thou canst not say I did it – never shake / Thy gory locks at me.

    Verb: 'did it' means murder and portrays his guilty conscience; imagery 'gory locks' emphasises Macbeth's fear and guilt over murdering Banquo.

History

This example relates to the A level history content on the 1450 timeline from the free recall test section earlier in Part 2.

Let's suppose I no longer had access to the text (or, at least, had it tucked away in a drawer) and was provided with a set of questions as a way of bringing this material to mind. Let's also suppose it had been a month or so since I'd read the passage, left it a couple of days, then did the free recall test to recall as much information as possible. A month or so later I am faced with the questions below, even though I have moved on to a different topic and have probably forgotten a fair bit of the material.

---

51 Paul Moss has written a brilliant blog on elaborative retrieval using quotations: 'Helping Students' Memories – Utilising Elaborative Retrieval', *Theories in Education* [blog] (21 March 2018). Available at: https://paulgmoss.wordpress.com/2018/03/21/helping-students-memories-utilising-elaborative-retrieval/.

I'll spare you my answers on this one, but if you're not a historian then please feel free to have a go at reading the passage, leaving some forgetting time, then in a week or so having a go at these questions:

1. What were the charges against Suffolk?

2. How did Henry VI respond to the charges against Suffolk?

3. What were the causes of Jack Cade's Rebellion?

4. Which evil councillors do the peasants target?

5. Who do the peasants describe as 'true' lords?

The next set of questions were written by history teacher Anna Hunt. Let's imagine that these questions appear at the end of a chapter in a history textbook which also features related questions earlier on in the same chapter. So, double-quizzing and no rereading!

1. Did economic or political causes lead to the American Civil War in 1861?

2. How far did economics cause the American Civil War?

3. Did the North and South go to war because of slavery?

4. 'The Southern States went to war because of the North's undue influence in their affairs.' How far do you agree?

5. 'Abraham Lincoln bears full responsibility for the outbreak of the American Civil War.' How far do you agree?

Some great research has been conducted by Oyku Uner and Henry Roediger on the placement of questions in textbooks.[52] They compared two groups who either read or reread chapter content, and found that the groups who practised retrieval with two sets of questions recalled the most in a final test. I am extremely grateful to Oyku Uner who responded so quickly to my request for some further information regarding this study. She said:

Research shows that retrieval practice typically enhances retention; however, prior studies mostly employ materials simpler than material that students study. We asked whether retrieval practice is effective for learning from

---

52 Oyku Uner and Henry L. Roediger III, 'The Effect of Question Placement on Learning from Textbook Chapters', *Journal of Applied Research in Memory and Cognition* (2017) [online]. Available at: https://doi.org/10.1016/j.jarmac.2017.09.002. I am grateful to Pooja Agarwal both for having brought this study to my attention and having taken the time to check the factual accuracy.

textbook chapters, and if so, which placement of questions would be most effective: during the chapter (after each section) or after the whole chapter?

Students studied a 40-page biology textbook chapter in one of three conditions: one group read the chapter once (read-only group, a control condition). A second group read the chapter and received short-answer questions either after each section of the chapter, after the whole chapter, or at both times (the tested group). Correct-answer feedback was provided after each practice question. A third group read the chapter and received the statements that served as feedback to the tested group in a similar regimen (a re-reading control group). All groups took a final test two days later.

Testing enhanced recall compared to the two control conditions. Whether students answered questions after a section or after the whole chapter did not affect recall in the final test, but answering questions at both times led to greatest recall. Students should test themselves when studying a textbook chapter and ideally, they should do so multiple times and with feedback.

Geography

A key theme in the AQA GCSE geography specification is the economic and environmental impact of deforestation. The extract on rainforests written by geography teacher Jon Haston (see the Rereading section in Chapter 3) shows how retrieval practice in the form of some good, old-fashioned quizzing might take place.

Jon has provided an idea of how many marks each question might attract based on questions from the draft new specification assessment material. However, he acknowledges that retrieval practice tends to work better with low- or no-stakes testing, so the marks are a slight betrayal of this view. Jon also says that he would normally go through this passage with the class using a visualiser to ensure the students understand the language that he, as a teacher, may take for granted (e.g. biodiversity, indigenous).

1. 'Natural environments should always be protected.' Using an example you have studied, to what extent do you agree? (6 marks)

2. Explain why it is important to sustain a biodiverse environment. (4 marks)

3. 'Natural environments are more important when left intact than destroyed by human actions.' Using a case study, do you support or challenge this statement? (9 marks)

4. Describe and explain how human intervention can lead to long-term economic and social benefits. (6 marks)

5. Explain how human actions can lead to the degradation of the Amazon rainforest's natural ecosystem. (4 marks)

A very useful technique is described by Pashler et al. for helping learners to accurately calibrate whether or not they have learned something.[53] Let's suppose that the content on deforestation was taught and these questions were shown to the students later on after the lesson. The students first attempt an answer and then provide a rating as to how well they think they knew the answers. For each question for which the students do not have 100% certainty, they are told the answer (or they find it out), they note this down on a different piece of paper and, after checking with the teacher that there aren't any misconceptions, spend some time reflecting on it. This is referred to as the 'cue-only delayed judgment of learning'.

Computer Science

Here is a passage on operating systems followed by some example questions (courtesy of head of computer science Joan Fuller).

Operating system (OS)

In order to think about what the OS does, start by thinking about your body and what controls that.

You control your body. Well, not consciously, not all the time. You have a system of nervous control and part of that manages most of the things you do without thinking (breathing, digesting) and the things that help you get out of trouble (fight, fright, flight). This is a sort of 'maintenance' OS. Then there is the bit of the nervous system which you do control which lets you move around and grasp things when you want to. This is a sort of 'interaction' OS.

So, the OS of a computer is similar to the nervous system of a human body. The nervous system is signals passed along nerves in the body; an OS is signals from a computer program being passed through the CPU of the computer. Both systems make things happen.

---

53 Pashler et al., *Organizing Instruction and Study to Improve Student Learning*, p. 23.

Different types of OS

There are lots of different types of OS. They all do much the same thing but they work in slightly different ways. Remember: an OS is a very specific program. Many people choose to have more than one OS on their computer, but most people are happy with just one.

Common OSs are:

- Linux – open source software

- Android – based on Linux/open source

- Windows – the most commonly used at the moment

- Mac OS X – used on Apple products

- iOS – used on Apple products

Games consoles can have different OSs as they are less multi-functional.

An embedded OS

An embedded computer system is designed to do a narrower range of things, but to do them very efficiently. Embedded computer systems are found in hardware that has a limited set of uses (washing machines, boilers, cars, etc.).

Functions of OS

These are the main things that an OS must have in order to be fully useful to both the CPU and the user.

1. **Interface** – this is what lets you communicate with the computer. It's the part which lets you tell the computer what to do. The most common PC interface we use is called a WIMP interface (W = windows, I = icons, M = menu, P = pointer) and these give us a wealth of different ways to interact.

   Because of smartphones and tablets we are also used to being able to communicate via touch control and this has been extended to many embedded systems, although these may have many older design features (buttons, knobs, etc.).

   These are both forms of a graphical user interface (GUI) which makes it easier to work out what to do to communicate with the computer.

   Originally there were only command line interfaces (CLI). These came before WIMP and were just a line of information (often called the C prompt, because it would end with 'C:'), after which you had to type in your instruction.

CLI is still available on Windows machines as many people like the absolute precision and control it offers. It only suits people who are prepared to learn the commands and how to use them.

2. **Memory management** – this is for the management of *main* memory. Remember: main memory is the RAM (the HDD is *secondary* storage).

    When a program is running it has to be in the main memory with the data it needs to run it. Think about the Little Man Computer and how each 'box' of the RAM has a label (the address). The memory management part of the OS keeps track of what is in each address, makes sure that enough space is kept to finish the work and then frees up the space when you have finished so it can be reallocated. This is especially important when more than one program (and its data) is sitting in the RAM at the same time.

3. **Multi-tasking** – some operating systems let you run more than one application at a time. Since a CPU can only do one thing at a time, multi-tasking can mean that more than one CPU is present and each CPU does something different, but it can also mean that there is only one CPU but that CPU keeps switching from one task to another so quickly that you feel it is doing lots of things at once. When a task is switched off, a signal called an 'interrupt' is used to help manage where something has stopped so it can be started again from the right place.

4. **Peripheral management** – these are the tasks which link the computer to its hardware (monitor, keyboard, printer, mouse) and allow it to store and retrieve from storage. In this situation peripheral means 'anything which isn't the CPU'. If you are using the computer and you save your document, you give an instruction which tells the peripheral management part of the OS to send the data from the RAM to the HDD. If you decide to print your document then the peripheral management sends the data from RAM to the device driver of the printer so that it can be printed. Because this is being controlled by the peripheral management part of the OS you can carry on printing.

5. **User management** – this controls the security of the system by allowing the person in charge of the computer/s (commonly a network manager in large organisations) to set up user accounts and organise who can look at/use what (access rights). Network managers also set the rules for passwords (their length, complexity, how often they must be changed, etc.). Many networks have a standard logout time which kicks in when you haven't

used the computer for a while (you can set your own option on your own computer). Basically, the network manager uses the interface for user management to enter values for these parts of the system, and then the user management part of the OS just follows the instructions that were entered and applies those rules.

6. **File management** – this enables you to not only create files and folders, but also to move them, search them, copy them, rename them and delete them. It is, however, cleverer than that:

   ● When you want to find a file you search for it and the file management part of the OS looks for it.

   ● When you have accidentally deleted a file the file management part of the OS will let you bring it back.

   ● When you are editing a file and someone else also wants to edit it, the file management locks them out.

   ● When you want to look at something you don't have access rights to (reread 'User management' if you can't remember what that means), the file management stops you.

   ● It knows how much free space is available and where it is.

   ● It knows what is stored and where it is all stored so that files can be retrieved when a program needs them.

7. **Utility software** – strictly speaking this is not part of the OS since utilities usually provide functions which tidy up the computer or make it easier to use. The OS is about controlling and managing the computer, and you don't really need a utility to do that. However, most modern OSs come equipped with utilities, and often they run automatically so we don't tend to get involved with them very often. They add value; they're worth knowing about.

   ● Disk organisation utilities are great for tidying up – they let you defragment the disk when you have scrappy bits of spare space in odd places which can't be used unless they are all put together. This has the benefit of making all the split parts of your files become 'glued' in one place which means it is easier to retrieve and use data. The disk organisation utility also lets you put your files into folders.

   ● File backup utilities help run your backup processes. Remember a *backup* is a copy of important or useful data, kept in a safe place, in case something goes wrong with the original. An *archive* is data you probably don't need any more, but don't want to throw away (in case you do need it again). It's also kept in a safe place; you just can't get at it easily.

● Data compression utilities let you reduce the amount of storage space used for a file. If you are short of space this is a good idea, but it's also helpful when transferring data from one place to another as it makes it quicker to transmit and means it uses less bandwidth during transfer.

● Security utilities are used to keep data safe. This is increasingly important. Commonly data encryption software finds ways of disguising your passwords, for example.

Time for the retrieval practice!

1. In a multi-tasking environment five programs are open at the same time, but the user is only working on one and looking at the others. What part of the operating system is enabling this, and what is the impact on the CPU and memory when the user changes to a different task?

2. There are several different kinds of interface when using a computer. When you login you generally have to use a graphical user interface to enter your user name and password. This enables the work you are doing to be logged. Why might this be needed on a networked system, and what kind of details would be logged?

3. What happens when you send a document that is not open on your computer to the printer?

4. Why is it important to have your work organised in a structured manner? Why is it important to the computer that its files are organised in a structured manner?

5. One of the utilities provided by the OS is the disk defragmentation tool. How does this relate to the system that organises files and directories?

6. What is the difference between the memory that is managed by the OS and the places where the file storage system is organised by the OS?

7. You are working on your desktop at school. You have a file open that you need to save to an external storage device and also print to hand in to your teacher. State what functions of the operating system are going to be used when you do those tasks and describe what they are going to be doing (you can choose the software you are using, but you must not use a manufacturer's name).

Interleaving and Distributed Practice

I have grouped together interleaving and distributed practice as these two strategies seem to go hand in hand.

Interleaving

Interleaving is effectively when you alternate between learning different things. According to James Lang, you spend some time learning one thing and then move on to a new one, before having completely mastered the first one, before then returning to it. You might then study a third or fourth thing before going back to secure your learning on the second thing and so on.[1]

Interleaving relates to what Jeroen van Merriënboer and Paul Kirschner write about in *Ten Steps to Complex Learning* in terms of variability of practice.[2] They describe a situation where students have to learn how to identify three distinct types of errors in a technical system. They are coached to spot error 1, then error 2 and then error 3. While it may appear that the students are learning how to identify each error quite quickly, this schedule won't promote transfer. Merriënboer and Kirschner suggest that a more effective strategy would be to train them to identify the errors in a random order.

It's tempting to compare how interleaving might help to mitigate the issues of 'rote performance'. In *Applying Cognitive Science to Education*, Frederick Reif relates the idea of rote performance to an incident when he had his blood taken.[3] The nurse was so used to taking blood from the left hand that when Reif requested that blood be taken from his right hand, the nurse asserted that she could only take blood from his left hand. She was disconcerted until finally accepting that she could take the blood from his right hand. According to Reif, the nurse was so used to performing the procedure in a particular way that she was unable to adapt when different circumstances were presented which required her to be more flexible. Reif likens this to those students who panic in exams

---

1 Lang, *Small Teaching*, loc. 1245.
2 Jeroen J. G. van Merriënboer and Paul A. Kirschner, *Ten Steps to Complex Learning: A Systematic Approach to Four-Component Instructional Design*, Kindle edn (Abingdon: Routledge, 2013), loc. 273–281.
3 Reif, *Applying Cognitive Science to Education*, loc. 317–326.

when they face a problem which differs from the practice problems they have encountered.

This helps to put into context the problems with teaching to the test, in the sense of designing practice tasks which mirror the exact style of those found in the exam and practising them over and over again. There is lack of variability in this kind of task practice which doesn't help to promote transfer. It is far more likely to promote a type of rote performance.

I used to adopt the blocked practice schedule of teaching French with my Year 11s, leaving some time from about March to revise with the class. Obviously, this assumed that the students' learning would fit into nice, chunky modules and that they would understand all of the grammar and retain all of the language. They would then take an end of module test which tested only that topic's content before moving on to the next blocked topic. It was almost like a macrocosm of the '20 minute window of progress' in lessons and the idea that progress should fit into discrete one-hour lesson chunks.

The problems with this as a learning schedule for the students are obvious and have been touched on already. The reason I mention it here is to emphasise how disastrous the blocked approach was for my students. As Dawn Cox observes: 'we need to forget following the textbook from the beginning to the end, and start planning for learning, not for teacher comfort or convenience'.[4]

Blocked practice meant that revision became an afterthought in lessons. Furthermore, even the revision/revisiting I did was blocked. I used to cut short the final module a little and then stressed about ensuring that I revised the content with the students in the order that it appeared in the textbook. Eventually, I shifted my approach to include the teaching and testing of what I had identified as key vocabulary and language, and incorporated this into lessons no matter what topic we were studying. The mantra changed to: it's not about how we cover the curriculum but how we recover the curriculum.

Dawn Cox presents an innovative way of planning a curriculum around the incorporation of other activities. The plan was based on the following spreadsheet.

4   Dawn Cox, 'Deliberate Recall – Don't Just Leave It To Chance', *missdcoxblog* [blog] (11 July 2016). Available at: https://missdcoxblog.wordpress.com/2016/07/11/deliberate-recall-dont-just-leave-it-to-chance/.

	Year 9	Year 10	Year 11	Total
Christianity: Beliefs & Teachings	4	2	2	8
Islam: Key beliefs	4	2	2	8
Theme B: Religion & life	3	1	3	7
Christianity: Worship & sacraments	2	2	2	6
Islam: Worship Five Pillars & Ten Obligatory acts	1	2	2	5
Theme E: Religion, Crime and punishment		3	2	5
Islam: Authority		2	2	4
Islam: Practice: Duties & festivals		2	2	4
Theme C: The existence of God & revelation		2	2	4
Christianity: Pilgrimage, celebrations & the worldwide church			3	3
Theme D: Religion, Peace & conflict			3	3

Key

Test ⬛

Homework quiz ⬜

Column headers (left to right):

- Theme D: Religion, Peace & conflict
- Christianity: Pilgrimage, celebrations & the worldwide church
- Theme C: The existence of God & revelation
- Islam: Practice: Duties & festivals
- Islam: Authority
- Theme E: Religion, Crime and punishment
- Islam: Worship Five Pillars & Ten Obligatory acts
- Christianity: Worship & sacraments
- Theme B: Religion & life
- Islam: Key beliefs
- Christianity: Beliefs & Teachings

Year	Term	No.
Year 9	Autumn a	1
	Autumn b	2
	Spring a	3
	Spring b	4
	Summer a	5
	Summer b	6
Year 10	Autumn a	7
	Autumn b	8
	Spring a	9
	Spring b	10
	Summer a	11
	Summer b	12
Year 11	Autumn a	13
	Autumn b	14
	Spring a	15
	Spring b	16
	Summer a	17
	Summer b	18
	Tests	
	HWs	

Thanks to this inventive approach, I started to encourage my GCSE languages students to practise writing longer and more structured pieces as part of the main topics. The plan now was to do the following with the Year 10 students and use the mocks at the end of the year as a review:

Topic	Year 10					
	1	2	3	4	5	6
	Autumn a	Autumn b	Spring a	Spring b	Summer a	Summer b
Me, my family and friends (**Autumn a**)	■				■	■
Home, town, neighbourhood and region (**Autumn a**)	■				■	■
My studies (**Autumn b**)		■	■			
Free-time activities (**Autumn b**)		■	■		■	
Social issues (Healthy/unhealthy living) (**Spring a**)			■		■	
Life at school/college (**Spring a**)			■		■	
Customs and festivals in Spanish-speaking countries/communities (**Spring b**)				■	■	
Travel and tourism (**Spring b**)				■	■	■
Education post-16 (**Summer a**)					■	■
Mocks						■

One caveat is that interleaving may be more applicable to some subject domains than others (giving learners the opportunity to compare and contrast different types of problems in maths, for example, has already been discussed). The tasks are not exactly problems to be solved; it is more about trying to apply some of the potential benefits of comparing and contrasting different tasks (and the language related to each) with a view to promote the transfer of language for whatever task is faced in a cumulative exam. Throughout the teaching plan, I will interleave topic tests on current and previous topics together with low-stakes writing tasks, again on current and previous topics. I then leave time for forgetting so more effortful retrieval takes place when I again revisit earlier topics.

One issue to bear in mind when taking advantage of interleaving and the spacing effect in the curriculum is striking a balance between curriculum coverage and retesting already taught material. It is always a trade-off. This is mentioned by Pooja Agarwal in a very interesting podcast led by Bonni Stachowiak in which she highlights the problem of delivering more content versus retrieval practice of previous content: students aren't going to remember the new content if you continue delivering it.[5]

Distributed Practice

Deputy head teacher Damian Benney (@Benneypenyrheol) describes how he adopts distributed practice and still finds the time to test material already covered with his Year 9 maths group. His students still do 20 questions on each topic, but they are distributed across the course in sets of five, rather than massed after the topic.[6] He has adopted an interesting approach which includes labelling the parts of the curriculum with letters and then using the letters in a 'do now' activity. The lettered tasks relate to different parts of the curriculum previously taught.

(The 'do now' is a great little activity from Doug Lemov's *Teach Like a Champion* and focuses either on previewing the lesson or recapping something previously taught. It should take no more than three to five minutes to complete and should need no explanation, with the same amount of time allotted to reviewing it.[7])

I have adopted a similar technique for a Key Stage 3 Year 9 languages group:

a) What is the 'they' form ending of the present tense for an 'er' verb?

  i) an   ii) en   iii) a   iv) emos

e) What is the 'I' form ending of the preterite tense for an 'ar' verb?

  i) aste   ii) í   iii) é   iv) o

5   Bonni Stachowiak, 'Pooja Agarwal – The Science of Retrieval Practice', *Teaching in Higher Ed* [podcast] (21 December 2017). Available at: http://teachinginhighered.com/podcast/science-retrieval-practice/.
6   Damian Benney, 'Spacing, Interleaving, the Testing Effect and Distributed Practice (the Diet Coke Version)', *mrbenney* [blog] (11 July 2016). Available at: https://mrbenney.wordpress.com/2016/07/11/spacing-interleaving-the-testing-effect-and-distributed-practice-the-diet-coke-version/.
7   Doug Lemov, *Teach Like a Champion 2.0: 62 Techniques that Put Students on the Path to College* (San Francisco, CA: Jossey-Bass, 2015), pp. 161–164.

g) Which word is the odd one out here?

    i) la natación   ii) el tenis   iii) la piscina   iv) el baloncesto

l)   From the 'Healthy living' topic, the anagram 'loopl' is what word?

Note that the last task (l) was based on a topic that I had taught the students much earlier in the year.

In a phenomenal follow-up blog post on spacing (this time in science), Benney describes using homework to revisit and test students, based around Joe Kirby's idea of 'lag and retrieve' homeworks.[8] Assistant head teacher and director of RE Andy Lewis (@AndyLewis_RE) has also written a fantastic post on how he has incorporated spaced practice in RE.[9]

An example of interleaving in the English curriculum comes from my brother, Jude Hunton, and Chris Peirce:

Quotation booklet exercises				
Autumn 1: 7 weeks	Autumn 2: 7 weeks	Spring 1: 8 weeks	Spring 2: 6 weeks	Summer 1: 5 weeks
Animal Farm knowledge organiser	Jekyll and Hyde knowledge organiser	Macbeth knowledge organiser		
Language terms: 1–6	Language terms: 7–12	Language terms: 13–18	Language terms: 19–24	Language terms: 24–27
Animal Farm GCSE Literature Paper 2	Jekyll and Hyde GCSE Literature Paper 1	English language Paper 1: Explorations in creative reading and writing	Poetry: Past and present and unseen GCSE Literature Paper 2	Revision for both Language and Literature

8   Damian Benney, '(Trying to Apply) Spacing in a Content Heavy Subject', *mrbenney* [blog] (16 October 2016). Available at: https://mrbenney.wordpress.com/2016/10/16/trying-to-apply-spacing-in-science/. He supplements this with another brilliant post: 'Optimal Time for Spacing Gaps (?)', *mrbenney* [blog] (3 November 2016). Available at: https://mrbenney.wordpress.com/2016/11/03/optimal-time-for-spacing-gaps/.

9   Andy Lewis, 'Forget Me Not: New GCSE Planning', *TDRE Boss* [blog] (28 February 2017). Available at: http://tdreboss.blogspot.co.uk/2017/02/forget-me-not-new-gcse-planning.html.

Quotation booklet exercises				
English Language Paper 2; Writers' viewpoints and perspectives	Poetry: Past and Present GCSE Literature Paper 2	Macbeth GCSE Literature Paper 1	English Language Revision	
Assessment point 1: GCSE Language Paper 2 full mock	Assessment point 2: Animal Farm question w/b 7th November Mock Exams 1: w/b 28th November Language Paper 1 Language Paper 2 Literature Paper 2	Assessment point 3: Writing assessment: Paper 2 Jekyll and Hyde question	Assessment point 4: Mock Exam 2: w/b 6th March Language Paper 1 and 2 Literature Paper 1 and 2	Assessment point 5: Writing assessment: Paper 1 Public Exams start 15th May

Year 11 English Curriculum 2016–2017

Chris adds:

This model has both interleaved and spaced practice as central principles. Firstly (and probably most commonly), each half-term interleaves language and literature study, meaning that students are learning and revising topics with gaps between first exposure, the follow-up lesson and formative assessment.

Secondly, running through these half-termly combined units are what we call 'language terms' (as in terminology) and the more familiar and popular 'knowledge organisers' for the literary text being studied. These 'language terms' are numbered progressively, following the theory of 'threshold concepts' from various writers on grammar and curriculum design. The thinking is that once a student masters the knowledge of a linguistic term they are in a position to move on to the next, eventually bringing about a cumulative bank of language knowledge that can improve both reading and writing abilities. Language concepts and the content of the knowledge organisers are interleaved and tested via multiple choice quizzes and memory platforms.

Thirdly, and perhaps most crucially, is the spaced practice assessments across the curriculum year. Where possible, students study a topic in one half term, are assessed formatively throughout this, and complete a summative assessment in the following half term. 'End of topic' assessment could be perceived as enabling a student's *performance* of knowledge, and can lead to a false sense of security amongst students and teachers alike; the aim with our spaced and interleaved curriculum design is to test and prioritise a student's *retention and recall* of knowledge. This gives teachers a more realistic measure of student knowledge, memory and applied skill, whilst also giving students a more challenging experience of linear exams. It is a curriculum designed to bring about learning and not just performance.

Rebecca Foster has kindly allowed me to reproduce a brilliant example of how interleaving is practised in the English department at her school for Key Stage 3 students.

English Threshold Concepts	Structure and coherence	Spelling, punctuation and grammar	Awareness of impact	Understanding context	Using evidence	Analysing technique	Structure and coherence	Spelling, punctuation and grammar	Awareness of impact	Understanding context	Using evidence	Analysing technique	Structure and coherence	Spelling, punctuation and grammar	Awareness of impact	Understanding context	Using evidence	Analysing technique
Year 7	*Of Mice and Men* – John Steinbeck									*The Tempest* – William Shakespeare								
	Analysing unseen non-fiction		Analysing unseen fiction		Weekly writing challenge		War poetry			Analysing unseen non-fiction		Analysing unseen fiction		Weekly writing challenge		War poetry		

English Threshold Concepts	Structure and coherence	Spelling, punctuation and grammar	Awareness of impact	Understanding context	Using evidence	Analysing technique	Structure and coherence	Spelling, punctuation and grammar	Awareness of impact	Understanding context	Using evidence	Analysing technique	Structure and coherence	Spelling, punctuation and grammar	Awareness of impact	Understanding context	Using evidence	Analysing technique
Year 8	*Animal Farm* – George Orwell								*Much Ado About Nothing –* William Shakespeare									
	Analysing unseen non-fiction	Analysing unseen fiction	Weekly writing challenge	Different writers' poetry					Analysing unseen non-fiction	Analysing unseen fiction	Weekly writing challenge	Different writers' poetry						
Year 9	*Jane Eyre* – Charlotte Brontë								*Romeo and Juliet* – William Shakespeare									
	Analysing unseen non-fiction	Analysing unseen fiction	Weekly writing challenge	Duffy and Armitage poetry					Analysing unseen non-fiction	Analysing unseen fiction	Weekly writing challenge	Duffy and Armitage poetry						

Rebecca adds:

A key feature of our KS3 and KS4 curriculum designs is that nothing is studied in isolation. For example, in Year 7, unit 1 lessons on *Of Mice and Men* are spaced out to about one per week. Although this has felt counterintuitive as teachers, and has necessitated a real change in our assessment practices, our students have not been fazed by the fact that no two English lessons within a week are the same.

In essence, the idea is that our girls are developing all of their key English skills all of the time rather than blocking one skill into a half term. Although the latter might lead to greater performance in the short term, we're interested in long-term learning. If I roll a piece of string out from point A it will reach point B far quicker than if I were to plait it. However, that speed is at the expense of dura-bility – we all know how easy it is to snap a single thread. In the same way, by interleaving and spacing study we're finding that our students' learning is more durable; they are retaining and developing their knowledge and skills over time. With regular retrieval practice built into our lessons, we're finding real success with this approach to curriculum design.

Cumulative Knowledge Testing

The idea of cumulative knowledge testing is a strategy that my own school has adopted to ensure that spaced and interleaved schedules are assessed with more validity than they would be by an end-of-unit test assessing the last half-term or current module.

According to the Belmont Teach blog, cumulative knowledge testing means that 'questions from units 1 + 2 also appear in a unit 3 test'.[10] The implication for assessment is clear: when students approach unit 3 or 4 they know that they will also have to revisit the content from the previous two units as well. This is also the case across a whole key stage. So, if a test at the end of a Key Stage 3 course assesses knowledge and skills which have been covered earlier on in Year 9, it will also assess knowledge and skills which have been covered in Years 7 and 8.

In terms of what content might be included in each assessment, here is a Year 9 language example which specifies that at least one question from previous content is included in the test.

Assessment term 1	Term 1 additional question	Assessment term 2	Term 2 additional question	Assessment term 3	Term 3 (end-of-year) additional question
Year 9 German Reading	**+ one question** from **Year 7 German term 1** (Introductory course, School and family members)	Year 9 German Grammar Assessment	**+ one question** from **Year 8 German term 1** (Celebrities and superheroes/ Berlin and German-speaking cities)	Year 9 German Speaking	**+ one role play** from **Year 7 German term 2** (Free time)

10 Belmont Teach, 'Using Cognitive Science to Inform Curriculum Design' [blog] (8 June 2014). Available at: https://belmontteach.wordpress.com/2014/06/08/ using-cognitive-science-to-inform-curriculum-design/.

Assessment term 1	Term 1 additional question	Assessment term 2	Term 2 additional question	Assessment term 3	Term 3 (end-of-year) additional question
Year 9 German Listening	+ one question from Year 7 German term 2 (Free time)	Year 9 Translation German into English	+ language from Year 8 German term 2 (TV and cinema)	Year 9 German integrated assessment (two reading questions, three grammar and one writing)	+ one question from Year 7 German term 3 (Town)
Year 9 German Grammar	+ one question from Year 7 German term 3 (Town)	Year 9 Translation English into German	+ language from Year 8 German term 3 (House and home)	Year 9 Spanish Speaking	+ one role play from Year 7 Spanish term 2 (Leisure activities)
Year 9 Spanish Reading	+ one question from Year 7 Spanish term 1 (Introductory course, school and family members)	Year 9 Spanish Grammar assessment	+ question from Year 8 Spanish term 1 (School – subjects/ description of teachers)	Year 9 Spanish integrated assessment (two reading questions, three grammar and one writing)	+ one question from Year 7 Spanish term 3 (Places in town)
Year 9 Spanish Listening	+ one question from Year 7 Spanish term 2 (Leisure activities)	Year 9 Translation Spanish into English	+ language from Year 8 Spanish term 2 (Holidays)		
Year 9 Spanish Grammar	+ one question from Year 7 Spanish term 3 (Places in town)	Year 9 Translation English into Spanish	+ language from Year 8 Spanish term 3 (House and home)		

When the curriculum is designed around cumulative knowledge testing combined with knowledge organisers, the ease with which students can access what they have to learn means that the assessments can test what it is they aim to test.

Joe Kirby's blog post on knowledge organisers proposes that students are given a knowledge organiser at the beginning of the year containing the core knowledge for each subject.[11] Knowledge organisers are also the subject of an article in the *TES* by Jon Brunskill and Mark Enser, in which they suggest that knowledge organisers can help to make what the students are learning clearer.[12] The aim is that by revisiting and testing the knowledge in the knowledge organisers through spaced retrieval practice, it becomes embedded in long-term memory. The students don't then come unstuck in tests which have a high level of content that may have been visited only once. It should be noted that they are more suited to cumulative than hierarchical subjects.

But which knowledge is the right knowledge? One of the issues Brunskill and Enser consider is choosing what knowledge to put in the knowledge organiser and what to leave out. They advise that the knowledge included should relate to what will be important to make sense of any future learning.

As part of promoting retrieval practice across the curriculum, James Lang refers to a 'retrieving syllabus' – that is, a syllabus containing as much detail in it as possible, a copy of which is provided to the students.[13] This opens up the opportunity to ask students to reflect on and recall elements of previously studied content – for example, noting down what they remember from the previous lesson and then checking this against the syllabus.

PE teacher David Fawcett (@davidfawcett27) recommends a similar idea to the one employed by Damian Benney to track the progress of distributed practice tasks: students numbering topics in chunks so they can monitor what they do and don't know more effectively when it comes to revisiting.[14]

As a department, we have noted the impact that the tests we have constructed using a common vocabulary with knowledge organisers have had on students' motivation – or more accurately, the effect that having a core body of knowledge has had on the students' self-efficacy. (Self-efficacy is a term from psychology, as defined by Albert Bandura, and could be interpreted as an individual's belief that they can be successful in accomplishing the task they are undertaking.) In *The Unified Learning Model*, Shell et al. describe a number of ways to enhance student self-efficacy, from the type of feedback given to a mastery method of teaching, which should present plenty of chances to be successful.[15]

11 Joe Kirby, 'Knowledge Organisers', *Pragmatic Education* [blog] (28 March 2015). Available at: https://pragmaticreform.wordpress.com/2015/03/28/knowledge-organisers/.

12 Jon Brunskill and Mark Enser, 'Are "Knowledge Organisers" Now Essential Tools in the Classroom?', *TES* (7 April 2017). Available at: https://www.tes.com/news/school-news/breaking-views/are-knowledge-organisers-now-essential-tools-classroom.

13 Lang, *Small Teaching*, loc. 767–777.

14 David Fawcett, 'Can I Be That Little Bit Better At … Using Simple Strategies To Make Content Stick?', *My Learning Journey* [blog] (19 February 2016). Available at: http://reflectionsofmyteaching.blogspot.co.uk/2016/02/can-i-be-that-little-bit-better-atusing.html.

15 Shell et al., *The Unified Learning Model*, pp. 126–127.

The idea of constructing tests which actually assess what has been taught might seem obvious, but the fact that the students know what content is coming up on a test could be a way to promote a sort of intrinsic motivation. In his thought-provoking blog post on using self-efficacy to motivate students, Gianfranco Conti describes a technique which involves teaching some of the vocabulary on a reading comprehension test beforehand so the students are somewhat 'freed up' to be able to concentrate their efforts on employing specific strategies to deal with the comprehension task, and as a result suffer less cognitive overload.[16]

In terms of promoting feelings of self-efficacy, one of the potential benefits to students of knowing the content ahead of each test is supported by Conti's view of construct validity of an assessment. Knowing key vocabulary is not a guarantee that a student knows how to use strategies to infer the meanings of unknown words:

A test requiring effective inference strategies is fair when the teacher has explicitly modelled and provided sufficient practice in those strategies prior to the test. In other words, we need to ensure that we are testing the students only on skills and linguistic items we have prepared them to cope effectively with.[17]

In the same post, Conti discusses another way of promoting self-efficacy among the students, and it is worth mentioning now as part of what underpins this book: in order to raise students' self-efficacy we should be modelling strategies which teach them how to learn the subject more effectively. Conti refers to the fact that if we were to teach students how to memorise vocabulary using even basic memory strategies, for instance, then this would help to reduce their levels of anxiety. And unlike the teaching of learning strategies by non-domain specialists, I like to think that what Conti recommends could transfer across to other domains.

In *Learn to Teach*, Catherine Scott discusses 'meta-memory': the more understanding a learner has about how memory functions, the greater the impact on their learning.[18] So, if a student knows why cumulative knowledge testing has been adopted, this will clearly help with their preparation and perhaps help to support their self-efficacy.

16 Gianfranco Conti, 'Self-Efficacy – the Most Neglected Motivational Factor in Foreign Language Instruction', *The Language Gym* [blog] (30 May 2015). Available at: https://gianfrancoconti.wordpress.com/2015/05/30/self-efficacy-the-most-neglected-motivational-factor-in-the-foreign-language-classroom/.
17 Conti, 'Self-Efficacy'.
18 Catherine Scott, *Learn to Teach: Teach to Learn*, Kindle edn (Melbourne, VIC: Cambridge University Press, 2015), loc. 2573.

My school's model of curriculum design and assessment is based around this simple idea:

Curriculum area 1	Curriculum area 2	Curriculum area 3	Curriculum area 4	Curriculum area 5
Test on 1	Test on 1 + 2	Test on 1 + 2 + 3	Test on 1 + 2 + 3 + 4	Test on 1 + 2 + 3 + 4 + 5

The idea is that curriculum area 1 is devoted to teaching some of the more difficult concepts – or 'frontloading'.[19] Our school's working party was inspired by a Joe Kirby blog post on mastery – in particular, the 80:20 principle (or Pareto's law) which he discusses in terms of 20% of the key concepts having 80% of the academic value.[20] His recommendation is to decide on which are the 20%, to teach these first and also to interleave them throughout the course.

Potential Difficulties with Spacing

Part of the problem with introducing interleaving and spacing into the curriculum is the concern over time constraints. As Didau asks, how do we fit optimal spaced sessions into an academic year of 160 days?[21]

In 'Memory and Recall', Paul Kirschner and Yana Weinstein refer to the need for a coordinated whole-school curriculum plan which would aim to ensure that scheduled tests for different subjects do not interfere with the studying for other subjects.[22] This would affect the application of the spacing for all subjects.

While it is important to have school-wide schedules which map out how the curriculum is going to take advantage of the spacing effect, the tasks which take place just before the point at which something is forgotten are key. In an interview about distributed practice, Sean Kang, assistant professor and director of the Cognition and Education Lab at Dartmouth College, says that practice on a topic which has been covered previously could be organised on a computer program so that students can take advantage of the program's capability to space out materials.[23]

19 Shaun Allison and Andy Tharby, *Making Every Lesson Count: Six Principles to Support Great Teaching and Learning* (Carmarthen: Crown House Publishing, 2015), p. 140.
20 Joe Kirby, 'Life After Levels: Who'll Create a Mastery Assessment System?', *Pragmatic Education* [blog] (30 November 2013). Available at: https://pragmaticreform.wordpress.com/2013/11/30/mastery/.
21 Didau, *What If Everything You Knew About Education Was Wrong?*, p. 223.
22 Kirschner and Weinstein, 'Memory and Recall', p. 136.
23 Aubrey Francisco, 'Ask the Cognitive Scientist: Distributed Practice' [interview with Sean Kang], *Digital Promise* (22 January 2015). Available at: http://digitalpromise.org/2015/01/22/

James Lang reports in *Small Teaching* that research shows that students who are revisiting/ revising find spacing and interleaving frustrating.[24] They would find it much easier if we were to cover material topic by topic in order. But that is perhaps the point: the more difficult it is, the better the learning is embedded.

In a brilliant blog post by psychology teacher Blake Harvard (@effortfuleduktr) on spaced practice, he discusses how to demonstrate spaced practice in the classroom so that students can see the tangible benefits of it.[25]

The process involves giving the students a table or chart to fill in first, like the example below:

Piaget's theory of cognitive development

Developmental stage	Approximate age range	Definition and description of tasks

1. Have students copy down the chart and the students should work **using only their brain** to fill in as much of the chart as possible.

2. Next, students need to highlight what they've written from step 1 in yellow.

3. Then, by using their notes or textbook, students should complete the rest of the chart.

4. Students next need to highlight what they've written down during step 3 in orange.

ask-the-cognitive-scientist-distributed-practice/.
24 Lang, *Small Teaching*, loc. 1251–1260.
25 Blake Harvard, 'Easy Application of Spaced Practice in the Classroom', *The Effortful Educator* [blog] (22 October 2017). Available at: https://theeffortfuleducator.com/2017/10/22/ easy-application-of-spaced-practice-in-the-classroom/.

Explicitly ask students how much of their chart is highlighted in yellow and how much is highlighted in orange. Certainly, the more yellow, the better. More yellow highlighting equates to more aspects of Piaget's theory known.

An important instruction next is to have the students keep their chart. Maybe ask the students to try and recreate the chart at home. They again should only use about 5–10 minutes to do this.

The next day, or maybe in a couple of days, have students follow all of the steps from above. Most of my students were able to remember more information for the chart during step 1, which required the notes and textbook being used less. Do this all over again another day. In my experience, my students continued to remember even more during step 1. To tie it all up, have the students view all of their charts. Ask them which chart has the least yellow highlighting? Which has the most? Again, most will see an increase in yellow highlighting, indicating they've remembered more information from day to day, or from retrieval to retrieval.

Finally, I ask my students a few questions about the exercise:

- Does this take more time than cramming?
- Does it work better than cramming?
- Does it literally show you what you know and what you don't know?
- Does it give you a better sense of what to study?

This blog made me consider how I might trial showing students the effect of spacing out learning. Instead of spending a 30-minute slot in a lesson practising the paradigm of *avoir* and *être*, and then moving on, I split up the practice into five-minute chunks over six lessons. The first lesson involves the students coming in and seeing the English already written up on the board (they have seen the French for this once at the beginning of term and this is just after half-term):

---

avoir = to have

I have

You have

He/she/one has

We have

You (plural) have

They have

être = to be

I am

You are

He/she/one is

We are

You (plural) are

They are

I ask them to pick up a pen and go to the Magic Whiteboard paper on the walls to write down as much as they can remember about the French in five minutes, followed by their name. I then use a Flip camera to record quickly what everyone has written. I tell them that in the next lesson we will do the same exercise. After they have retrieved the knowledge for the second time, I will show them the short video to compare what was known then after five minutes of recall versus what was recalled after one day and five further minutes of recall. I repeated this a number of times, with the final five-minute slot showing markedly greater recall.

This type of spaced learning could just as easily take place in books, of course. However, I've found that this way of modelling the spacing technique – where the students can clearly see that the same amount of time has been spent but distributed rather than massed – can lead to more effective learning.

Final Thoughts

In a review of Fiorella and Mayer's *Learning as a Generative Activity*, Bruce Henderson points out that 'Most, if not all, of the eight generative learning strategies require more effort than those less effective strategies preferred by many learners, such as rereading, recopying, and highlighting' and that therefore we need to 'convince learners of the benefits of what Bjork and his colleagues call "desirable difficulties," including those learning strategies that require time and effort'.[1] This summarises well some of the key points made throughout this book. Put simply, revisiting and revision techniques that involve hard, mental activity are more beneficial than those which feel easy.

Genuinely effective learning and revision doesn't always feel good, so if you're getting a nice, warm and comfortable feeling when you're revising, then it's probably time to try something more difficult, or at least to test yourself on the material to find out if you do actually know it. Rereading and highlighting can create that feeling of fuzzy, cognitive ease whereas retrieval practice (while not a panacea) is a more effortful revision activity.

But there are a fair number of grey areas, as well as some fence-sitting …

We have seen that it is beneficial to teach students how to use more effective revision techniques and explain how the benefits of retrieval practice and distributed practice work in the domain in which students are being taught. If transfer of more effectual learning strategies is the aim, then domain-specific teaching will probably do this better than more generic techniques.

However, suggesting that all revision or revisiting should be hard is possibly a little reductionist. If the cognitive load is too heavy, and the students are having to think too hard in a way that is not conducive to promoting germane load, then arguably that is not going to be an effective learning strategy.

I used to believe that you could improve students' outcomes by doing lots of past papers, especially at a relatively early stage. It still might be the most successful way to teach to the test, but it encompasses a very narrow view of learning and promotes a level of rote performance. It did not occur to me that this early over-reliance on an exam-focused summative approach might also cause working memory overload.

---

1   Bruce B. Henderson, 'Learning as Thinking and Thinking as Learning: A Review of *Learning as a Generative Activity: Eight Learning Strategies That Promote Understanding* by Logan Fiorella and Richard E. Mayer', *PsycCRITIQUES*, 60(37) (2015). Available at: https://www.apa.org/pubs/highlights/psyccritiques-spotlight/PSQ_a0039516.pdf, p. 3.

One of the approaches I used was to explicitly teach some of the content on the paper and then test on it, using the students' high retrieval strength as a way of showing them that they could do well. However, the conclusion of this book is that the strategies involved in successful exam preparation don't necessarily look like the exam itself.

We have explored elaboration and other revisiting/revision techniques which promote deep processing during which learners make meanings and connections for themselves. Bruce Goldstein touches on the merits of elaborative rehearsal over maintenance rehearsal (i.e. saying something over and over to yourself, like trying to remember a new phone number). The latter simply maintains the information in working memory without it transferring into long-term memory.[2] Saying GCSE German vocabulary over and over again to myself didn't make it stick for me in the summer of 1997.

Goldstein links the benefits of elaborative rehearsal to Fergus Craik and Robert Lockhart's work on levels of processing: the more deeply processed information is, the greater the encoding and retrieval.[3] This point is supported by David Didau and Nick Rose in *What Every Teacher Needs to Know About … Psychology* where they make clear that activities which demand only shallow processing do not lead to the deeper understanding required for strong long-term recall of the material.[4]

Learning strategies such as revisiting and revision have been blurred throughout. Many of the subject-specific strategies could be used in class or as revision tasks that students use away from the classroom.

Other useful resources on learning and teaching include the Learning Scientists' website (especially the 'Six Strategies for Effective Learning' which are downloadable[5]); the brilliant visuals from Oliver Caviglioli;[6] Barak Rosenshine's 'Principles of Instruction: Research-Based Strategies That All Teachers Should Know';[7] Benassi et al.'s *Applying Science of Learning in Education* and Pashler et al.'s *Organizing Instruction and Study to Improve Student Learning*. There is always another study, point of view or practical-looking example out there which will challenge your thinking, which can make developing your practice a bit like painting the Forth Bridge.

2   Goldstein, *Cognitive Psychology*, pp. 173–174.
3   Fergus Craik and Robert Lockhart, 'Levels of Processing: A Framework for Memory Research', *Journal of Verbal Learning and Verbal Behavior*, 11 (1972), 671–684.
4   Didau and Rose, *What Every Teacher Needs to Know About … Psychology*, p. 47.
5   See http://www.learningscientists.org/downloadable-materials.
6   See https://teachinghow2s.com/docs/HOW2_ResearchED_Rugby.pdf.
7   Barak Rosenshine, 'Principles of Instruction: Research-Based Strategies That All Teachers Should Know', *American Educator* (Spring 2012), 12–39. Available at: https://www.aft.org/sites/default/files/periodicals/Rosenshine.pdf.

I have tried to avoid including any wild claims and occasionally added the proviso that the strategy *might* work better than others. I certainly didn't know any of this as an NQT, so hopefully if some of these ideas help to spark a more developed interest in one or more of these areas then I am happy with that. My summary and views on all of this will be open to bias as much as anyone's. As David Didau advises, 'seek to *explore* rather than *confirm* your biases'.[8]

If nothing else, I hope that a collaborative discussion ensues around domain-specific learning strategies delivered in the context of a lesson and how these might transfer to students when revisiting and revising.

8   David Didau, 'Five Techniques for Overcoming Overconfidence and Improving Decision-Making', *The Learning Spy* [blog] (3 November 2015). Available at: http://www.learningspy.co.uk/leadership/five-techniques-for-overcoming-overconfidence-improving-decision-making/.

References

Adragna, Rachel (2016). 'Be Your Own Teacher: How to Study with Flashcards', *The Learning Scientists* [blog] (18 February). Available at: http://www.learningscientists.org/blog/2016/2/20-1.

Alcock, Lara (2014). *How to Think About Analysis* (Oxford: Oxford University Press).

Allison, Shaun (2015). 'Supporting Learning Through Effective Revision Techniques', *Class Teaching* [blog] (29 January). Available at: https://classteaching.wordpress.com/2015/01/29/supporting-learning-through-effective-revision-techniques/.

Allison, Shaun and Andy Tharby (2015). *Making Every Lesson Count: Six Principles to Support Great Teaching and Learning* (Carmarthen: Crown House Publishing).

Ambrose, Susan A., Michael W. Bridges, Michele DiPietro, Marsha C. Lovett and Marie K. Norman (2010). *How Learning Works: Seven Research-Based Principles for Smart Teaching* (San Francisco, CA: Jossey-Bass).

Ashman, Greg (2016). 'When Quizzing Fails', *Filling the Pail* [blog] (13 May). Available at: https://gregashman.wordpress.com/2016/05/13/when-quizzing-fails/.

Ashman, Greg (2017). 'Cognitive Load Theory – "The Single Most Important Thing for Teachers to Know"', *Filling the Pail* [blog] (27 January). Available at: https://gregashman.wordpress.com/2017/01/27/cognitive-load-theory-the-single-most-important-theory-for-teachers-to-know/.

Baddeley, Alan, Michael W. Eysenck and Michael C. Anderson (2009). *Memory* (Hove and New York: Psychology Press).

Bahrick, Harry P. and Elizabeth Phelps (1987). 'Retention of Spanish Vocabulary Over 8 Years', *Journal of Experimental Psychology: Learning, Memory, and Cognition*, 13(2), 344–349. Available at: https://www.gwern.net/docs/spacedrepetition/1987-bahrick.pdf.

Bahrick, Harry P., Lorraine E. Bahrick, Audrey S. Bahrick and Phyllis E. Bahrick (1993). 'Maintenance of Foreign Language Vocabulary and the Spacing Effect', *Psychological Science*, 4(5), 316–321. Available at: http://www.psych.utoronto.ca/users/shkim/Bahrick%20et%20al.%20(1993)%20spacing%20effect.pdf.

Balota, David A., Janet M. Duchek and Jessica M. Logan (2007). 'Is Expanded Retrieval Practice a Superior Form of Spaced Retrieval? A Critical Review of the Extant Literature'. In James S. Nairne (ed.), *The Foundations of Remembering: Essays in Honor of Henry L. Roediger III* (New York: Psychology Press), pp. 83–105.

Bambrick-Santoyo, Paul (2012). *Leverage Leadership: A Practical Guide to Building Exceptional Schools* (San Francisco, CA: Jossey-Bass).

Barnett, Susan and Stephen Ceci (2002). 'When and Where Do We Apply What We Learn? A Taxonomy for Far Transfer', *Psychological Bulletin*, 128(4), 612–637.

Barton, Craig (2017a). 'Dylan Wiliam – Author, Researcher, Trainer and Assessment for Learning Expert', *Mr Barton Maths* [podcast] (3 November). Available at: http://www.mrbartonmaths.com/blog/dylan-wiliam-author-researcher-trainer-and-assessment-for-learning-expert/.

Barton, Craig (2017b). 'Kris Boulton – Part 1: Planning Lessons, Engelmann and Differentiation', *Mr Barton Maths* [podcast] (17 July). Available at: http://www.mrbartonmaths.com/blog/kris-boulton-part-1-planning-lessons-engelmann-and-differentiation/.

Barton, Craig (2017c). 'Robert and Elizabeth Bjork – Memory, Forgetting, Testing, Desirable Difficulties', *Mr Barton Maths* [podcast] (29 June). Available at: http://www.mrbartonmaths.com/blog/robert-and-elizabeth-bjork-memory-forgetting-testing-desirable-difficulties/.

Barton, Craig (2018). *How I Wish I'd Taught Maths: Lessons Learned from Research, Conversations with Experts, and 12 Years of Mistakes*, Kindle edn (Woodbridge: John Catt Educational).

Belmont Teach (2014). 'Using Cognitive Science to Inform Curriculum Design' [blog] (8 June). Available at: https://belmontteach.wordpress.com/2014/06/08/using-cognitive-science-to-inform-curriculum-design/.

Benassi, Victor A., Catherine E. Overson and Christopher M. Hakala (eds) (2014). *Applying Science of Learning in Education: Infusing Psychological Science into the Curriculum*. Available at: https://scholars.unh.edu/cgi/viewcontent.cgi?article=1286&context=psych_facpub.

Benney, Damian (2016a). 'Optimal Time for Spacing Gaps (?)', *mrbenney* [blog] (3 November). Available at: https://mrbenney.wordpress.com/2016/11/03/optimal-time-for-spacing-gaps/.

Benney, Damian (2016b). 'Spacing, Interleaving, the Testing Effect and Distributed Practice (the Diet Coke Version)', *mrbenney* [blog] (11 July). Available at: https://mrbenney.wordpress.com/2016/07/11/spacing-interleaving-the-testing-effect-and-distributed-practice-the-diet-coke-version/.

Benney, Damian (2016c). '(Trying to Apply) Spacing in a Content Heavy Subject', *mrbenney* [blog] (16 October). Available at: https://mrbenney.wordpress.com/2016/10/16/trying-to-apply-spacing-in-science/.

Berry, Dianne C. (1982). 'Metacognitive Experience and Transfer of Logical Reasoning', *Quarterly Journal of Experimental Psychology*, 35A, 39–49.

Bilbrough, Emma and Danielle Walters (2016). 'Teaching Tier 2 Vocabulary', *Class Teaching* [blog] (8 December). Available at: https://classteaching.wordpress.com/2016/12/08/teaching-tier-2-vocabulary/.

Birbalsingh, Katharine (ed.) (2016). *Battle Hymn of the Tiger Teachers: The Michaela Way* (Woodbridge: John Catt Educational).

Bjork, Elizabeth L. and Robert Bjork (2009). 'Making Things Hard on Yourself, But in a Good Way: Creating Desirable Difficulties to Enhance Learning'. In Morton A. Gernsbacher and James Pomerantz (eds), *Psychology and the Real World: Essays Illustrating Fundamental Contributions to Society* (New York: Worth), pp. 59–68. Available at: https://bjorklab.psych.ucla.edu/wp-content/uploads/sites/13/2016/04/EBjork_RBjork_2011.pdf.

Boulton, Kris (2015). 'What Rote Knowledge Isn't – A Short Introduction to Inflexible and Flexible Knowledge', … *To the Real* [blog] (25 April). Available at: https://tothereal.wordpress.com/2015/04/25/what-rote-knowledge-isnt-a-short-introduction-to-inflexible-and-flexible-knowledge/.

Boulton, Kris (2017). 'The 80:20 Principle – 5 – Mental Models for Education', … *To the Real* [blog] (11 February). See https://tothereal.wordpress.com/2017/02/11/the-8020-principle-5-mental-models-for-education/?wref=pil.

Boxer, Adam (2017). 'The Retrieval Roulette', *Adam Boxer* [blog] (4 May). Available at: https://achemicalorthodoxy.wordpress.com/2017/05/04/the-retrieval-roulette/.

CGP (2010). *GCSE D&T Product Design: AQA Specification (The Revision Guide)* (Broughton-in-Furness: CGP Books).

CGP (2011). *GCSE Business Studies Revision Guide (A*–G Course)* (Broughton-in-Furness: CGP Books).

CGP (2016). *GCSE Physics for AQA (Grade 9–1): The Revision Guide* (Broughton-in-Furness: CGP Books).

Brown, Peter C., Henry L. Roediger and Mark A. McDaniel (2014). *Make It Stick: The Science of Successful Learning*, Kindle edn (Cambridge, MA: Harvard University Press).

Brunskill, Jon and Mark Enser (2017). 'Are "Knowledge Organisers" Now Essential Tools in the Classroom?', *TES* (7 April). Available at: https://www.tes.com/news/school-news/breaking-views/are-knowledge-organisers-now-essential-tools-classroom.

Bruyckere, Pedro De, Paul A. Kirschner and Casper D. Hulshof (2015). *Urban Myths about Learning and Education* (London: Academic Press).

Camden, Billy (2016). 'Headteacher Scraps "Mad" Year 11 Revision Classes to Protect Pupil Mental Health', *SchoolsWeek* (4 March). Available at: http://schoolsweek.co.uk/head teacher-scraps-mad-year-11-revision-classes-to-protect-pupil-mental-health/.

Carey, Benedict (2014). *How We Learn: The Surprising Truth About When, Where and Why It Happens*, Kindle edn (London: Macmillan).

Carpenter, Shana K. (2011). 'Semantic Information Activated During Retrieval Contributes to Later Retention: Support for the Mediator Effectiveness Hypothesis of the Testing Effect', *Journal of Experimental Psychology: Learning, Memory, and Cognition*, 37(6), 1547–1552.

Caviglioli, Oliver (2017). 'My researchED Cheshire Presentation', *HOW2* (19 March). Available at: http://linkis. com/teachinghow2s.com/bl/BfbYM.

Chandler, Paul, Annishka Oksa and Slava Kalyuga (2010). 'Expertise Reversal Effect in Using Explanatory Notes for Readers of Shakespearean Text', *Instructional Science*, 38(3), 217–236.

Chi, Michelene T. H. (2009). 'Active-Constructive-Interactive: A Conceptual Framework for Differentiating Learning Activities', *Topics in Cognitive Science*, 1(1), 73–105.

Chi, Michelene T. H. and Kurt A. VanLehn (1991). 'The Content of Physics Self-Explanations', *Journal of the Learning Sciences*, 1(1), 69–105. Available at: http://www.public.asu.edu/~mtchi/papers/ChiVanLehn.pdf.

Chiu, Jennifer and Michelene Chi (2014). 'Supporting Self-Explanation in the Classroom'. In Victor A. Benassi, Catherine E. Overson and Christopher M. Hakala (eds), *Applying Science of Learning in Education: Infusing Psychological Science into the Curriculum*. Available at: https://scholars.unh.edu/cgi/viewcontent. cgi?article=1286&context=psych_facpub.

Christodoulou, Daisy (2013a). 'Closed Questions and Higher Order Thinking', *The Wing to Heaven* [blog] (6 October). Available at: https://thewingtoheaven.wordpress.com/2013/10/06/ closed-questions-and-higher-order-thinking/.

Christodoulou, Daisy (2013b). 'Research on Multiple Choice Questions', *The Wing to Heaven* [blog] (30 October). Available at: https://thewingtoheaven.wordpress.com/2013/10/30/research-on-multiple-choice-questions/.

Christodoulou, Daisy (2014). 'Why Teaching to the Test is So Bad', *The Wing to Heaven* [blog] (19 January). Available at: https://thewingtoheaven.wordpress.com/2014/01/19/why-teaching-to-the-test-is-so-bad/.

Christodoulou, Daisy (2015). 'Assessment Alternatives 1: Using Questions Instead of Criteria', *The Wing to Heaven* [blog] (7 June). Available at: https://thewingtoheaven.wordpress.com/2015/06/07/ assessment-alternatives-1-using-questions-instead-of-criteria/.

Christodoulou, Daisy (2016). *Making Good Progress? The Future of Assessment for Learning* (Oxford: Oxford University Press).

Clark, Ruth C., Frank Nguyen and John Sweller (2006). *Efficiency in Learning: Evidence-Based Guidelines to Manage Cognitive Load*, Kindle edn (San Francisco, CA: Pfeiffer).

Clark, Ruth Colvin and Richard E. Mayer, (2016). *E-Learning and the Science of Instruction: Proven Guidelines for Consumers and Designers of Multimedia Learning*, Kindle edn (Hoboken, NJ: John Wiley).

Conti, Gianfranco (2015). 'Self-Efficacy – the Most Neglected Motivational Factor in Foreign Language Instruction', *The Language Gym* [blog] (30 May). Available at: https://gianfrancoconti.wordpress. com/2015/05/30/self-efficacy-the-most-neglected-motivational-factor-in-the-foreign-language-classroom/.

Conti, Gianfranco (2016). 'How to Enhance Your Students' Chances of Succeeding at Listening (Part 1)', *The Language Gym* [blog] (3 October). Available at: https://gianfrancoconti.wordpress.com/2016/10/03/ how-to-enhance-your-students-chances-of-succeeding-at-listening-part-1/.

Conti, Gianfranco (2017). 'Patterns First – Why You Should "Ditch" Word Lists, Traditional Grammar Rules and … Your Textbook', *The Language Gym* [blog] (21 May). Available at: https://gianfrancoconti.wordpress. com/2017/05/21/why-you-should-ditch-word-lists-and-traditional-grammar-rules/.

Cook, Jo (2014). 'Is It About Time We Forget Ebbinghaus?', *HRZone* (30 September). Available at: http://www. hrzone.com/talent/development/is-it-about-time-we-forget-ebbinghaus.

Cowley, Sue (2017). 'What Works for What?', *Freeing the Angel* [blog] (28 February). Available at: https:// suecowley.wordpress.com/2017/02/28/what-works-for-what/.

Cox, Dawn (2016a). 'Deliberate Recall – Don't Just Leave It To Chance', *missdcoxblog* [blog] (11 July). Available at: https://missdcoxblog.wordpress.com/2016/07/11/deliberate-recall-dont-just-leave-it-to-chance/.

Cox, Dawn (2016b). 'Ditch Revision. Teach It Well', *missdcoxblog* [blog] (9 January). See https://missdcoxblog. wordpress.com/2016/01/09/ditch-revision-teach-it-well/.

Cox, Dawn (2016c). 'Using Research to Design a Revision Session', *missdcoxblog* [blog] (12 January). Available at: https://missdcoxblog.wordpress.com/2016/01/12/using-research-to-design-a-revision-session/.

Craik, Fergus and Robert Lockhart (1972). 'Levels of Processing: A Framework for Memory Research', *Journal of Verbal Learning and Verbal Behavior*, 11, 671–684.

Crehan, Lucy (2016). *Cleverlands: The Secrets Behind the Success of the World's Education Superpowers* (London: Unbound).

Davies, Gary (2016). 'Why Don't Teachers Engage with Research?', *Gary Davies* [blog] (5 June). Available at: http://garydavies.org/2016/06/05/why-dont-teachers-engage-with-research/.

Davies, Jamie (2014). 'No More Highlighting – Improving Learning with Effective Techniques', *Jamie Davies* [blog] (15 March). Available at: http://jamiedavi.es/no-more-highlighting-improving-learning-with-effective-techniques-575.php.

Deans for Impact (2015). *The Science of Learning* (Austin, TX: Deans for Impact). Available at: http://deansforimpact.org/the_science_of_learning.html.

Didau, David (2013). 'Redesigning a Curriculum', *The Learning Spy* [blog] (25 March). Available at: http://www.learningspy.co.uk/english-gcse/redesigning-a-curriculum/.

Didau, David (2015a). 'Five Techniques for Overcoming Overconfidence and Improving Decision-Making', *The Learning Spy* [blog] (3 November). Available at: http://www.learningspy.co.uk/leadership/five-techniques-for-overcoming-overconfidence-improving-decision-making/.

Didau, David (2015b). 'Intelligent Accountability', *The Learning Spy* [blog] (4 October). Available at: http://www.learningspy.co.uk/featured/intelligent-accountability/.

Didau, David (2015c). 'The Testing Effect is Dead! Long Live the Testing Effect!', *The Learning Spy* [blog] (20 May). Available at: http://www.learningspy.co.uk/featured/the-testing-effect-is-dead-long-live-the-testing-effect/.

Didau, David (2015d). *What If Everything You Knew About Education Was Wrong?* (Carmarthen: Crown House Publishing).

Didau, David (2017a). 'Further Problems with the "Thinking Hard" Proxy for Learning?', *The Learning Spy* [blog] (11 January). Available at: http://www.learningspy.co.uk/learning/problems-thinking-hard-proxy-learning/.

Didau, David (2017b). 'How To Start a Lesson', *The Learning Spy* [blog] (29 July). Available at: http://www.learningspy.co.uk/featured/how-to-start-a-lesson/.

Didau, David (2017c). 'What Do Teachers Believe?', *The Learning Spy* [blog] (16 March). Available at: http://www.learningspy.co.uk/research/what-do-teachers-believe/.

Didau, David (2017d). 'What Do Teachers Think Differentiation Is?', *The Learning Spy* [blog] (24 April). Available at: http://www.learningspy.co.uk/research/teachers-think-differentiation/.

Didau, David and Nick Rose (2016). *What Every Teacher Needs to Know About ... Psychology* (Woodbridge: John Catt Educational).

Dunlosky, John (2013). 'Strengthening the Student Toolbox: Study Strategies to Boost Learning', *American Educator*, 37(3), 12–21.

Dunlosky, John, Katherine A. Rawson, Elizabeth J. Marsh, Mitchell J. Nathan and Daniel T. Willingham (2013). 'Improving Students' Learning with Effective Learning Techniques: Promising Directions from Cognitive and Educational Psychology', *Psychological Science in the Public Interest*, 14(1), 4–58.

Dunlosky, John, Katherine A. Rawson, Elizabeth J. Marsh, Mitchell J. Nathan and Daniel T. Willingham (2015). 'What Works, What Doesn't', *Scientific American Mind*, 24(4), 46–53.

Dunlosky, John, Katherine A. Rawson and Erica L. Middleton (2005). 'What Constrains the Accuracy of Metacomprehension Judgments? Testing the Transfer-Appropriate-Monitoring and Accessibility Hypotheses', *Journal of Memory and Language*, 52, 551–565.

Durrington High School (2016). 'What Will Improve a Students' Meomory [sic]?', *Research Bulletin*, Issue 8, Spring 2. Available at: https://twitter.com/atharby/status/699211606102839296.

Dyer, Olivia (2016). 'Drill and Didactic Teaching Work Best'. In Katharine Birbalsingh (ed.), *Battle Hymn of the Tiger Teachers: The Michaela Way* (Woodbridge: John Catt Educational), pp. 28–39.

Emeny, William (2012). *100 Things Awesome Teachers Do* (n.p.: CreateSpace).

Emeny, William (2013). *The Magic of Pineapples: A Brain Tingling Adventure Through Amazing Mathematics* (n.p.: CreateSpace).

Emeny, William (2015). 'Building Interleaving and Spaced Practice Into Our Pedagogy', *Great Maths Teaching Ideas* [blog] (1 February). Available at: http://www.greatmathsteachingideas.com/2015/02/01/building-interleaving-and-spaced-practice-into-our-pedagogy/.

Emeny, William (2016). 'A Week Working at UCLA in the Bjork Learning and Forgetting Lab', *Great Maths Teaching Ideas* [blog] (26 August). Available at: http://www.greatmathsteachingideas.com/2016/08/26/a-week-working-at-ucla-in-the-bjork-learning-and-forgetting-lab/.

Emeny, William (2017). 'Spaced and Interleaved Retrieval Practice Using Flashcards', *Great Maths Teaching Ideas* [blog] (13 April). Available at: http://www.greatmathsteachingideas.com/2017/04/13/spaced-and-interleaved-retrieval-practice-using-flashcards/.

Enser, Mark (2017a). 'The Ritual of Teaching', *Teaching It Real* [blog] (15 October). Available at: https://teachreal.wordpress.com/2017/10/15/the-ritual-of-teaching/.

Enser, Mark (2017b). 'Schools Must Say "No" to Out-of-Hours Revision Sessions, for the Collective Good of the Profession', *TES* (10 December). Available at: https://www.tes.com/news/school-news/breaking-views/schools-must-say-no-out-hours-revision-sessions-collective-good.

Epstein, Robert (2016). 'The Empty Brain', *Aeon* (16 May). Available at: https://aeon.co/essays/your-brain-does-not-process-information-and-it-is-not-a-computer.

Ericsson, K. Anders and Robert Pool (2016). *Peak: Secrets from the New Science of Expertise*, Kindle edn (London: Bodley Head).

Fawcett, David (2016). 'Can I Be That Little Bit Better At … Using Simple Strategies To Make Content Stick?', *My Learning Journey* [blog] (19 February). Available at: http://reflectionsofmyteaching.blogspot.co.uk/2016/02/can-i-be-that-little-bit-better-atusing.html.

Fearn, Heather (2016). 'Developmentalism vs Mastery: Should Teachers Be "Flinging Mud at the Wall"?', *SchoolsWeek* (22 October). Available at: http://schoolsweek.co.uk/developmentalism-vs-mastery-should-teachers-be-flinging-mud-at-the-wall/.

Fiorella, Logan and Richard E. Mayer (2015). *Learning as a Generative Activity: Eight Learning Strategies That Promote Understanding* (New York: Cambridge University Press).

Fletcher-Wood, Harry (2013). '28 Hinge Questions to Use, Adapt and Refine', *Improving Teaching* [blog] (17 August). Available at: https://improvingteaching.co.uk/2013/08/17/28-hinge-questions/.

Fordham, Michael (2017). 'Resisting the Pull of the Generic: Knowledge, Specificity and Teaching', *Clio et cetera* [blog] (20 October). Available at: https://clioetcetera.com/2017/10/20/resisting-the-pull-of-the-generic-knowledge-specificity-and-teaching/.

Fowler, Robert L. and Anne S. Barker (1974). 'Effectiveness of Highlighting for Retention of Text Material', *Journal of Applied Psychology*, 59(3), 358–364.

Francisco, Aubrey (2014). 'Ask the Cognitive Scientist: Retrieval Practice' [interview with Henry Roediger], *Digital Promise* (15 October). Available at: http://www.digitalpromise.org/blog/entry/ask-the-cognitive-scientist-retrieval-practice.

Francisco, Aubrey (2015). 'Ask the Cognitive Scientist: Distributed Practice' [interview with Sean Kang], *Digital Promise* (22 January). Available at: http://digitalpromise.org/2015/01/22/ask-the-cognitive-scientist-distributed-practice/.

French, Toby (2016). 'Summarising with Y9', *MrHistoire.com* [blog] (1 October). (This post is no longer available.)

French, Toby (2017). 'How to Create a Knowledge Organiser', *MrHistoire.com* [blog] (25 January). Available at: https://mrhistoire.com/2017/01/25/createkos/.

Gerrard, Sue (2017). 'Cognitive Science: The Wrong End of the Stick', *logicalincrementalism* [blog] (25 October). See https://logicalincrementalism.wordpress.com/2017/10/25/cognitive-science-the-wrong-end-of-the-stick/.

Gilbert, Kelsey (2016). 'Guest Post: Self-Explanation as a Study Strategy for Math', *The Learning Scientists* [blog] (10 July). Available at: http://www.learningscientists.org/blog/2016/7/12-1.

Goldstein, E. Bruce (2010). *Cognitive Psychology: Connecting Mind, Research, and Everyday Experience* (Belmont, CA: Cengage Learning).

Harris, Robert (2014). 'Learning Strategy 5: Self Explanation', *VirtualSalt* (27 February). Available at: http://www.virtualsalt.com/learn5.html.

Harvard, Blake (2017). 'Easy Application of Spaced Practice in the Classroom', *The Effortful Educator* [blog] (22 October). Available at: https://theeffortfuleducator.com/2017/10/22/easy-application-of-spaced-practice-in-the-classroom/.

Hattie, John, John Biggs and Nola Purdie (1996). 'Effects of Learning Skills Interventions on Student Learning: A Meta-Analysis', *American Educational Research Association* 66(2), 99–136.

Henderson, Bruce B. (2015). 'Learning as Thinking and Thinking as Learning: A Review of *Learning as a Generative Activity: Eight Learning Strategies That Promote Understanding* by Logan Fiorella and Richard E. Mayer', *PsycCRITIQUES*, 60(37). Available at: https://www.apa.org/pubs/highlights/psyccritiques-spotlight/PSQ_a0039516.pdf.

Hendrick, Carl and Robin Macpherson (2017). *What Does This Look Like in the Classroom? Bridging the Gap Between Research and Practice* (Woodbridge: John Catt Educational).

Herbert, Wray (2011). *On Second Thought: Outsmarting Your Mind's Hard-Wired Habits* (New York: Broadway Books).

Herbert, Wray (2012). 'Two Cheers for Multiple-Choice Tests', *Association for Psychological Science* (29 March). Available at: http://www.psychologicalscience.org/index.php/news/full-frontal-psychology/two-cheers-for-multiple-choice-tests.html.

Hilton, Rhiannon (2011). Alsager School GCSE Results, *Crewe Chronicle* (31 August). Available at: http://www.crewechronicle.co.uk/news/local-news/alsager-school-gcse-results-5607224.

Hochman, Judith and Natalie Wexler (2017). *The Writing Revolution: A Guide to Advancing Thinking Through Writing in All Subjects and Grades* (San Francisco, CA: Jossey-Bass).

Hunton, Jake (2015). *Fun Learning Activities in Modern Foreign Languages: A Complete Toolkit for Ensuring Engagement, Progress and Achievement* (Carmarthen: Crown House Publishing).

Jones, Gary (2016). *Evidence-Based Practice: A Handbook for Teachers and School Leaders* (n.p.: Gary Jones and CEBMa).

Jones, Pete (2016). 'Beautifully Dull', *Where's Your Head At?* [blog] (23 October). Available at: http://deeplearning.edublogs.org/2016/10/23/beautifully-dull/#.WBJpOuArK01.

Kahneman, Daniel (2011). *Thinking, Fast and Slow* (London: Allen Lane).

Kapp, Karl (2014). 'Spaced Retrieval, Retrieval Practice, and Knowledge Guru: What Research Tells Us', *The Knowledge Guru* (19 March). Available at: http://www.theknowledgeguru.com/spaced-retrieval-retrieval-practice-knowledge-guru-research-tells-us/.

Karpicke, Jeffrey D. and William R. Aue (2015). 'The Testing Effect Is Alive and Well with Complex Materials', *Educational Psychology Review*, 27(2), 317–326. Available at: http://link.springer.com/article/10.1007/s10648-015-9309-3/.

Karpicke, Jeffrey D., Andrew C. Butler and Henry L. Roediger III (2009). 'Metacognitive Strategies in Student Learning: Do Students Practice Retrieval When They Study On Their Own?', *Memory*, 17(4), 471–479.

Kirby, Joe (2013a). 'Life After Levels: Who'll Create a Mastery Assessment System?', *Pragmatic Education* [blog] (30 November). Available at: https://pragmaticreform.wordpress.com/2013/11/30/mastery/.

Kirby, Joe (2013b). 'Why Don't Students Remember What They've Learned?', *Pragmatic Education* [blog] (16 November). Available at: https://pragmaticreform.wordpress.com/2013/11/16/memory/.

Kirby, Joe (2015a). 'A 5 Year Revision Plan', *Pragmatic Education* [blog] (3 May). Available at: https://pragmaticreform.wordpress.com/2015/05/03/a-5-year-revision-plan/.

Kirby, Joe (2015b). 'Knowledge Organisers', *Pragmatic Education* [blog] (28 March). Available at: https://pragmaticreform.wordpress.com/2015/03/28/knowledge-organisers/.

Kirschner, Paul A., John Sweller and Richard E. Clark (2006). 'Why Minimal Guidance During Instruction Does Not Work: An Analysis of the Failure of Constructivist, Discovery, Problem-Based, Experiential, and Inquiry-Based Teaching', *Educational Psychologist*, 41(2), 75–86.

Kirschner, Paul A. and Yana Weinstein (2017). 'Memory and Recall'. In Carl Hendrick and Robin Macpherson (eds), *What Does This Look Like in the Classroom? Bridging the Gap Between Research and Practice* (Woodbridge: John Catt Educational), pp. 122–142.

Koretz, Daniel (2009). *Measuring Up: What Educational Testing Really Tells Us* (Cambridge, MA: Harvard University Press).

Kuepper-Tetzel, Carolina (2017). 'How To Improve Your Metacognition and Why It Matters', *The Learning Scientists* [blog] (28 March). Available at: http://www.learningscientists.org/blog/2017/3/30-1.

Lang, James M. (2016). *Small Teaching: Everyday Lessons from the Science of Learning*, Kindle edn (San Francisco, CA: Jossey-Bass).

Lemov, Doug (2015). *Teach Like a Champion 2.0: 62 Techniques that Put Students on the Path to College* (San Francisco, CA: Jossey-Bass).

Lemov, Doug (2016). 'My Favorite No: Mistaking Knowledge Problems for Skill Problems', *Teach Like a Champion* [blog] (12 December). Available at: http://teachlikeachampion.com/blog/favorite-no-mistaking-knowledge-problems-skill-problems/.

Lemov, Doug, Erica Woolway and Katie Yezzi (2012). *Practice Perfect: 42 Rules for Getting Better at Getting Better* (San Francisco, CA: Jossey-Bass).

Leutner, Detlev, Claudia Leopold and Elke Sumfleth (2009). 'Cognitive Load and Science Text Comprehension: Effects of Drawing and Mentally Imagining Text Content', *Computers in Human Behavior*, 25(2), 284–289.

Lewis, Andy (2017). 'Forget Me Not: New GCSE Planning', *TDRE Boss* [blog] (28 February). Available at: http://tdreboss.blogspot.co.uk/2017/02/forget-me-not-new-gcse-planning.html.

Lindner, Reinhard W., Wayne I. Gordon and Bruce R. Harris (1996). 'Highlighting Text as a Study Strategy: Beyond Attentional Focusing'. Paper presented at the American Educational Research Association Annual Meeting, New York, 8–12 April. Available at: https://files.eric.ed.gov/fulltext/ED401320.pdf.

Marzano, Robert J. (2007). *The Art and Science of Teaching: A Comprehensive Framework for Effective Instruction* (Alexandria, VA: Association for Supervision and Curriculum Development).

Marzano, Robert J. and John L. Brown (2009). *A Handbook for the Art and Science of Teaching* (Alexandria, VA: Association for Supervision and Curriculum Development).

Mathur, Pranay, Aman Gill and Aayush Yadav (2017). 'Text Summarization in Python: Extractive vs. Abstractive Techniques Revisited', *Rare Technologies* [blog] (5 April). Available at: https://rare-technologies.com/text-summarization-in-python-extractive-vs-abstractive-techniques-revisited/.

Mayer, Richard E. (2017). 'Instruction Based on Visualizations'. In Richard E. Mayer and Patricia A. Alexander (eds), *Handbook of Research on Learning and Instruction*, Kindle edn (New York: Routledge), ch. 22.

Mayer, Richard E. and Alexander, Patricia A. (eds) (2017), *Handbook of Research on Learning and Instruction*, Kindle edn (New York: Routledge).

Mccrea, Peps (2017). *Memorable Teaching: Leveraging Memory to Build Deep and Durable Learning in the Classroom* (n.p.: Peps Mccrea).

McDaniel, Mark A. and Carol M. Donnelly (1996). 'Learning with Analogy and Elaborative Interrogation', *Journal of Educational Psychology*, 88(3), 508–519. Available at: http://ldt.stanford.edu/~educ39105/paul/articles_2006/Learning%20with%20analogy%20and%20elaborative%20interrogation.pdf.

McGill, Ross Morrison (2014). '10 Tips for Tweeting Teachers', *Teacher Toolkit* [blog] (1 August). Available at: https://www.teachertoolkit.co.uk/2014/08/01/10-tips-for-tweeting-teachers-by-teachertoolkit/.

McGill, Ross Morrison (2017). *Mark. Plan. Teach.: Save Time. Reduce Workload. Impact Learning.*, Kindle edn (London: Bloomsbury Education).

Miller, George (1956). 'The Magical Number Seven, Plus or Minus Two: Some Limits on Our Capacity for Processing Information', *Psychological Review*, 63(2), 81–97.

Morgan, Kelly (2011). 'Teaching with Worked Examples – Save Learner Time and Effort While Increasing Performance!', *Kelly Morgan* [blog] (10 February). Available at: http://kellymorganscience.com/teaching-with-worked-examples-save-learner-time-and-effort-while-increasing-performance/.

Moss, Paul G. (2018). 'Helping Students' Memories – Utilising Elaborative Retrieval', *Theories in Education* [blog] (21 March). Available at: https://paulgmoss.wordpress.com/2018/03/21/helping-students-memories-utilising-elaborative-retrieval/.

Newmark, Ben (2016). 'Verbal Feedback: Telling Them What To Do', *Learning History* [blog] (26 September). Available at: http://bennewmark.edublogs.org/2016/09/26/227/.

Newmark, Ben (2017). 'Nothing New, It's a Review – On Why I Killed My Starters', *Learning History* [blog] (13 November). Available at: https://bennewmark.wordpress.com/2017/11/13/nothing-new-its-a-review-on-why-i-killed-my-starters/.

Nuthall, Graham (2007). *The Hidden Lives of Learners* (Wellington: New Zealand Council for Educational Research Press).

Pashler, Harold, Patrice Bain, Brian Bottge, Arthur Graesser, Kenneth Koedinger, Mark McDaniel and Janet Metcalfe (2007). *Organizing Instruction and Study to Improve Student Learning* (NCER 2007–2004) (Washington, DC: National Center for Education Research, Institute of Education Sciences, US Department of Education). Available at: https://ies.ed.gov/ncee/wwc/PracticeGuide/1.

Pawlak, Mirosław (ed.) (2011). *Extending the Boundaries of Research on Second Language Learning and Teaching* (Heidelberg: Springer).

Peal, Robert (2014). *Progressively Worse: The Burden of Bad Ideas in British Schools* (London: Civitas).

Peal, Robert (2017). 'The Art of the Paragraph', *Robert Peal* [blog] (14 October). Available at: https://robertpealhistory.wordpress.com/2017/10/14/the-art-of-the-paragraph/.

Perkins, David N. and Gavriel Salomon (1992). 'Transfer of Learning' [contribution to the *International Encyclopaedia of Education*, 2nd edn (Oxford: Pergamon Press)]. Available at: http://jaymctighe.com/wordpress/wp-content/uploads/2011/04/Transfer-of-Learning-Perkins-and-Salomon.pdf.

Petty, Geoff (2009). *Evidence-Based Teaching: A Practical Approach*, 2nd edn (Cheltenham: Nelson Thornes).

Petty, Geoff (2014). *Teaching Today: A Practical Guide* (Oxford: Oxford University Press).

Petty, Geoff (2015a). 'The Uses and Abuses of Evidence in Education' (April). Available at: http://geoffpetty.com/wp-content/uploads/2015/04/The-uses-and-abuses-of-evidence.pdf.

Petty, Geoff (2015b). 'What is High Quality Teaching and Learning?' [video] (9 December). Available at: https://www.youtube.com/watch?v=g-DKu7Q5_wA&feature=youtu.be.

Powley, Ruth (2015). 'Meaningful Manageable Revision', *Love Learning Ideas* [blog] (25 March). Available at: http://www.lovelearningideas.com/blog-archive/2015/3/25/meaningful-manageable-revision.

Pressley, Michael, Mark A. McDaniel, James E. Turnure, Eileen Wood and Maheen Ahmad (1987). 'Generation and Precision of Elaboration: Effects on Intentional and Incidental Learning', *Journal of Experimental Psychology: Learning, Memory, and Cognition*, 13, 291–300.

Quigley, Alex (2015). 'Why I Hate Highlighters!', *The Confident Teacher* [blog] (17 January). Available at: https://www.theconfidentteacher.com/2015/01/hate-highlighters/.

Quigley, Alex (2016). *The Confident Teacher: Developing Successful Habits of Mind, Body and Pedagogy*, Kindle edn (Abingdon: Routledge).

Quigley, Alex (2017). 'The Problem with Past Exam Papers', *The Confident Teacher* [blog] (8 April). Available at: http://www.theconfidentteacher.com/2017/04/the-problem-with-past-exam-papers/.

Raichura, Pritesh (2018). 'Retrieval Cues: Do Your Questions Help or Hinder?', *Bunsen Blue* [blog] (19 March). Available at: https://bunsenblue.wordpress.com/2018/03/19/retrieval-cues-do-your-questions-help-or-hinder/.

Rawson, Katherine A., John Dunlosky and Sharon M. Sciartelli (2013). 'The Power of Successive Relearning: Improving Performance on Course Exams and Long-Term Retention', *Educational Psychology Review*, 25(4), 523–548.

Reed, Stephen K. (2006). *Cognition: Theory and Applications* (San Diego, CA: Wadsworth Publishing).

Reif, Frederick (2008). *Applying Cognitive Science to Education*, Kindle edn (London: MIT Press).

Renkl, Alexander and Robert K. Atkinson (2010). 'Learning from Worked-Out Examples and Problem Solving'. In Jan L. Plass, Roxana Moreno and Roland Brünken (eds), *Cognitive Load Theory*, Kindle edn (New York: Cambridge University Press), ch. 5.

Rickards, John P. and Gerald J. August (1975). 'Generative Underlining Strategies in Prose Recall', *Journal of Educational Psychology*, 67(8), 860–865.

Robinson, Martin (2016). 'Don't Panic About Tests', *Trivium21c* [blog] (17 May). Available at: https://martinrobborobinson.wordpress.com/2016/05/17/dont-panic-about-tests/.

Roediger III, Henry L. and Jeffrey D. Karpicke (2006a). 'The Power of Testing Memory: Basic Research and Implications for Educational Practice', *Perspectives on Psychological Science*, 1(3), 181–210. Available at: http://journals.sagepub.com/doi/10.1111/j.1745-6916.2006.00012.x.

Roediger III, Henry L. and Jeffrey D. Karpicke (2006b). 'Test-Enhanced Learning: Taking Memory Tests Improves Long-Term Retention', *Psychological Science*, 17(3), 249–255.

Roediger III, Henry L., Adam L. Putnam and Megan A. Smith (2011). 'Ten Benefits of Testing and Their Applications to Educational Practice', *Psychology of Learning and Motivation*, 55. Available at: http://psych.wustl.edu/memory/Roddy%20article%20PDF%27s/BC_Roediger%20et%20al%20(2011)_PLM.pdf.

Rogers, Ben (2017). 'Retrieval Practice and Sentence Practice All in One!', *Reading for Learning* [blog] (7 October). Available at: https://readingforlearning.org/2017/10/07/retrieval-practice-donows-are-great-but-lets-not-forget-sentence-practice/.

Rogers, Timothy B., Nicholas A. Kuiper and Willam S. Kirker (1977). 'Self-Reference and the Encoding of Personal Information', *Journal of Personality and Social Psychology*, 35(9), 677–688.

Rohrer, Doug and Kelli Taylor (2007). 'The Shuffling of Mathematics Problems Improves Learning', *Instructional Science*, 35(6), 481–498.

Rose, Nick (2014). 'Does Visual Mapping Help Revision?', *Evidence Into Practice* [blog] (25 August). Available at: https://evidenceintopractice.wordpress.com/2014/08/25/does-visual-mapping-help-revision/.

Rose, Nick (2015). 'Can We Teach Students Effective "Revision Skills"?', *Evidence Into Practice* [blog] (8 February). Available at: https://evidenceintopractice.wordpress.com/2015/02/08/can-we-teach-students-effective-revision-skills/.

Rose, Nick (2016). 'Germane Load: The Right Kind of Mental Effort?', *Evidence Into Practice* [blog] (26 January). Available at: https://evidenceintopractice.wordpress.com/2016/01/26/germane-load-the-right-kind-of-mental-effort/.

Rose, Nick and Susanna Eriksson-Lee (2017). *Putting Evidence to Work: How Can We Help New Teachers Use Research Evidence to Inform Their Teaching?* (London: TeachFirst).

Rosenshine, Barak (2012). 'Principles of Instruction: Research-Based Strategies That All Teachers Should Know', *American Educator* (Spring), 12–39. Available at: https://www.aft.org/sites/default/files/periodicals/Rosenshine.pdf.

Ross, Brian H., Peter F. Delaney, Peter P. J. L. Verkoeijen and Arie Spirgel (2010). *The Psychology of Learning and Motivation: Advances in Research and Theory* (Burlington, VT: Academic Press).

Scott, Catherine (2015). *Learn to Teach: Teach to Learn*, Kindle edn (Melbourne, VIC: Cambridge University Press).

Sealy, Clare (2017). 'Memory Not Memories – Teaching for Long Term Learning', *primarytimerydotcom* [blog] (16 September). Available at: https://primarytimery.com/2017/09/16/memory-not-memories-teaching-for-long-term-learning/.

Seifert, Tim (1993). 'Learning Strategies in the Classroom', *Memorial University*. Available at: http://www.mun.ca/educ/faculty/mwatch/vol2/seifert.html.

Sellgren, Katherine (2016). 'Harsh Marks "Put Pupils Off Languages"', *BBC News* (18 April). Available at: http://www.bbc.co.uk/news/education-36027905.

Shell, Duane F., David W. Brooks, Guy Trainin, Kathleen M. Wilson, Douglas F. Kauffman and Lynne M. Herr (2010). *The Unified Learning Model: How Motivational, Cognitive, and Neurobiological Sciences Inform Best Teaching Practices* (New York: Springer).

Sherrington, Tom (2015). 'FACE It. A Formula for Learning', *teacherhead* [blog] (19 September). Available at: https://teacherhead.com/2015/09/19/face-it-a-formula-for-learning/.

Sherrington, Tom (2017a). 'Accountability "Stick" Is Taking Us to the Brink: Time for Radical Change', *teacherhead* [blog] (13 December). Available at: https://teacherhead.com/2017/12/13/accountability-stick-is-taking-us-to-the-brink-time-for-radical-change/.

Sherrington, Tom (2017b). 'Teaching and Assessment for Top-End Success in New GCSEs', *teacherhead* [blog] (12 March). Available at: https://teacherhead.com/2017/03/12/teaching-and-assessment-for-top-end-success-in-new-gcses/.

Sherrington, Tom (2017c). *The Learning Rainforest: Great Teaching in Real Classrooms* (Woodbridge: John Catt Educational).

Singh, Ravi Pratap (2014). 'Beating the Forgetting Curve with Distributed Practice', *eLearning Industry* (16 March). Available at: https://elearningindustry.com/beating-the-forgetting-curve-with-distributed-practice.

Smith, Megan (2017). 'How to Create Retrieval Practice Activities for Elementary Students', *The Learning Scientists* [blog] (6 April). Available at: http://www.learningscientists.org/blog/2017/4/6-1.

Smith, Megan A., Henry L. Roediger III and Jeffrey D. Karpicke (2013). 'Covert Retrieval Practice Benefits Retention as Much as Overt Retrieval Practice', *Journal of Experimental Psychology: Learning, Memory, and Cognition*, 39(6), 1712–1725.

Smith, Megan and Yana Weinstein (2016a). 'Learn How to Study Using … Dual Coding', *The Learning Scientists* [blog] (30 August). Available at: http://www.learningscientists.org/blog/2016/9/1-1.

Smith, Megan and Yana Weinstein (2016b). 'Learn How to Study Using … Elaboration', *The Learning Scientists* [blog] (5 July). Available at: http://www.learningscientists.org/blog/2016/7/7-1.

Smith, Steve (2016). 'The Terrible State of MFL Timetabling in England', *Language Teacher Toolkit* [blog] (2 August). See http://frenchteachernet.blogspot.co.uk/2016/08/the-terrible-state-of-mfl-timetabling.html.

Smith, Steven and Gianfranco Conti (2016). *The Language Teacher Toolkit* (n.p.: CreateSpace).

Smith, Steven, Arthur Glenberg and Robert Bjork (1978). 'Environmental Context and Human Memory', *Memory & Cognition*, 6, 342–353.

Soderstrom, Nicholas C. (2016). *Study Smart: 10 Ways to Master the SAT/ACT Using the Science of Learning* (n.p.: Lasting Learning Press).

Solity, Jonathan (2008). *Michel Thomas: The Learning Revolution* (Abingdon: Hodder Education).

Stachowiak, Bonni (2017). 'Pooja Agarwal – The Science of Retrieval Practice', *Teaching in Higher Ed* [podcast] (21 December). Available at: http://teachinginhighered.com/podcast/science-retrieval-practice/.

Stafford, Tom (2016). 'The Way You're Revising May Let You Down in Exams – And Here's Why', *The Guardian* (7 May). Available at: https://www.theguardian.com/education/2016/may/07/the-way-youre-revising-may-let-you-down-in-exams-and-heres-why.

Stock, Phil (2016). 'Five Strategies for Encouraging More Effective Independent Study', *Must Do Better* [blog] (24 March). Available at: https://joeybagstock.wordpress.com/2016/03/24/five-strategies-for-encouraging-more-effective-independent-study/.

Sweller, John, Paul Ayres and Slava Kalyuga (2011). *Cognitive Load Theory (Explorations in the Learning Sciences, Instructional Systems and Performance Technologies)*, Kindle edn (New York: Springer).

Tharby, Andy (2014). 'Memory Platforms', *Reflecting English* [blog] (12 June). Available at: https://reflectingenglish.wordpress.com/2014/06/12/memory-platforms/.

Thomas, David (2017). 'How Exams Took the Joy, and the Learning, Out of Our Classrooms', *David Thomas' Blog* [blog] (29 May). Available at: http://davidthomasblog.com/2017/05/how-exams-took-the-joy-and-the-learning-out-of-our-classrooms/.

Tierney, Stephen (2016a). 'It's the High Stakes Accountability Not the Testing', *@LeadingLearner* [blog] (3 May). Available at: https://leadinglearner.me/2016/05/03/reduce-high-stakes-accountability-not-testing/.

Tierney, Stephen (2016b). 'Teaching in a Terminal Testing World', *@LeadingLearner* [blog] (31 January). Available at: https://leadinglearner.me/2016/01/31/teaching-in-a-terminal-testing-world/.

Tomsett, John (2015). 'This Much I Know About … the Sutton Trust/EEF Toolkit and the Golden Thread from Evidence to Student Outcomes, Via Deliberate Intervention', *johntomsett* [blog] (13 February). Available at: https://johntomsett.com/2015/02/13/this-much-i-know-about-the-golden-thread-from-evidence-to-student-outcomes/.

Tullis, Jonathan and Aaron Benjamin (2015). 'Cue Generation: How Learners Flexibly Support Future Retrieval', *Memory & Cognition*, 43(6), 922–938. Available at: https://doi.org/10.3758/s13421-015-0517-3.

Uner, Oyku and Henry L. Roediger III (2017). 'The Effect of Question Placement on Learning from Textbook Chapters', *Journal of Applied Research in Memory and Cognition* [online]. Available at: https://doi.org/10.1016/j.jarmac.2017.09.002.

Van Merriënboer, Jeroen J. G. and Paul A. Kirschner (2013). *Ten Steps to Complex Learning: A Systematic Approach to Four-Component Instructional Design*, Kindle edn (Abingdon: Routledge).

Van Merriënboer, Jeroen J. G. and John Sweller (2010). 'Cognitive Load Theory in Health Professional Education: Design Principles and Strategies', *Medical Education*, 44, 85–93. Available at: http://sites.uci.edu/medsim/files/2015/03/Cognitive-Load-Theory-in-Health-Professions.pdf.

Wade, Carole, Carol Tavris and Maryanne Garry (2013). 'The Nine Secrets of Learning', *American Psychological Association*. Available at: http://www.apa.org/ed/precollege/psn/2013/09/learning-secrets.aspx.

Weinstein, Yana (2017). 'Are Our Memories Like Libraries?', *The Learning Scientists* [blog] (2 March). Available at: http://www.learningscientists.org/blog/2017/3/2-1.

Wiliam, Dylan (2016a). 'Learning Styles: What Does the Research Say?', *Deans for Impact* [blog] (28 April). Available at: https://deansforimpact.org/learning-styles-what-does-the-research-say/.

Wiliam, Dylan (2016b). 'Why Teaching Isn't – and Probably Never Will Be – a Research-Based Profession'. Presentation at researchED Washington, Columbia Heights Education Campus, Washington, DC, 29 October.

Wiliam, Dylan and Daisy Christodoulou (2017). 'Assessment, Marking and Feedback'. In Carl Hendrick and Robin Macpherson (eds), *What Does This Look Like in the Classroom? Bridging the Gap Between Research and Practice* (Woodbridge: John Catt Educational), pp. 35–40.

Williams, Dan (2016). 'Making Maths Work', *furtheredagogy* [blog] (4 April). Available at: https://furtheredagogy.wordpress.com/2016/04/04/making-maths-work/.

Williams, Dan (2017). 'Cognitive Load Theory', *furtheredagogy* [blog] (20 May). Available at: https://furtheredagogy.wordpress.com/2017/05/20/cognitive-load-theory/.

Willingham, Daniel (2002). 'Ask the Cognitive Scientist: Allocating Student Study Time: "Massed" versus "Distributed" Practice', *American Educator*, 26(2), 37–39. Available at: https://www.aft.org/periodical/american-educator/summer-2002/ask-cognitive-scientist/.

Willingham, Daniel (2008). 'Ask the Cognitive Scientist: What Will Improve a Student's Memory?', *American Educator*, 32(4), 17–44. Available at: https://www.aft.org/sites/default/files/periodicals/willingham_0.pdf.

Willingham, Daniel (2009). *Why Don't Students Like School? A Cognitive Scientist Answers Questions About How the Mind Works and What It Means for the Classroom* (San Francisco, CA: Jossey-Bass).

Willingham, Daniel and Gail Lovette (2014). 'Can Reading Comprehension Be Taught?', *Teachers College Record* (26 September). Available at: http://www.danielwillingham.com/uploads/5/0/0/7/5007325/willingham&lovette_2014_can_reading_comprehension_be_taught_.pdf.

Wooldridge, Cindy and Yana Weinstein (2016a). 'What's Transfer, and Why Is It so Hard to Achieve? (Part 1)', *The Learning Scientists* [blog] (31 May). Available at: http://www.learningscientists.org/blog/2016/6/2-1.

Wooldridge, Cindy and Yana Weinstein (2016b). 'What's Transfer, and Why Is It so Hard to Achieve? (Part 2)', *The Learning Scientists* [blog] (9 June). Available at: http://www.learningscientists.org/blog/2016/6/9-1.

Yan, Veronica (2016). 'Guest Post: Retrieval Strength vs. Storage Strength', *The Learning Scientists* [blog] (8 May). Available at: http://www.learningscientists.org/blog/2016/5/10-1.

Yue, Carole L., Benjamin C. Storm, Nate Kornell and Elizabeth L. Bjork (2014). 'Highlighting and Its Relation to Distributed Study and Students' Metacognitive Beliefs', *Educational Psychology Review*, 27(1), 69–78.